Laboratory Total Quality Management for Practitioners and Students of Medical Laboratory Science

Laboratory Total Quality Management for Practitioners and Students of Medical Laboratory Science

Osaro Erhabor (Ph.D, FIBMS, CSci)

Associate Professor of Haematology and Transfusion Medicine Usmanu Danfodio University Sokoto Nigeria.

Teddy C Adias (Ph.D, FIBMS)

Provost, College of Health Technology, Bayelsa State, Nigeria

authorHOUSE®

AuthorHouse™
1663 Liberty Drive
Bloomington, IN 47403
www.authorhouse.com
Phone: 1-800-839-8640

Published by AuthorHouse   10/01/2012

ISBN: 978-1-4772-3108-1 (sc)
ISBN: 978-1-4772-3109-8 (hc)
ISBN: 978-1-4772-3110-4 (e)

Library of Congress Control Number: 2012917760

Any people depicted in stock imagery provided by Thinkstock are models, and such images are being used for illustrative purposes only.
Certain stock imagery © Thinkstock.

PREFACE

With the increasing emphasis on accountability within the public sector, the requirement to satisfy the accreditation criteria of several scrutinising regulatory bodies, and the need to meet the changing customer requirements, it is imperative that the laboratory as an organisation adopt a systematic approach to quality management issues. Hitherto the emphasis on achieving accreditation has meant that the concept of quality and quality systems in general have received less attention. However a properly managed quality system can form the framework to address many accreditation issues, as well as provide real opportunities for reducing waste, errors, enhancing staff morale, productivity, optimizing profitability and fostering a culture of continual quality improvement and customer satisfaction. This book amongst others will help practitioners and students in the field of medical laboratory science, other allied medical professions and medicine understand the peculiar role of laboratory total quality management in the delivery of a continually improving quality diagnostic service that meet customer and regulatory requirements as well as enhance the profitability of the laboratory as a business.

Erhabor Osaro

ACKNOWLEDGEMENTS

Our sincere thanks goes to AuthorHouse Publishers, for their assistance and contribution to the publication of this book; to our father in the Lord, Bishop David O. Oyedepo for being an inspiration in our lives through his teachings; to Pastor David Oladosu, Pastor Cyriacus Ekweme and Pastor T Davies for their spiritual oversight; to Chief Aibangbee Erhabor and Mrs Rose Erhabor; to Prof D.E. Agbonlahor, Prof O.A. Emeribe, Prof Uko E.K., Prof O.A. Ejele, Prof C.A. Nwauche, Prof A. Ojule, Prof C. Akani, Prof S.D. Abbey, Prof R.A. Shehu, Prof L.S. Bilbis, Prof J Lori, Dr E.A.D. Alikor, Dr FI Buseri, Dr C Onwuka, Dr ZA Jeremiah, Dr A. Mainasara, Dr M.K. Dallatu, Dr H. Opurum and Mr O. Azuonwu for all their support and encouragement over the years. Our sincere thanks go to our families and friends for the encouragement while we wrote this book that will help build a culture of continuous quality improvement and create a quality consciousness among all those involved in diagnostic service delivery all over the world. To the Almighty God alone be all the glory.

CONTENTS

CHAPTER 1

WHO IS A MEDICAL LABORATORY SCIENTIST AND PRINCIPLE OF GOOD PROFESSIONAL PRACTICE

Medical laboratory scientists or Biomedical Scientist work in healthcare to diagnose disease and evaluate the effectiveness of treatment through the analysis of body fluids and tissue samples from patients. They provide the "engine room" of modern medicine with 70% of diagnoses based on the laboratory results provided by laboratory scientist. Medical Laboratory Scientist are at the heart of the medical team providing other professionals with vital scientific information that allows them to make medical judgements needed for the effective management of the patient medical condition. When a major incident occurs it is Medical Laboratory Scientists that ensure the right amount of blood reaches the right patient at the right time. We measure vital blood chemicals to monitor patient conditions and detect signs of internal bleeding, we determine coagulation analysis to determine patients prone to thrombosis and will require anticoagulation, we screen blood and blood product for transfusion to patients to ensure they are free from transfusion transmissible diseases, we carry out blood cultures to determine patients with septicaemia and require antibiotics treatment, we determine the specific antibiotics that is required to treat infective processes in patients and we study biopsies to determine if patients have cancers or are predisposed to cancers

Without the important and life saving services provided by Medical Laboratory Scientist, accident and emergency wards would shut down, blood transfusion services will be unavailable, there will be inadequate management of hospital associated infections (MRSA), Coagulation clinics to provide thrombosis patients with anticoagulation would shut, premature babies would struggle to survive without our support. Whenever you have a sample taken from you by a doctor or nurse, it is usually analysed by a biomedical scientist. Quite simply, without the services and support of these oracles of modern medicine, doctors would frequently be unable to diagnose diseases properly or treat their patients effectively.

Registration requires completion of an academic degree plus a period of training in a any of the government approved laboratory to develop your practical skills and ensure your competence to allow for the protection of the vulnerable public and for patient safety. This may occur as part of an integrated degree (laboratory attachment) or may be completed post-graduation (Internship). The trainee's progress and competence is recorded and should be assessed on completion of training. Trainees whose training meets the requirement of regulatory institute or council are issued with a license to practice as a Medical Laboratory Scientist.

SPECIALISING IN THE FIELD OF MEDICAL LABORATORY SCIENCE

Training of the Laboratory Scientist is generic in the first 4 years of training and often covers a broad spectrum of courses in; haematology and blood transfusion, chemical pathology, immunology, histology, cytology medical microbiology, virology and parasitology.

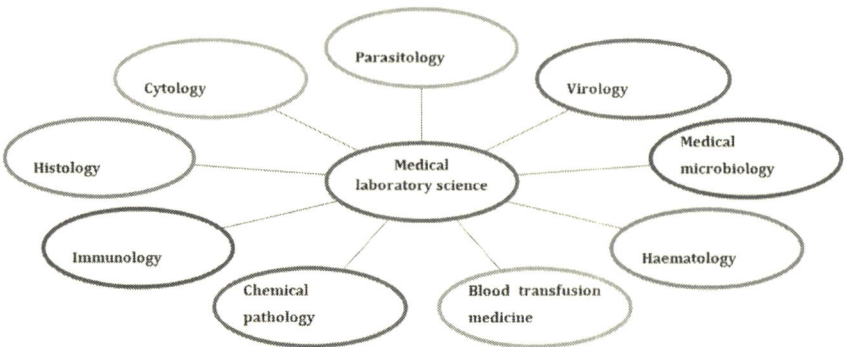

Figure: Field of specialisation in medical laboratory science

However in the final year of study the student medical laboratory scientist is expected to specialize in any of the field of speciality in medical laboratory science. They are usually expected to do specialist courses in their chosen field of speciality as well as carry out a research work and present a project report which is presented before a departmental examination board in the presence of an external examiner who is a specialist in the speciality.

After qualifying as a Medical Laboratory Scientist, you are expected to be actively involved in Continuous Professional Development (CPD) by being involved in a mixture of learning activities (attendance of seminars, workshops, paper presentation, book review, publication of articles and books, top up training, training of subordinate staff and other relevant training activities that is relevant to your work). Medical Laboratory Science is a dynamic science-based profession. The only way to be up-to-date is to engage in Continuous Professional Development.

MEDICAL MICROBIOLOGY

As a medical laboratory scientist in microbiology you will study micro-organisms such as bacteria, fungi and parasites which cause disease. You will identify these organisms and establish the antibiotic treatment required to effectively eliminate them therefore stopping the disease. Diseases diagnosed in the microbiology laboratory include meningitis, tuberculosis, gonorrhoea and other sexually transmitted diseases (STD's) and food poisoning. Medical microbiology includes the study of microbial pathogenesis and epidemiology and is related to the study of disease pathology and immunology. In the medical laboratory, these microbiologists also work in a sub-department dedicated to parasitology. The discipline consists primarily of four major spheres of activity:

- The provision of laboratory investigation, diagnosis, and treatment of patients suffering from infectious diseases.
- The establishment and direction of infection control programs across the continuum of care.
- Public health and communicable disease prevention and epidemiology.
- The scientific and administrative direction of a diagnostic microbiology laboratory.

CHEMICAL PATHOLOGY

In clinical chemistry also known as chemical pathology, medical laboratory scientists analyse blood, body fluids and other biological materials to help the diagnosis of diseases (such as renal failure, diabetes). They also carry out toxicological studies, test kidney and liver functions and help to monitor therapies. The discipline originated in the late 19th century with the use of simple chemical tests by medical Laboratory Scientists for various components of blood and urine. Subsequently other techniques were introduced including the use and measurement of enzyme activities, spectrophotometry, electrophoresis and immunoassay. Most current laboratories are now highly automated analyzers and use assays that are closely monitored and quality controlled. Chemical Pathology test are performed on any kind of body fluid, but mostly on serum or plasma. Serum is the yellow watery part of blood that is left after blood has been allowed to clot and all blood cells have been removed. This is most easily done by centrifugation which packs the denser blood cells and platelets to the bottom of the centrifuge tube, leaving the liquid serum fraction resting above the packed cells. Plasma is essentially the same as serum, but is obtained by centrifuging anticoagulated blood. Plasma therefore contains all of the clotting factors, including fibrinogen. The chemical pathology laboratory carry out a large array of tests can be further sub-categorized into sub-specialties of:

- General or routine chemistry
- Endocrinology (the study of hormones)
- Immunology (the study of the immune system and antibodies)
- Pharmacology or Toxicology (the study of drugs)

TRANSFUSION SCIENCE

In this discipline you will identify blood groups for blood donation, screen transfusion recipients for atypical antibodies, ensure the correct grouped blood is matched to the patient due to receive a red cell transfusion and make certain there is enough blood available in case of emergency such as road traffic accidents, operations and cancer treatments, screen donors for transfusion transmissible infections, screen patients for presence of alloantibodies, select antigen negative units for patients with alloantibodies. Manage stock levels of blood and blood products, prepare blood components (packed red cells, fresh frozen plasma (FFP), platelets and cryoprecipitate, stock and manage batch products like anti D for prophylactic use in Rhesus negative pregnant women, tranaxemic acid for the management of major haemorrhage and prothrombin complex concentrate (PCC) for the management of patients prone to thrombosis who are on anticoagulant therapy such as warfarin., carry out investigation for feto-maternal haemorrhage (FMH) in Rhesus negative women delivered of Rhesus positive babies to enable the effective dosing of prophylactic anti-D to prevent incidence of haemolytic disease of the foetus and newborn (HDFN) in subsequent Rhesus positive pregnancies as well as investigate transfusion reactions and other unexpected negative outcome associated with transfusion of blood and blood products.

HAEMATOLOGY

Haematology is the study of blood. In this discipline you will be involved with the formation, composition, functions and diseases of the blood. Some of the diseases diagnosed in haematology are leukaemia, malaria and anaemia. Haematology is concerned with the study of blood, the blood-forming organs, and blood diseases. Hematology includes the study of etiology, diagnosis, treatment, prognosis, and prevention of blood diseases. The laboratory work that goes into the study of blood is frequently performed by a medical laboratory scientist. *Blood diseases* affect the production of blood and its components, such as blood cells (red cells, white cells and platelets), hemoglobin, and blood proteins. Routine work in the Haematology laboratory includes routine complete blood count estimation, viewing blood films and bone marrow slides under the microscope, diagnosis of haemoglobinopathies, carrying out of coagulation investigations such as prothrombin time, APTT, Fibrinogen and D-Dimer, factor assays, thrombophilia screen, prothrombin gene variants and factor 5 Leiden for the management of hypercoagulable patients, patients prone to thrombosis on anticoagulant therapy and in determining patients disposition to bleeding, interpreting various hematological test results.

Hematology also includes specialist areas such as:

- Diagnosis of bleeding disorders such as haemophilia and idiopathic thrombocytopenic purpura
- Diagnosis of hematological malignancies such as lymphoma and leukemia
- Diagnosis of haemoglobinopathies like sickle cell disease (SCD) and thalassaemia

- Examination of bone marrow and stem cell transplantation

HISTOLOGY

In histology also called anatomical pathology, tissue samples are studied microscopically to establish the cause of illness. Tissue may be taken during surgery or at post mortem. Diseases such as cancer are diagnosed by looking for abnormal features in tissue cells. Anatomical pathology is a medical laboratory science specialty that is concerned with the diagnosis of disease based on the gross, microscopic, chemical, immunologic and molecular examination of organs, tissues, and whole bodies (autopsy).

CYTOLOGY

This discipline is often part of histology or anatomical pathology in most countries in Africa. However in most developed countries it is a speciality of its own. Cytology is best known for its work in screening cervical smears, but it also provides a non-gynaecological service. Like histology, specialised techniques are used to prepare and study samples of cellular materials. Cytology involves carrying out cervical screening programmes which involves cervical smears investigations to test women for the presence of cytological abnormalities in the cervix (neck of the womb) that can potentially develop into cancer. This test is performed regularly and routinely as a preventive measure to reduce mortality from cervical cancers.

VIROLOGY

Virology is the study of viruses and the disease caused by them such as German measles, HIV, Hepatitis B, Hepatitis C, Herpes Simplex virus and chickenpox. You will also be involved in monitoring the effects of vaccines. The virology laboratory also performs your viral studies, experimentation, testing, analysis and research. Clinical virology is becoming increasingly complex, rapidly developing in areas such as nucleic acid technology, antiviral chemotherapy, new viral vaccines, identification of new human viruses, and management of infection control problems in both the hospital and local community.

IMMUNOLOGY

Medical Laboratory scientists in immunology deals with the body's immune system and its role in infectious diseases, parasitic infestations, allergies, tumour growth, tissue grafts and organ transplants. Their work is particularly important in the monitoring and treatment of patients living with HIV and AIDS. Medical laboratory science is an evolving science moving into new areas such as cytogenetics and molecular biology.

CYTOGENETICS

Cytogenetics involves the processing and analysis of the chromosomes of different types of sample with the purpose of detecting and interpreting chromosomal abnormalities. Five decades ago the first recognized the correct chromosome number in man was said to be 46. Shortly thereafter, several chromosome aneuploid syndromes were identified. In the early 1970s, various chromosomal-banding techniques were developed that allowed the recognition of individual chromosomes and deletions and duplications as aetiologies for numerous chromosome syndromes. The roles of a cytogeneticist include:

- Analysis of blood from individuals from a variety of chromosomal syndromes such as congenital abnormalities, learning difficulties, reproductive difficulties and sexual development-related problems.
- Prenatal diagnosis of chromosomal abnormalities such as Down's syndrome from the amniotic fluid or chorionic villus samples.
- Analysis of bone marrow and blood samples from patients with haematological malignancies such as leukaemia to aid diagnosis ans management.

MOLECULAR BIOLOGY

Molecular biology is the branch of biology that deals with the molecular basis of biological activity. This field overlaps with other areas of biology and chemistry, particularly genetics and biochemistry. Molecular biology chiefly concerns itself with understanding and the interactions between the various systems of a cell, including the interactions between the different types of DNA, RNA and protein biosynthesis as well as learning how these interactions are regulated.

PRINCIPLE OF GOOD PROFESSIONAL PRACTICE

It is the responsibility of every regulatory laboratory professional body to provide information (good professional practice) to help her members practice safely and effectively in the interest of the vulnerable public. Good professional practice outlines how, as a profession, medical laboratory science can aim to provide the highest quality of service to ensure that patients and clients get the best possible diagnostic service and care. It defines the level of practice expected from every medical laboratory scientists and their duty of care they have to patients as well as their responsibilities to professional colleagues, other healthcare professionals and the profession. Medical laboratory science is an important part of the medical family. Several health professionals work as a team to provide patients with the best possible medical service. Good Professional Practice also provides information on additional professional and specific guidance provided by the regulatory professional bodies. First and foremost practising medical laboratory scientists must abide by the legal and statutory requirements regulating the profession. Failure to do so could result in a scientist being suspended or removed from the council's register. Medical laboratory scientist should note that failure to adhere to legal requirements of practice and recommended principles of professional good practice could affect an individual's cover under the council professional indemnity insurance scheme, and may result in expulsion from the council register.

CODE OF CONDUCT FOR LABORATORY SCIENTIST

The ethical framework within which medical laboratory scientists should practise is concerned with:

• Professional competence
• Personal conduct
• Professional relationships with other healthcare colleagues
• Public duties—confidentiality, honesty, diligence, integrity.

All members of the Medical Laboratory Science profession shall always:

- Exercise their professional knowledge and skill with judgement and care for the benefit of the vulnerable wider general public and in the best interests of the users of the service.
- Demonstrate the highest standards of conduct, honesty and integrity in their personal and professional behaviour.
- Understand, recognise and work within the limits of their professional knowledge, skills and experience.
- Recognise the beliefs and values of the wider general public, the users of the service and professional colleagues, treating them on a fair and equitable basis.
- Ensure their own beliefs and values do not prejudice or compromise their ability to carry out their professional roles and duties.
- Maintain, improve and keep up to date their professional knowledge and skills.
- Aid and support the development of medical laboratory science by education or training of their professional colleagues, the users of the service and the wider general public.
- Promote the study and activity of laboratory science by promotion of the values, aims and objectives of the Institute of Biomedical Science.
- Be involved in continuing professional development (CPD) as a way of being up-to-date in their professional knowledge and skills.
- Promote the aims, objectives and values of the profession.

Usually failure by a member of a professional group to abide by the code of conduct of an organization can result in the member being struck off the profession's register

PROFESSIONALS INVOLVED IN THE HOSPITAL AND DIAGNOSTIC LABORATORY

There are a variety of skilled and educated laboratory professionals who you may never encounter as a patient. However, these individuals play a very important role in diagnostic service delivery. People working in the clinical laboratory are responsible for conducting tests that provide crucial live saving information to the clinician. Apart from detecting the presence of infective agents, they are also involved in disease monitoring, research and public health. These skilled professionals use specialized equipment and techniques to analyze patients' samples, such as blood, urine, body fluids and tissue, and stool. They may be working in the hospital, clinic or a reference laboratory. Professionals involved in laboratory include medical laboratory scientist, laboratory technicians and laboratory attendants. Biomedical scientists work and supervise a complex mix of professional staff groups who interact and work together in delivering clinical laboratory services. They include scientific, technical and support staff (laboratory technicians, attendants, phlebotomy staff, secretarial and administrative staff. The medical laboratory science profession is regulated by the Institute of Biomedical Science in the case of the UK. In most countries the diagnostic laboratory is headed by the Director of medical laboratory services or the Chief Medical Laboratory scientist who is in charge of day to day running of the laboratory (budgeting, planning inventory control, personnel management, training).These cadres of laboratory staff manages other subordinate staff in the laboratory (laboratory technicians, attendants, trainees, phlebotomy staff and secretarial staff).They manage the laboratory revolving funds and ensure an uninterrupted delivery of a continually improving quality diagnostic service that meet the needs of the laboratory customers. Other categories of an autonomous professional group that work in the laboratory are pathologist. They are clinician whose training is regulated by Royal College of pathologist as in the UK or the Medical and Dental Councils. This cadre of laboratory professions have a parallel organogram. They are responsible for managing patients with conditions in the area of specialty using results generated by laboratory scientist, running their clinics, training of their residents as well as talking consult from their medical colleagues and managing their clinical laboratory budget. However, there has been a widespread breakdown in working relationships between Medical Laboratory Scientist and Pathologist in some countries because of the failure of Pathologist in those countries to appreciate the fact that both professions are autonomous, have different regulatory bodies and have different schemes of service even though they work as a team to ensure that patients receive the best possible diagnostic and clinical care.

CHAPTER 2

RECRUITMENT, COMPETENCE, AND APPRAISAL OF MEDICAL LABORATORY STAFF

RECRUITING THE BEST MEDICAL LABORATORY STAFF FOR YOUR TEAM

In theory, recruitment should be simple. Many managers perform the same routine: they write a job description, put an advertisement in the newspaper or online, wait for applicants to apply, and then hire the person they deem fit for the job. Care is required to ensure that the selected candidate is likely to get on with the rest of the team, is in tune with the organization's continuous improvement culture, and is likely to stay with the organization rather than get employed, become fully trained, and immediately leave to work for another organization. Recruitment mistakes waste time, money, and organizational resources, and they can really hold a team back. Organizations must realize that it is not just a function of employing the best candidate for a job; it is also their responsibility that staff welfare and motivation is taken seriously. Staff members who are not motivated are likely to be less productive and are more likely to seek greener opportunities elsewhere.

EFFECTIVE RECRUITMENT (WHAT A LABORATORY MANAGER MUST LOOK OUT FOR)

There are several reasons why it is extremely important that recruitment is done properly.

- The right people in the right roles will be more productive. Employing the right persons for the right roles is critical if an organization must be productive and result-oriented. The right persons are not likely to leave the organization. High staff turnover is a serious problem that can put a lot of stress on staff on the ground and can affect morale among teams.

- A poor hiring decision may cause stress, low morale, and conflict within your team. If a new employee is not a team player (has personality issues), this may lower productivity for members of the team.

Proper hiring saves costs and helps an organization maximize resources. Organizations spend many resources (money, time, and energy) in hiring and training to bring new employees up to speed in the tasks they are expected to perform. When new staff members are hired and trained and subsequently leave, they take with them the time, money, and energy that the organization has invested in them. The organization also then needs to grapple with the responsibility of going through the recruitment process all over again.

COMPETENCE AND APPRAISAL OF THE MEDICAL LABORATORY SCIENTIST

Competence

At a minimum. all laboratory staff should be appraised annually so that further education and/or training needs can be identified, discussed, and incorporated into a Personal Development Plan (PDP). The appraisal of competence itself should evolve and respond to professional and scientific changes and influences, as well as the requirements of the individual employer. Continuing professional development is integrated within the Medical Laboratory Science Council registration and other healthcare professions as one method of ensuring that staff retains the capacity to practise

- Safely,
- Effectively,
- And legally within their evolving scope of practice.

Medical laboratory scientists working outside organisations with a formal appraisal system are encouraged to seek out an appropriately experienced and qualified colleague as a professional mentor.

Laboratory Staff Appraisals

One of the key roles of a laboratory manager is to carry out annual appraisals and provide feedback to his or her team members on their performance. Without feedback, one cannot expect people to know where improvements are needed. The outcomes of the appraisal process help an organization to do the following:

- Assess the competence of the workforce
- Plan training and development activities
- Pay people according to the value of their contribution

Note that while there is a clear link between appraisal and pay, this is not the primary purpose of the appraisal. Laboratory managers should not underestimate the importance of regular appraisal. The abilities of managers are expressed in the performance of their staff, and they will ultimately be judged on this. A manager may be seen not to have provided an enabling environment and to be performing sub-optimally if his subordinate staff:

- Complains
- Portrays discontented attitude
- Underperforms
- Shows lack of pride and joy at work
- Becomes unproductive

There are many benefits to conducting staff reviews (appraisals). Reviews allow management to do the following:

- Identify areas where laboratory staff needs improvement with the intention of removing stumbling blocks to performance
- Identify the training-related needs of staff
- Review staff performance in the previous year, agree on a set of achievable objectives for the current year, and review staff commitment to service development
- Encourage open communication with the hope of possibly improving the service delivery in the laboratory based on quality improvement suggestions made by the staff being appraised

- Identify potential that staff members have that can be harnessed to the benefit of the organization (untapped staff potential is a potential waste from lean-management perspectives)
- Determine and make career and development plans to help facilitate the objectives of the department
- Improve performance and productivity and ensure that staff have pride and joy in their service delivery in the department

PREPARING TO APPRAISE

Data Collection: In order to ensure fairness and objectivity toward the person who is being appraised, a thorough preparation in terms of information gathering is essential. A manager must always note that the appraisal process is an official procedure and not about personal vendettas or whether or not you like someone. Rather, it is a way to measure staff performance as well as to identify the peculiar role the department can play in supporting the staff to be productive and support the overall objectives and goals of the department. This process includes

- looking at current staff job descriptions, standards, objectives, and competencies required;
- and examining the staff appraisal from the previous year to identify major outcomes or achievements and personal development tasks that were not achieved that must be carried over to the current year.

Identifying Situational Factors: There are situational factors that can negatively affect staff performance and productivity. A laboratory manager must be aware of these and take them into consideration when preparing to appraise. Examples of such situational factors include the following.

- If new technology, new assay, new management, or new equipment has been introduced during the year and staff has not been adequately trained on these new procedures, the staff performance is likely to be affected.
- Were new standards or operating procedures produced, or were new targets set within the period under review for which the staff

has not been appropriately trained? All staff must be adequately trained to the SOP, competency tested, and certified.

- Organizational changes or moves to new locations can affect the staff.
- Organization in which staff turnover is high can affect staff morale and productivity.
- If an organization is having problems retaining staff, the staff on the ground may be doing more than is statutorily required. This can negatively affect the productivity of the staff.
- If the workload increases over a period and the staff strength has not increased to match the increased workload (negative workloads), staff morale and productivity are likely to be low. Also, the stress level and error rate in such a laboratory is likely to be high.
- Staff members may sometimes have personal (marital, debt, alcohol, mental health, and drug-related) issues or relationship problems that may be impacting on performance.

These factors may constitute the reasons for under-achievement that may be outside the appraisee's control. The laboratory management must be able to identify these issues during staff appraisal and be able to determine the possible ways the laboratory can assist the staff in overcoming these challenges.

Identifying Staff Potential: Unidentified or untapped staff potential is considered as waste to an organization and can affect the productivity of staff. Every staff has a potential (things they are good at). It is the responsibility of the laboratory manager to ensure that these potentials are identified and used to the advantage of the organization (nurtured towards meeting the organizational goals and objectives).

- It is the responsibility of the lab manager to identify the potential of staff and to provide an enabling environment and set personal development objectives to ensure that staff subsequently blossom.
- Managers should be able to identify whether staff members are operating at their peak performance and are demonstrating that they can achieve more than is required. Are they receptive to change and to learning new skills? Are certain staff members seen

as role models by other staff? Can staff potentially help with the training of new staff? Are there any knowledge and skills that the staff members have acquired, from a recent training, workshop, conference attendance, or completion of a course of study, that they have not been given the opportunity to practice or share with colleagues?

- Does staff have qualities and experience that can be used in other departments within the organization (multi-tasking)?

PREPARING AND THE APPRAISAL PROPER

- Prepare a basic meeting plan incorporating a detailed review of past performance with examples against objectives or standards.
- Include situational factors that you have identified as affecting performance, major strengths, and areas for development with some ideas about how to address them.
- Arrange a mutually convenient time and a quiet place to meet and inform the staff of the purpose of the appraisal.
- An excellent technique to instil in your staff is self-appraisal. Give staff the opportunity to think about their own performance in advance of the meeting. This will often provide new insights into their performance.
- Allow staff to focus on their achievements and identify areas where they believe achievements or shortfalls occurred.
- Allow staff an opportunity to ask questions they may have about the job, their career aspirations, and their training needs, and include time for a discussion on future performance and career needs.
- It is often counterproductive to complete the appraisal form in advance; this will negate the purpose of the meeting.

REVIEWING STAFF PERFORMANCE

- Start by asking the appraisee to provide an overall review of their performance. This will give you a feel for how they see their contribution and will indicate the extent to which their perception varies from your own.

- If appropriate, confirm your performance ratings for each key area as you go along.
- When you reach a performance problem area, be sure to focus on the work problem rather than the person or their characteristics. If you cannot reach agreement through questioning, then confront the issue constructively and assertively.
- Try to get a commitment that will lead to an improvement in the future and confirm that you do not hold a grudge.
- Remember to mention some factors that may have affected the appraisee's performance over the period of the review, positively or negatively. Note these factors and mention them later in the process.

THE APPRAISAL DOCUMENT

Appraisal of staff is made under seven broad headings.

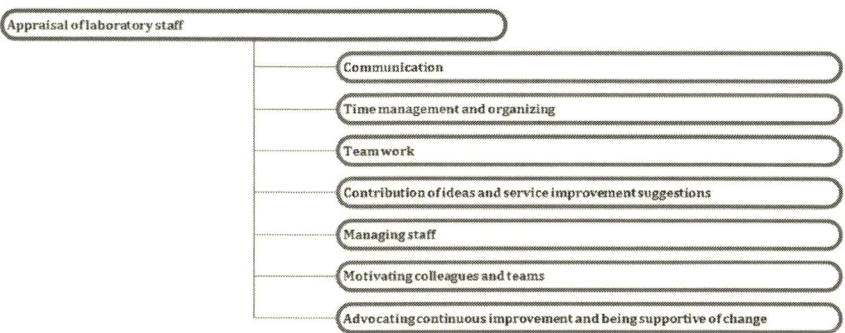

Figure: Broad Headings Under Which Staff Is Appraised

ACTION PLANNING

The purpose of the action plan is to bring together all aspects of the appraisal, confirm the areas of performance to be addressed and agree an end result for each, look for ways of achieving these end results that are practical and economical to the organization and staff, and establish a time frame for all activities in the plan. Set the start date, the likely duration, key follow-up dates, and finish times. Acton planning also includes:

- Addressing areas for which staff requires improvement
- Building on the area of strengths of the staff
- Setting new attainable objectives
- Planning for future known or envisaged changes in the way the laboratory is run or the service is provided
- Helping build an enabling environment and support for the appraisee to meet his or her career aspirations

Appraisal Report Writing: It is good practice to write up the appraisal report straight after the appraisal meeting. A quick turnaround of the appraisal document also shows the appraisee that their performance is a priority to the organization. The report should be well structured and should reflect the quality of the discussion. The appraisee should receive a draft of the document to review to allow them to make any corrections and to add their comments. Show the appraisal to the line manager and have them add their comments to the document. Sign the document and ask your line manager to sign as well as the appraisee. The appraisee should receive a signed copy of the report, and a copy should be placed in the appraisee's file. Finally, the appraiser should agree with the appraisee when to schedule a review.

APPRAISAL FORM

Appraisal Parameter	Requirement	Scoring Characteristics
Communication	Communication when dealing with colleagues, staff, supervisors, patients, and other service users	1. Shows the ability to listen and understand information 2. Presents information in a clear and concise manner. 3. Knows appropriate ways of communicating with all staff, management, and service users 4. Demonstrates respect for all individuals in all forms of communication, regardless of their background or culture 5. Maintains confidentiality as appropriate

Time Management and Organising	Organisation of self and management of workload (accuracy, thoroughness, and effectiveness)	1. Is able to work under pressure and meet standards of quality. 2. Uses time appropriately and accomplish suitable volume of work. 3. Work output matches the expectations established. 4. Arranges work schedules and prioritises work to meet deadlines. 5. Knows when to ask for clarification before proceeding when appropriate.
Teamwork	Ability to work as part of a team and contribute to team objectives	1. Establishes and maintains effective working relationships with others 2. Shares information and resources with others. 3. Follows instructions of supervisor and responds to requests from others in a helpful manner 4. Is aware of organization's priorities, aims, and values
Contributing Ideas/Service Improvement Suggestions	Contribution of ideas for improvement and new ways of working	1. Challenges old traditions and cultures that are not fit for purpose 2. Makes constructive suggestions as to how services can be improved for staff, users, and/or the public 3. Completes work to deadlines alerting others of barriers/delays in advance 4. Participates in change events 5. Adapts to agreed change, altering practice as necessary
Managing or Supervising Staff	Being a role model (a good example) to subordinate staff	1. Delivers timely appraisals and completion of personal development plans (PDPs) 2. Provides clear and effective constructive feedback to team members 3. Delegates authority to people as appropriate, agreeing clear achievable outcomes/targets 4. Develops and recognises levels of performance in the team 5. Is willing to make necessary and immediate decisions given incomplete information

		6. Makes effective decisions; identifies and anticipates problems
		7. Role models appropriate ethical behaviours
Motivating Colleagues/Team	Engaging team to achieve shared local/ departmental objectives linked to organization's values	1. Establishes/supports a positive culture of teamwork and cooperation
		2. Provides guidance and supports development of staff.
		3. Involves staff in decision-making opportunities where appropriate
		4. Provides regular opportunities for shared communication of performance and direction
		5. Delegates authority to others when required and monitors against agreed achievable outcomes
		6. Recognises and shares achievements with team/colleagues/department
		7. Supports and encourages others in understanding the need for and in making agreed changes
		8. Identifies and evaluates areas for potential service improvement
		9. Undertakes own role in improving services, supporting others effectively during times of change, and works to overcome problems and tensions as they arise
Advocating Continuous Improvement and Supporting Change		1. Is a self-starter, recommending/ developing and implementing new methods, procedures, solutions, concepts, designs, and applications of existing designs or procedures
		2. Accepts additional challenges and responsibilities and willingly assists others; is self-reliant
		3. Ensures own and team's awareness of and involvement in continuous improvement activities

CHAPTER 3

QUALITY ASSURANCE AND CONTINUOUS QUALITY IMPROVEMENT

A quality management system (QMS) is the sum total of all the processes that allow for the effective control of the whole operation. It includes the use of a documented set of policies and procedures that define how you achieve a defined quality of product or service. In the laboratory, a quality product or service is a service that meets the customer's requirements. It is providing the right result on the right specimen from the right patient in a way that is cost effective (value for money), reliable, accurate, reproducible (best possible care), timely (improving health), communicated effectively and appropriately by a highly motivated laboratory professional (joy and pride at work) to the users of the service. It enhances the quality of care offered to the customer.

INDICATORS TO MONITOR THE QUALITY OF YOUR LABORATORY'S PERFORMANCE

- Turnaround times
- Internal quality assessment
- External quality assessment

It is not sufficient to sit back and assume that we are doing fine in terms of quality. In fact, since no system is perfect, there is every likelihood that we do make mistakes. If we do, then it is extremely important to have data on the following:

- How many mistakes do we make on a monthly basis and why?
- Are there trends in the number of mistakes we make as a laboratory?
- How often do we exceed our turnaround times?
- How often does our Laboratory Information Management System (LIMS) go down?

- How often do we produce an incorrect result or send the correct result but for the wrong patient?

It is vital for every laboratory organization to measure their performance. Measuring our performance is the only way to monitor and measure improvements.

WHAT CONSTITUTES QUALITY FROM A CUSTOMER'S PERSPECTIVE?

The customer:

- Sees the response time for a lab test as critical to the quality of care
- Wants to be informed about the turnaround times
- Expects that laboratory results are reliable
- Expects simple and easy-to-follow instructions on sample collection and handling
- Requires a prompt, customer-focused, and friendly phlebotomy service
- Wants a continually improving service
- Requires a cost-effective quality service
- Wants a safety, environment and infection control conscious laboratory service
- Likes a process-oriented diagnostic service with a feedback system

WHAT IS QUALITY ASSURANCE?

Quality Assurance includes all arrangements put in place by a laboratory organization to ensure that products and services meet the quality required. Other elements of quality assurance include:

- Staff training
- Proactive maintenance of equipment
- Use of internal quality control (IQC)
- Enrolment in external quality assessment programmes (EQA). External Quality Assessment is an essential aspect of any laboratory

operation providing laboratories with a means of assessing their analytical performance compared to other laboratories utilising the same methods and instruments.

- Use of standard operating procedures (SOPs)
- Regular performance of quality audits (vertical, horizontal, and examination)
- Submission to accreditation by accreditation agencies (Clinical Pathology Accreditation (CPA), Medicine and Healthcare Product Regulatory Agency (MHRA), and United Kingdom Regulatory Service (UKRS) and Medical Laboratory Science Council of Nigeria (MLSCN) and others.
- Carrying out of regular user (patients and other users of services) satisfaction surveys

BENEFITS OF A QUALITY SYSTEM

- Helps a laboratory achieve accreditation
- Allows for a better control of processes
- Drives continuing quality improvement (documented quality system is a mechanism for improvement)
- Is a proof (particularly in case of litigation) that adequate procedures are in place to allow for the provision of a safe, effective, and high-quality diagnostic service
- Facilitates an improved service delivery to customers
- Increases efficiency through reduction of mistakes and waste
- Can potentially improve the profitability of the diagnostic laboratory as a business

CONTINUOUS QUALITY IMPROVEMENT (CQI)

Continuous quality improvement (CQI) is also known as *Kaizen,* a Japanese word for improvement or change for the better. *Kaizen* is made up from *koi* (change) and *zen* (good or improvement). It refers to activities (small and continuous changes to the process) that continually improve all functions and processes. It is often driven by staff involved in the actual process. It is the workforce that drives a process. They are the ones responsible for the day to day running of the process. They know where the bureaucracies and waste are. The suggestion on possible ways to improve the process lies in the hands of staffs that daily runs this process. Management do not necessarily grow an organization. They merely makes policy decisions and changes while staff involve in the process drive the policy implementation. Managers often responsible for the following:

- Implementation
- Delivery process
- Design of the delivery process

Continuous quality improvement (CQI) is a system that seeks to improve the provision of services with an emphasis on a future state or a result from the current state. It involves the use of a set of statistical tools to understand the process and uncover problems. It's emphasis is on maintaining quality in the future not just controlling a process. Once a process that needs improvement is identified, each step of that process is identified, specific expectations are arrived at, a procedure is put in place to measure output, and suggested changes are implemented with the aim of preventing future failures and setting future goals. Education of staff to implement the change is vital. The success achieved must be measurable. The process will need to be reviewed to determine to what extent the process has been improved, to determine whether change being implemented is associated with any bureaucracy, and to determine whether new changes will need to be implemented. CQI is an on-going effort to improve:

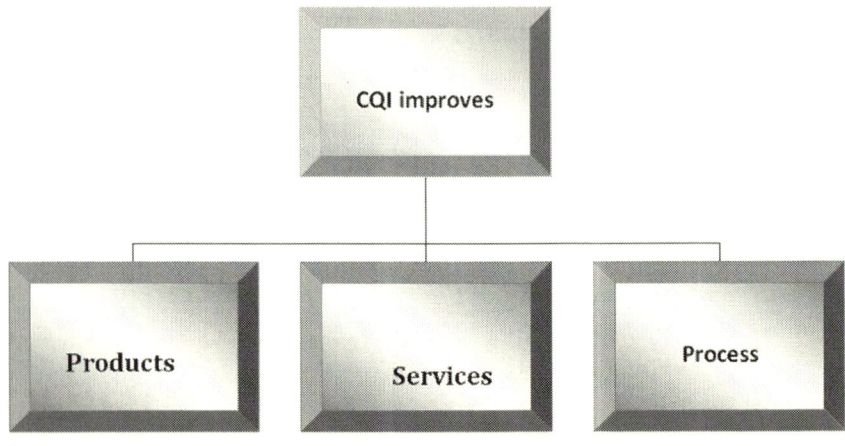

Figure: Role of CQI

CQI involves small incremental changes aimed at improving service delivery and customer satisfaction over time. It requires a constant evaluation of the process, with the hope of improving the process by removing all non-value added (from the customer's perspective) steps from the processes. It is aimed at improving:

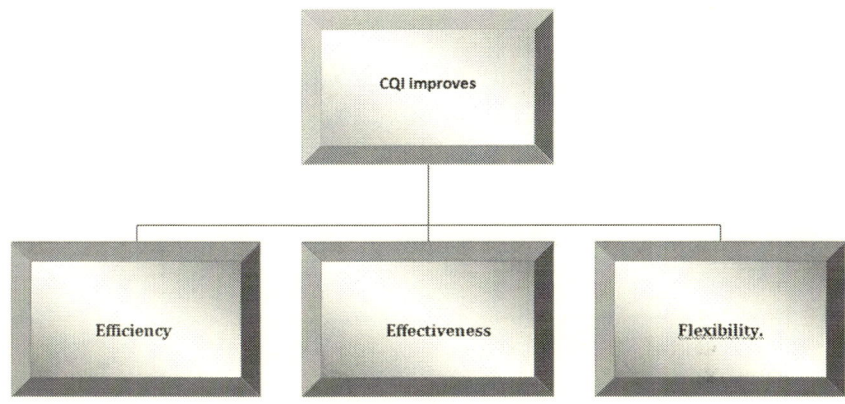

Figure: Role of CQI

While *kaizen* (at Toyota) usually delivers small improvements, the culture of continual aligned small improvements and standardization yields large results in the form of compound productivity improvement. CQI involves improving standardized activities and processes by eliminating waste (*muda*). The core principles of CQI are described below.

- It creates an opportunity for self-reflection on the processes as well as promotion of effective feedback mechanisms.
- It facilitates the identification, reduction, and elimination of suboptimal processes (waste and inefficiency).
- It is not a fire-brigade approach but rather an implementation of small and continuous changes (evolution) that bring about significant improvement in the process and, by extension, the service delivered (small continual steps rather than giant leaps) and profitability to the business.

Key Features of CQI

- Improvements are based on many small but continual changes rather than the radical changes that might arise from quality improvement suggestions, findings from customer satisfaction surveys and brainstorming by the research and development team.
- Implementation of small quality improvement suggestions and ideas come from the workers who are involved daily in the process. Changes tend to be simple suggestions for making things better and the process smoother. They are unlikely to be radically different from the normal process, and thus they tend to be easier to implement.
- Changes tend not to be capital-intensive. They are usually small improvements that involve doing things differently from the usual.
- These small improvements are usually staff-driven (those involved in the process). The ideas come from the talents of the existing workforce rather than from consultants or equipment which can be very expensive to implement.
- All employees should continually be seeking ways to improve their own performance.
- CQI gives staff a sense of belonging. It encourages the workforce to take responsibility and ownership for their work and the process, and it can potentially help in team building and increased productivity and job satisfaction and motivation for staff.
- It is all about increasing the value of improving the service delivery to the customer (effectiveness) and a measure as to what extent the introduction of flexibility in the process can help meet the changing needs of customers.

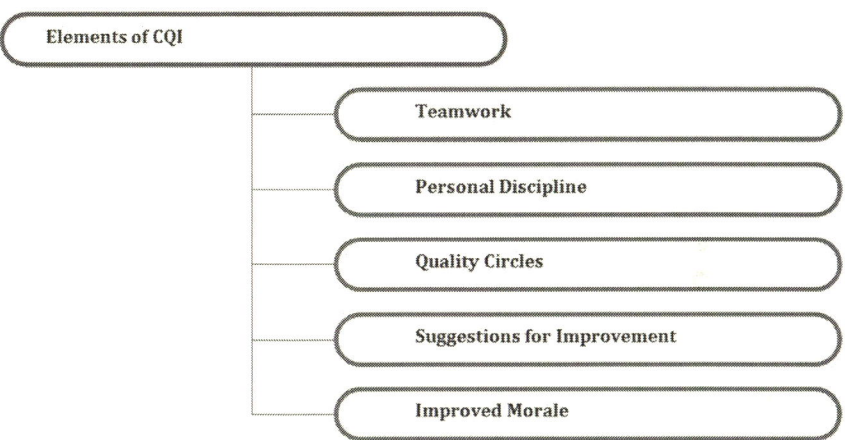

Figure: Elements of CQI

The Toyota approach to CQI involves the identification of any abnormality, identifying the root causes, and arriving at corrective and preventive measures to remove the root causes. The cycle of *kaizen* activity involves; plan, do, check, and act (PDCA cycle). The cycle is defined below.

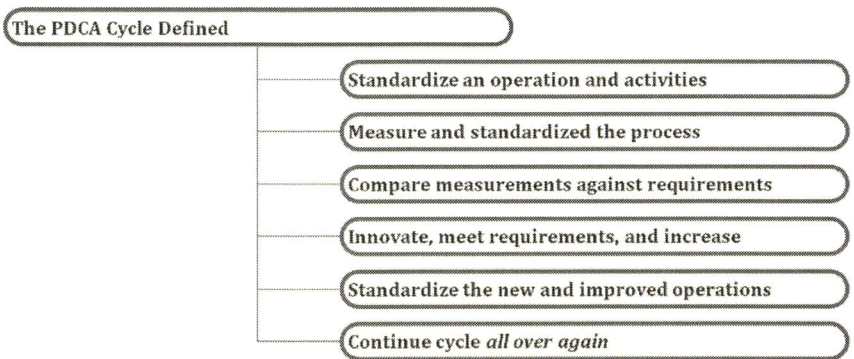

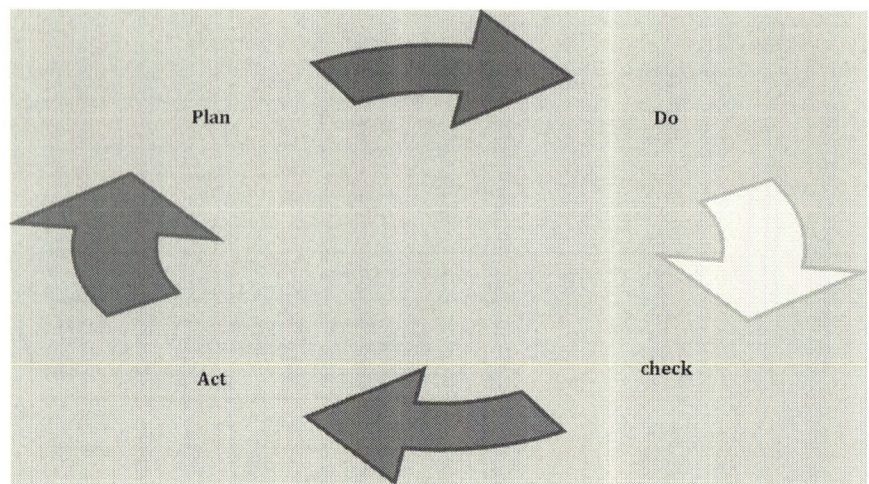

Figure: PDCA Cycle

IMPLEMENTING CQI

The successful implementation of CQI requires:

- The involvement of all workers involved in the process from management to the least subordinate staff
- Adequate training and competency testing of all staff involved in the process
- It requires a concerted effort of identifying problems and doing a root-cause analysis of the problems rather than dealing with the symptoms.
- Effort must be made to distinguish between symptom and ailment so that efforts are concentrated on solving the root causes of the problem and putting in place an improved process to prevent the recurrence of the root causes.

WHAT IS CONTINUOUS QUALITY IMPROVEMENT (CQI?)

Continuous Quality Improvement (CQI) is a theory-based management system that looks critically at processes and determines if processes meet outcomes (are fit for purpose or are good enough). It accomplishes the following:

- Builds a culture of proactive change (a desire to do things differently to achieve a different outcome from the usual)
- Renders a continually improving and measurable customer-focused service
- Involves the identification of a process, generating tools to measure what we do and how many mistakes we make, identifying root causes and arriving at corrective and preventive actions to eliminate the root cause and improve service delivery
- Offers shared success by all those involved in process change and the resultant improved service delivery to customers, improved profit to the organization, better staff remuneration, and improved productivity of staff
- Deliberately searches for common causes of variation in production (goods or services)
- Brings change that is based on evidence (accurate and data driven)
- Thrives on the process and customer satisfaction surveys (customer feedbacks)
- Although it's not a quick fix, it involves building a proactive culture of long-term approaches of implementing small but continuous changes to improve the production process and improve service delivery and customer satisfaction

KEY ELEMENTS OF CQI

- CQI requires accountability by all involved at different levels of the production process (goods or services).
- CQI is driven by a good management team and subordinate workforce. Management makes policy changes but requires the cooperation of the subordinate staff to drive the process and arrive at the desirable result required by management.
- CQI requires team spirit; quality improvement suggestions come from positive inputs of all levels of staff and stakeholders involved in the process.
- CQI requires a continuous review of progress made, setting of new targets, and working from the present state and putting measures in place.

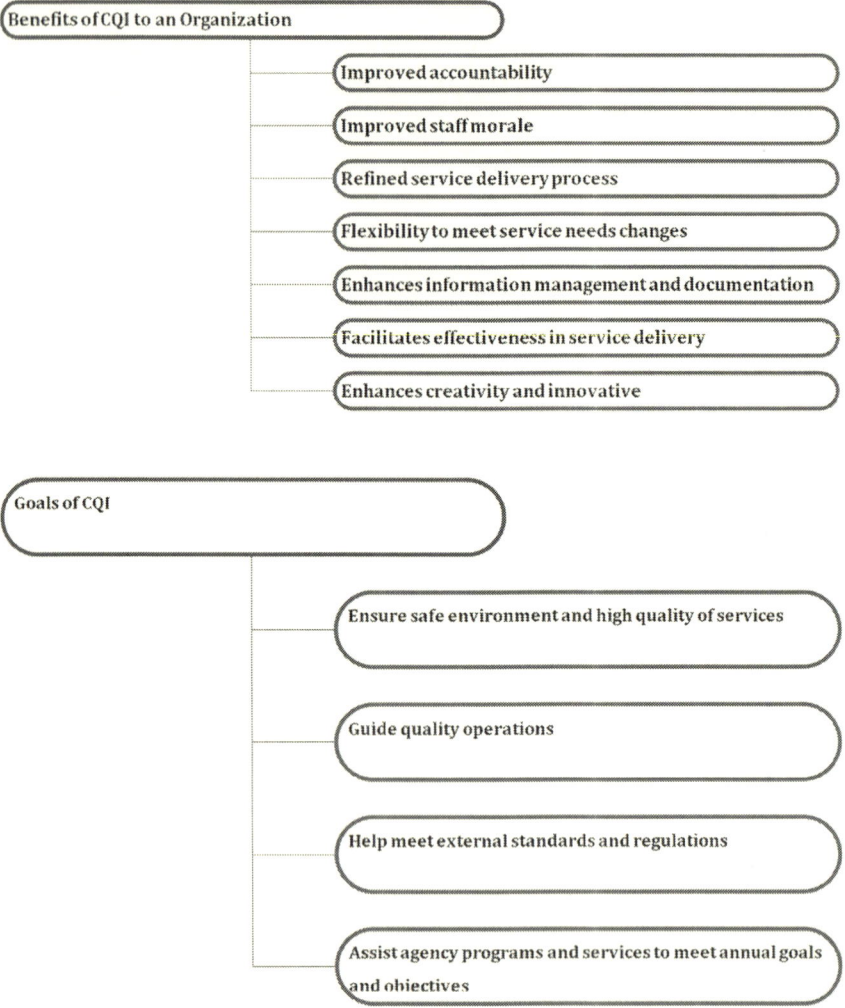

Figure: Goals of CQI

Individuals Involved in CQI

- Customers and clients (from results of customer satisfaction surveys and complaints)
- Quality improvement suggestions from employees, volunteers, and consultants
- Useful advice from members of advisory boards
- Feedback from consumer advocates

- Findings from rapid improvement events (RIE) carried out in the department

COMPOSITION OF QUALITY IMPROVEMENT TEAMS

Quality improvement teams should ideally include staff members from all levels and should include representatives from all stages of the process. Customer representatives and community stakeholders should also be included.

CQI TEAMS

- The CQI team should be led by a quality manager. His responsibility should be to head quality improvement meetings, to champion the Continuous Quality Improvement process, and to coordinate input and feedback to staff.
- There should be a secretary, whose responsibility it is to schedule meetings, book venues, and take detailed meeting minutes.
- Other members should cut across all units involved in the process. They participate in review of issues referred to the Continuous Quality Improvement team and also provide feedback to peers, stakeholders, and consumers.

STEPS INVOLVED IN A CQI PROCESS

- Identify a need, issue, or problem and develop a problem statement.
- Define the current situation. Break down the process or problem into component manageable parts. Identify major (capital-intensive) and minor problem areas. Develop a target improvement goal.
- Do a root-cause analysis of the problem, identify the root causes and arrive at corrective actions needed.
- Draw up a step-by-step plan aimed at eliminating the root causes of the problem. The plan must contain:

  - specific actions to be taken (what is to be done);
  - identification of how it is to be done;

- why action is to be taken; identification of whose responsibility it is to carry out the task;
- and the time needed to carry out the task.

- Audit the process to confirm that the problem and its root causes have decreased or have been eliminated.
- Identify whether the target has been met and display results in graphic format (before and after the change) to show at a glance the effect the change has had on the process.

- Start over again and use the same process to solve the next problem.

CHAPTER 4

LABORATORY QUALITY AUDITS

Sops are being followed
↘
↗ materials required to get work done are in place.
↘ statutory requirements in place.

A quality audit is a systematic, independent, and documented process of evaluating selected elements of a quality system. It is a systematic examination of a quality system. It is carried out either by an internal or external quality auditor or an audit team. It is an important part of an organization's quality management system and a key element in the ISO quality system standard, ISO 9001 and 15189. It is a requirement of most accreditation bodies (CPA, MHRA, and MLSCN). Audits are an essential management tool used for verifying that standard operating procedures are being followed, that materials required to get work done are in place, and that statutory requirements for carrying out a process are in place. They assess how successfully processes have been implemented and judge the effectiveness of achieving any defined target levels in order to provide evidence concerning the reduction and elimination of problems and waste. Audit should report any non-conformances identified. The root causes of the non-conformances should be identified and corrective actions should be determined and implemented. The process should be audited again at a set time in the future to ensure that the identified root causes have indeed been eliminated.

Audits should also highlight areas of good practice (praise). This allows other departments to learn from those areas of good practice, while the audited department amends their problematic practices. The audit is one way of building a culture of proactive continuous improvement. Quality audits are typically performed at pre-defined time intervals and ensure that the institution has clearly defined internal system monitoring procedures linked to effective action. This can help determine if the organization complies with the defined quality system processes and can involve procedural or results-based assessment criteria. Audits ensure that systems being implemented are effective and are being complied with. Regular audits are essential to sustain or improve a quality system. They verify that non-compliance notes raised against identified shortfalls are being addressed and will be reviewed in subsequent audits.

There are three types of audits:

- The *horizontal audit* involves the assessment of one element of the quality system.
- The *examination audit* involves a process whereby the assessor watches a test being performed to ascertain if the Standard Operating Procedure (SOP) is being followed. It is used to confirm competence of the staff and level of training.
- The *vertical audit* involves a process whereby a sample is tracked from receipt to the issue or result.

Quality audits re-emphasize the following:

- The importance of proper record-keeping and documentation
- The need to work to defined standards and procedures
- The importance of effective and appropriate storage and monitoring of temperature-dependent reagents.
- The need for proactive maintenance of equipment
- The need to develop a culture of continuous improvement
- The need for an enabling and safe laboratory environment
- The need for high morale among staff
- The need to investigate all incidents, accidents and near misses
- The need for competencies and appraisals of staff
- The need for good laboratory practice
- The need for effective housekeeping in the laboratory

Figure: Examples of horizontal audits (audits of an element of the process)

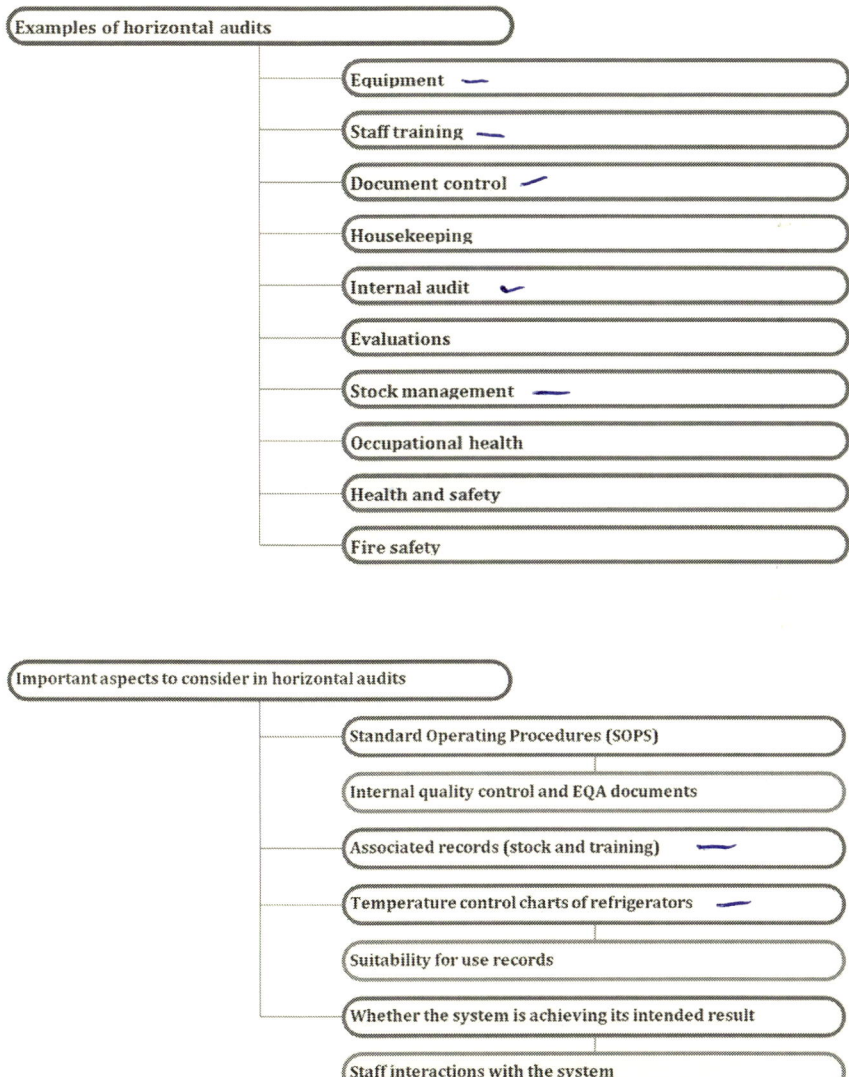

Vertical audits cuts across the entire process from sample collection to results availability to requesting clinicians. Vertical audits involve:

- Storage of reagents
- Health and safety issues
- Staff training
- Infection control

- Competences
- Equipment maintenance
- Internal and external quality assessments
- Premises
- Corrective actions
- Pre, examination and post examination
- Evidence that staff members who performed specific tasks were trained to do so. *Competency logs*
- Whether equipment that was used was suitable for use (clean, monitored, calibrated and maintained).
- Whether reagents that were used were suitable for use (in date, correctly stored).
- Infection control, manual handling, fire safety and health and safety issues. — *Mandatory training* ~

IMPORTANCE OF QUALITY AUDITS

- Quality audits can provide a mechanism for improvements by generating evidence-based data to monitor quality improvements.
- By carrying out regular and objective audits and implementing corrective and preventive action
- By building a culture of continual improvement.
- The only thing that adds value from the customers perspectives is the transformation of raw material into something that meets customer's requirement.

PERFORMING A QUALITY AUDIT

Performing an effective audit requires the following steps:

- Preparation of a checklist.
- The better the checklist is, the easier and more standardised audits become.
- A checklist prepared for one audit may be updated and used for repeat audits of the same topic.
- Organise a pre-audit meeting.

- Consult relevant SOPs since you will need to ensure staff members are compliant to the SOP.
- Draw up quality improvement notes arising from the audit to facilitate a continually improving process.
- Organize a post audit meeting to discuss non-compliances and quality improvement issues arising.
- Implement suggested change.
- Set a date for a post implementation audit to justify that the root causes initially identified has been eliminated and to ensure that implemented change has not introduced new bureaucracies into the process.

EXAMPLES OF NON-COMPLIANCES

- Someone is doing a routine test for which there is no SOP.
- Equipment temperature monitoring forms are filled in haphazardly.
- Temperature reading has regularly gone out of set limits and there is no evidence of action taken.
- A diagnostic kit in the refrigerator is beyond its expiry date.
- There is a bottle of clear liquid on the bench with no label on. A member of staff says it is only water.
- A diagnostic kit in the refrigerator is beyond its expiry date.
- The training record of a junior member of staff has not been filled in for some time.
- Reagents being used for analysis of patient's sample have gone out of date.
- A patient has recently reacted to a red cell transfusion and there is no evidence that it was investigated.
- Life dependent coagulation drug (Octaplex and Novo 7) has run out of stock for a week and it was not detected by staff.
- A staff whose is not occupational health compliant (has not be vaccinated against HBV) is seen handling potentially infectious samples (screening samples for HBV).
- Staff seen attending to a spill (blood sample) without protective equipments (hand gloves and lab coat).
- Staff not manual handling compliant (found carrying heavy equipment without appropriate aid (trolley)

- Lunch for a staff in the laboratory was found in the refrigerator used for storing reagents.
- There is no evidence of training of internal auditors.
- The internal quality control used for a test run was out of limits and there is no evidence that any action was taken.

NON-CONFORMANCE NOTES

Non-compliance notes (NCNs) are used to report any deficiencies found during an audit. The purpose of the non-compliance notes is to:

- Convey findings in a clear and accurate manner to the audited (what was wrong and what to do next).
- To advise the next auditor on what you have found in a previous audit so that they can follow it up.
- To present a record that can be re-assessed at a later date during management review.
- To enable auditee to determine root cause, development of remedial, corrective and prevention action to eliminate root causes.

DEALING WITH NON CONFORMANCES

- What remedial action (Quick fix) you would take.
- Consider the further corrective action to eliminate root causes.
- Implement corrective action.
- Audit the process to ensure that root cause have been eliminated.
- Continuously solving root problems drives organizational learning and improvement.
- Sophisticated technique for solving problems is to: ask "why?" this problem objectively five times. Normally at the end of the 5th way, you have gotten to the root cause of the problem.

PERFORMING A QUALITY AUDIT

1. Preparation of a checklist.
2. The better the checklist is, the easier and more standardised audits become.
3. A checklist prepared for one audit may be updated and used for repeat audits of the same topic.
4. Organise a pre-audit meeting.
5. Consult relevant SOPs since you will need to ensure staff members are compliant to the SOP.
6. Draw up quality improvement notes arising from the audit to facilitate a continually improving process.
7. Organize a post audit meeting to discuss non-compliances & quality improvement issues arising.
8. Implement suggested change.

EXAMPLE OF AN AUDIT CHECK LIST

Audit type/number and details (Vertical audit/AUD 100: General duties in transfusion)/Completed by/completion date: Dr Osaro/3/11/2011		
Number	**Audit question**	**Response**
1.	Identify test, processes, procedure being audited.	
2.	Are there SOP available for sample examination processes?	
3.	Have procedures been validated for use prior to introduction. List document examined	
4.	Are SOP current, signed and dated	
5.	Are SOP be followed by staff performing task	
6.	Is there evidence of document control in place? State last revision date	
7.	Are there COSHH (control of substances hazardous to health) risk and general assessment s available for all tasks?	

8.	Are there procedure in place for reporting and monitoring of accidents and incidents	
9.	Are staff responsible clearly identified and are there evidence of training and education.	
10.	Are there procedures for sample receipt, transport and booking in?	
11.	What is the specimen number of the sample being audited? Is there sufficient information to uniquely identify patient. Is there evidence of date and time of sample collection? Does request form contain required clinical information?	
12.	Is there process in place for handling urgent sample? Is there criteria for rejection of sample	
13.	Is there record available for each stage of the process such that there is complete audit trail of staff, equipment reagents and quality control procedures involved? List document examined?	
14.	Is there evidence that equipment used is routinely maintained, daily checks done and quality controlled? List equipment checked	
15.	Is the lab enrolled into and EQA. Are EQA report reviewed? Indicate scheme	
16.	Does lab report contain time and date of report, results and reason if no examination done. Are there interpretive comments and are abnormal results highlighted	
17.	Does lab has turnaround time for test/process being audited. Is set turnaround time feasible and are target being met	

EXAMPLES OF NON-CONFORMANCES THAT CAN BE INCLUDED ON THE NON-CONFORMANCE NOTE

- The internal quality control used for a test run was out of limits and there is no evidence that any action was taken.
- Purpose is to convey findings in a clear and accurate manner to the auditee (what was wrong and what to do next)
- Fridges used for storage of temperature dependent reagents have gone outside ambient temperature several and there is no remedial action taken.
- Incidents, near misses and complaint are not investigated
- Staff satisfaction surveys are not being done
- Staff performing task have not been trained or competency tested
- There are no standard work for task being performed
- The transfusion lab is not registered for any EQA scheme
- There are no policy in place for infection control, manual handling and there are no personal protective equipment for staff
- Staff occupational health-related vaccination is not up to date.
- Someone is doing a routine test for which there is no SOP.
- There is a bottle of clear liquid on the bench with no label on. A member of staff says it is only water.

AIM OF NON-CONFORMANCE NOTES

1. To advise the next auditor what you have found so that they can follow it up.
2. To present a record that can be re-assessed at a later date during management review.
3. To enable auditee to determine root cause, determine remedial, corrective and prevention action to eliminate root causes.
4. Non-compliance notes (NCNs) are used to report any deficiencies found during an audit.

DEALING WITH NON CONFORMANCES

1. What remedial action (Quick fix) you would take.
2. Consider the further corrective action to eliminate root causes.
3. Implement corrective action.
4. Audit the process to ensure that root cause have been eliminated.
5. Continuously solving root problems drives organizational learning and improvement.
6. Sophisticated technique for solving problems is to : ask "why?" objectively five times.

PERFORMING 6 S AUDITS

The 6 S is a systematic way of creating of improving the productivity in a laboratory by identifying and reducing waste. It is a way of creating a safe, clean, tidy, orderly, uncluttered and more productive (enabling) environment and sustaining it that way. It is a way of having an organized work place. Even small improvements achieved by implementing 6S can have a very positive impact on overall productivity. 6S is derived from 5S the method of workplace organization and visual controls made popular by Hiroyuki Hirano (1990). The origin of 5S seems rooted in the works of two American pioneers; Frederick W. Taylor's *Scientific Management* (1911) and Henry Ford (1922). The five S's refer to five Japanese words:

TABLE: JAPANESE MEANING OF THE 5S'S

Japanese word	English Meaning
Seiri	Separation of needed and unneeded materials and removal of the unneeded.
Seiton	Neatly arranging and identifying needed materials for ease of use and to minimize time wasted looking for or getting it.
Seiso	To conduct a cleanup campaign
Seiketsu	Means to do (seiri, seiton, and seiso) at frequent intervals
Shitsuke	Means to form the habit (build a culture) of always following the first four Ss.

IMPORTANCE OF 6S AUDIT

- Cluttered and untidy work benches
- Stacks of files
- A team having to spend a great deal of time searching for the tools and resources that they need to get their jobs done.
- Disorganization (wastes time and reduces productivity and morale).
- It introduces orderliness, eliminating unneeded materials
- Establishing self-discipline and enhances effective time management.

WHY PERFORM 6S AUDIT

- Cluttered, untidy and dirty work areas are unsafe and staff waste valuable time searching for needed material and information.
- It is not about routine cleaning, it is rather putting a sustainable system in place to ensure safe, waste free, clean and more productive work places. Routine cleaning without put a sustainable process and conditions in place will not yield the desired result. Application of 6S enables the identification and removal of waste form the value stream processes. The pillars of 6S include:

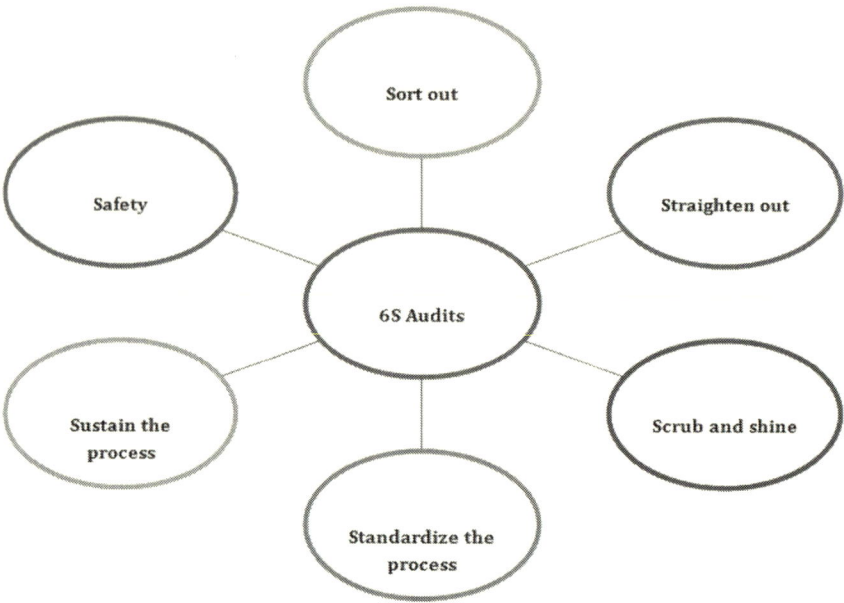

Figure: 6 pillars of 6 S

The following pillars (sort out, straightening out, shine and safety) helps to create a clean safe and efficient workplace) while the standardize and sustain are necessary to ensure that the culture is maintained and that the conditions do not fall back to previous state.

EXPLANATION OF THE 6 PILLARS OF 6S

Sort out: It involves distinguishing between what is needed and not needed and to remove the latter. It Involves remove materials (equipment, reagents, spares, files) that are not needed. The work area in the laboratory should only contain items required to perform task in the laboratory. Every other items not required to perform task or that belong to other work areas are clutter and should be removed from the work area. During 6S audit, auditors walk through the work areas and identify any material that does not belong to the area are tagged and removed to the red tag area for sorting (disposal of if still functional and usable in another area should be allocated to other areas where it is requires in the organization).

Straighten out: Straightening out means finding a home for everything and ensure that everything in its place. It involves organising what is needed. Every equipment and items used in the laboratory should be allocated a space where they sit or are located and within reach to perform the required task performed in that work area and to allow for a smooth and unhindered flow and un-necessary travel to perform task. It involves the use of visual management to ensure orderliness in the work area. It facilitates the removal of waste associated with non-value added motion and transportation of material and equipment.

Scrub or shine: Clean up the workplace and put a process in place to keep it consistently clean. It is an expectation under the principle of good laboratory practice that work benches and the environment in the laboratory are kept clean and left uncluttered. Daily cleaning and disinfection of work benches is evidence of good housekeeping. Doing it daily help build a culture of proactive (preventive) cleanliness. As benches are cleaned daily, you are looking for clutter and removing them.

Standardize: Maintain and monitor adherence to the first three Ss (sort out, straighten and standardize). Work done in the laboratory should be process driven. The roles and responsibilities of all staff involved in the process must be identified. There must be a validated system (standard operating procedures) in place to ensure that the process is performed in the same correct way by all staff involved in the task and that there is no room for user-related variation. The task required and its status should be clearly set out and visual.

Sustain: Follow the rules to keep the workplace 6S-right.Build a culture aimed at maintaining the standard already achieved. Sustain involves putting a system in place to ensure that that the standard work is being followed and that staff are keeping up to the standard of work already achieved. It means ensuring that the quality of work done continually improve. This is achieved by carrying out regular audits to maintain and improve on standards already achieved.

Safety: Eliminate hazards and ensure that work environment are safety compliant and that staff are safety conscious. It is a general expectation under the principle of GLP that work areas in the laboratory is safe, clean and tidy (for staff, service users and the environment). Effort should be made to regularly identify and prevent unsafe conditions in the laboratory. It is part of the laboratory responsibility that their activity does not put the environment at risk for the vulnerable public.

PERFORMING A 6S AUDIT

- A 6S audit should ideally be performed by a minimum of 2 members of staff (one from the immediate work area and one from another area).
- The laboratory should have an audit sheet that contains the audit check list.
- The 6S auditors take a good look around the work area and agree for each audit question if the expected condition has been met (Yes) or not (No).
- Add up all the yes answers in which audit condition has been met and work out the % compliance at the end of the sheet.
- If the conditions have not been met for any item on the audit check list, it may be worthwhile to take a photograph of the problem as a way of putting in perspective what the present state is.
- Discuss the outcome of the non-compliance in the staff meeting
- Carry out a root cause analysis (5 whys) or use the cause and effect (fish bone diagram) to arrive at the root causes and identify immediate remedial actions, preventive and corrective actions to remove the root causes.

WASTE FROM 6 S PERSPECTIVE

- Drafts of materials stacked on each other
- Edited copy on the floor around my desk
- Project reference materials stacked up on office table
- Obsolete equipment left lying in the laboratory
- Non-value added search, travel, transporting materials, inventory, and hazards.
- Cluttered work benches
- Un-attended sample spillage
- Daily temperature log not up to date
- Items to achieve a task on the bench not available in the designated home position.
- Daily process board not updated
- Suboptimal waste segregation. Clinical waste found among clean waste. Sharps bins found overfilled.
- Confidential waste containing patient's details found in the clean waste bin.
- Centrifugation being carried out without the caps in place
- Laboratory staff was found attending to sample spillage without necessary protective equipment.

Nelson Biomedical Limited 6S Audit Check List (Worksheet)				
Date:			Work area:	
S/no	Audit question/item		Yes	No
Sorting out(Removal of items not required)				
1.	Has any defective and un-needed items or equipment (clutter) been identified and removed from the work area.			
2.	Are there items in the audited work area that belong to other work area?			
3.	Are there items required to carry out the task in the work area missing or in the wrong places.			
Straighten out (Set materials in order to allow for free flow of process)				

4.	Are all equipments, storage areas, reagent storage fridges and freezers clearly marked in their marked areas		
5.	Is the layout of work area clearly marked and organized to facilitate flow		
6.	Are process control boards updated		
7.	Are there evidence of effective stock control (Are Kanban signals available and being used), are there out of date reagents in reagent storage fridges and freezers.		
Scrub or Clean			
8.	Are floors, work benches, equipment, and storage areas clean and tidy? Is there evidence to show that they are being done regularly as stipulated in the standard work?		
9.	Are there sign of effective management and segregation of waste? Check that sharps containers are not overfull, that confidential waste is not found with clinical waste, that clinical waste are not put with non-contaminated waste and that that waste are being emptied regularly.		
Standardise (Required Task)			
10.	Are there standards work available for task		
11.	Are standard work up-to-date		
12.	Are checklist for equipment available and up-to-date		
13.	Are there signs of adequate visual management (Does visual management board show the task expected and their status).		
Sustain (Maintain the standard already achieved)			
14.	Are standard work up-to-date and being complied with		
15.	Are there any uncontrolled and hand written document in use		
16.	Are process control boards up-to-date		

Safety			
17	Are required safety information clearly sign posted (fire exit, health and safety notices).		
18	Safety and PAT testing stickers are in place on analyzers and other appliances and up to date.		
19	Are protected equipment being appropriately used		
20	Are there adequate materials for dealing with spills		
21	Are staff up-to-date with their protective vaccination		
22	Are inflammable chemical box available and sign posted		
23	Is work environment safety compliant (lightening, air quality, temperature).		
24	Are risk assessment of the workplace regularly done		
Calculation: % Compliance = number of compliance (yes)/Total number of audit questions x 100.			

DEALING WITH NON-COMPLIANCES FROM THE 6S AUDIT

All non-compliances from a 6 S audit must have a root cause analysis carrying out with the hope of arriving at immediate remedial action to obviate the immediate effect of the root cause as well as arriving at corrective action to eliminate the root causes. Findings from the audit and root cause analysis will need to be put on a defect control and improvement form (an action plan of action that needs to be implemented to eliminate the root cause, preventive action to be put in place to prevent a future re-occurrence, whose responsibility it is to implement the action, when the action is to be implemented, any feedback on implementation and the status of implementation (defect identified, root causes determined, action assigned, problem resolved).

Nelson Biomedical Limited 6S Defect management and improvement form								
S/No	Date	Area and Non-compliance observed	Root cause	Corrective action to eliminate root cause	Who by	When by	Feedback	Status
1.	12/2/08							
2.	13/3/09							

Issue Resolved   Non-compliance observed

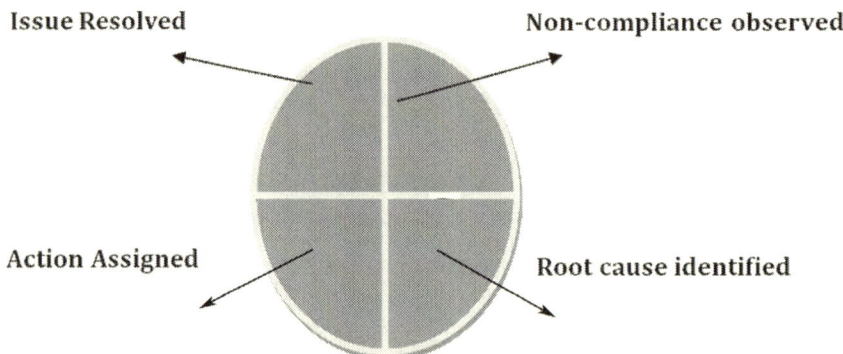

Action Assigned   Root cause identified

Figure: Status of action from 6S Audit

MAKE IMPROVEMENTS AND MEASURING RESULTS

Once the 6S audit has been completed, all the non-compliances identified, root cause analysis carried out to determine root causes, and corrective actions arrived at, the team takes each goal, looks at the observations associated with it, and generates ideas to eliminate the waste and improve workplace organization and the display of important information. For example, the team may propose removing unnecessary items in the work area (Sort), arranging necessary items in an orderly manner that places them nearest to their points of use (Stabilize), replacement of health and safety signs, replacement of broken chairs (Shine and Safety); and write job aids to remind workers of tasks to do to keep the workplace environment enabling (Sustain).It is vital to credit the workers in the work area for any good practices, note the non-compliances observed and finally emphasize the importance of sustaining the event's gains.

AUDITS REPORT

A quality audit has been defined as a systematic, independent and documented process for obtaining evidence and evaluating objectively the extent to which audit criteria are fulfilled (ISO 9001: 2000). Audit criteria include set of policies, procedures or requirements used as a reference.

WHY CONDUCT AN AUDIT?

The purpose of an audit is to establish whether all activities that affect quality (as defined by audit criteria) are carried out correctly. This is necessary to maintain existing quality systems. It also enables managers to have a better understanding of the day to day work of their department and to give them the opportunity to make management decisions based on information obtained from the process.

TYPES OF AUDITS:

Internal audit process involves three different types of audits:

- Horizontal audit:—Involves the assessment of one element of the quality system for example; equipment maintenance, Staff training, Document control, Housekeeping, Internal audit and Evaluations. By this type of audit, individual elements of the quality system are examined to make sure they are functioning properly.
- Examination audit:—Involves a process whereby the assessor watches a test being performed, to ascertain whether or not an SOP is being followed. It is an opportunity to find out the competence of the staff and level of training needed or received for the task being performed.
- Vertical audit:—Involves a process whereby a sample is tracked from receipt to the issue of result (or the other way round), checking each step associated with processing of the sample. A vertical audit cuts across cuts across different phases within a system and shows how the processes are interlinked and function as a whole.

In conducting an internal audit, relevant information is obtained by checking records, work sheets, and procedures relevant to the audit criteria.

EXAMPLE OF A HORIZONTAL AUDIT (AUDIT OF THE SYSMEX HAEMATOLOGY ANALYZER)

Audit Check list	Records and Procedures examined	Findings	Remarks
Is equipment appropriate for purpose used?	Laboratory daily work load is on the average 1000 samples/day	Analyzer throughput is 150 test/hr. Analyzer is fit for purpose	Compliant
Is there a procedure for the procurement and management of equipment? Those procedures include: Assessment & justification, Selection, Acceptance, Training, Maintenance/service & repair, Decontamination, Record of equipment failure & subsequent corrective action, Planned replacement & disposal, Adverse incident & vigilance reporting.	Procurement documents and user operational manual	Yes	Compliant
Is there an Operator/Service manual for the equipment?	There is operator service manual	Yes	Compliant
Is there record for equipment down time?	Equipment down time log examined	Yes	Compliant

Are there associated evidence that staff members who perform specific analyzer-associated task are adequately trained	Departmental training log examined.	Yes	Compliant
Is there evidence of routine equipment maintenance?	Analyzer maintenance log examined.	Yes	Compliant
Is daily checks performed on equipment? Daily maintenance, daily QC run and weekly maintenance	Daily, weekly maintenance log and QC log examined	Yes	Compliant
Is there an operational, up-to-date SOP in use for this analyzer?	Analyzer SOP Observed and found up to date.	Yes	Compliant
Is there evidence of temperature measurement of refrigerator for storing temperature-sensitive reagents/QC materials	Daily temperature log observed	Fridge temperature was suboptimal severally and no corrective action was taken	Non-compliance to Standard D (equipment information systems and materials) sub standard D3 (Management of reagents, calibrations and quality control).
Is there appropriate and adequate storage of bulk reagent for use on this analyzer?	Departmental store examined	Yes	Compliant

Are the associated Health and safety issues as well as infection control issues with this analyzer adequately met	Health and safety associated issues are adequately taken care of as evidenced in Sterilization SOP and log.	Yes	Compliant
Is there an up to date procedure for dealing with analyzer-related flags.	SOP exist for dealing with analyzer-related flags	Yes	Compliant
Does a standard work exist for dealing with disposal of analyzer-related waste materials?	Yes	Yes	Compliant
Is there evidence of Inventory control of reagents used on analyzer	Inventory control log examined	Yes.	Compliant
Is there a standard work for technical validation of results on analyzer	SOP exist	Yes	Compliant
Is there documentation on analyzer down time	Log exist	Analyzer seems fit for purpose indeed.	Compliant

HORIZONTAL AUDIT-MAIN FINDINGS:

The audit helped to re-emphasize:

- The importance of proper record keeping and documentation
- The need to work to defined standards
- The importance for effective and appropriate storage and monitoring of temperature-dependent reagents.

An important lesson learnt was that good maintenance culture can sustain the life of equipment. Equipment maintenance records checked revealed good maintenance culture. However issues regarding health and safety, infection control, management of reagents (storage) and reporting of laboratory results raised from this audit constitute non-compliances to CPA standards C, D and G. Corrective measures to these non-compliances need to be addressed soonest.

VERTICAL AUDIT OF SAMPLE (REF: T46740B) FROM SAMPLE RECEPTION TO RESULT DELIVERY.

Sample reception

Audit Check list	Records/Methods/Procedures checked	
Sample Received labelled and booked onto LMIS:		
Is the a standard work in place for this activity	Sample reception SOP examined	Yes up to date and current
Are staff members who performed task appropriately trained	Training records	Yes
Are staff members who performed appropriately trained on infection control/ health and safety to include dealing with spillages and remedial action to take following accidental exposure to body fluids	SOP on dealing with spillages and Discussion with staff	Staff did not seem to know what the procedure is for dealing with accidental exposure to body fluids
Is there an operational work schedule and load levelling and sequencing.	Work schedule observed	Yes

Is a procedure available for dealing with stranger samples	SOP for dealing with stranger samples examined	Yes
Is there adequate endowment human and materials to facilitate performance of task (materials and equipment)	Duty roster and stocking log endowment checked	Yes

SAMPLE LOADED ON THE SORTING ANALYZER:

Audit Check list	Records / Procedures checked	Audit Finding (Yes/No)	Remarks
Is there a standard work on use of the OLA	SOP examined	Yes	Compliant
Is there evidence of regular daily and weekly maintenance on OLA	Maintenance log examined	Yes	Compliant
Are the health and safety issues associated with analyzer strictly adhered to?	Visual observation on running of the OLA	The protective glass which is supposed to be down was observed up all day. Staff operating the	

		OLA did not seem to appreciate the health and safety risk associated with running the OLA without the protective glass door being in position as prescribed by the manufacturers	Non compliance to standard C (Premises and environment) Sub standard C5 (Health and safety).
Is there a designated and appropriately trained staff to perform task	Training records examined	Yes	Compliant
Is there a procedure in place decontamination following spillages	No SOP exists for decontamination of the OLA following spillage of samples.	No SOP for dealing with spillage on the OLA	Non compliance to CPA standard C (Premises and environment) Sub standard C5 (Health and safety).
Is there a maintenance log and documentation on down time of the Olympus OLA sample sorter	Fault documentation log examined	Yes	Compliant

Sample Loaded and Analyzed on Analyzer

Audit Check list	Records / Procedures checked	Audit Finding	Remarks
Is there an operational standard procedure for use for this analyzer?	SOP current and operational	Yes	Compliant
Is daily checks performed on equipment? • Daily Maintenance • Weekly maintenance	Maintenance Log	Yes	Compliant
Is there a procedure for internal quality control of test?	QC log on analyzer examined	Results consistently within manufacturer set limits.	Compliant
Is there evidence that laboratory participate in EQA/ are report discussed in departmental meetings	EQA report observed	Yes results discussed at departmental meetings	Compliant
Is there appropriate and adequate storage facility for bulk reagents for use on this analyzer	Departmental store examined	Yes	Compliant

Is there appropriate and adequate storage facility for temperature-dependent reagents/QC materials for use on this analyzer	Daily temperature log observed	Fridge temperature is higher on several occasions than manufacturer's defined storage temperature	Non-compliance to Standard D (equipment information systems and materials) sub standard D3 (Management of reagents, calibrations and quality control).
Are the associated Health and safety issues as well as infection control issues with this analyzer adequately met?	Analyzer disinfection log examined	Yes	Compliant
Is there associated evidence that staff members who perform specific analyzer associated task are adequately trained and competency tested?	Departmental staff training log examined	Yes	Compliant
Is the analyzer achieving its intended results/fit or purpose	Daily work load log observed. On the average 1000 samples ran on analyzer daily	Yes	Compliant
Is there a maintenance log and records of analyzer down time?	Analyzer down time log examined	Yes	Compliant
Is there an Operator/Service manual for the equipment	Operator service manual seen	Yes	Compliant

Is there a procedure for the procurement and management of equipment? Those procedure include: Assessment & justification, selection, acceptance, training, maintenance, service & repair, planned replacement and disposal	Procurement documents all inclusive of relevant information	Yes	Compliant
Is there a procedure in place for Decontamination	SOP exist for sterilization of analyzer	Yes	Compliant
Are there procedures for handling urgent work?	SOP exist for running emergency samples	Yes	Compliant
Are there procedures for sample referrals & are records kept for such samples?	Records exist of LIMS on samples referred, referral centre to which sample was referred and expected date results is expected.	Yes	Compliant

TECHNICAL VALIDATION OF RESULT ON ANALYZER

Audit Check list	Records /Procedures checked	Audit Finding	Remarks
Is there a procedure in place for attending to analyzer flags	SOP exist	Yes	Compliant
Is there any documentation for dealing with analytical problems associated with analyzer	Sop exist	Yes	Compliant
Is there a procedure in place for dealing with requesting further testing based on results from analyzer	SOP exist on factor that should trigger the request for further testing (blood films, optical platelet count, NRBC and reticulocyte count)	Yes	Compliant

Result validated on LMIS and Result reported and dispatched to requesting clinician

Audit Check list	Records /Procedures checked	Audit Finding	Remarks
Are there procedure for transcription of result between worksheets and entry into LMIS?	Discussion with staff. Verbal instruction said to exist on need for a second staff to check result transcribed onto the LIMS before validation. No standard work is available for performing this task.	No	Non-compliance to standard G (Post examination processes) and sub section G1 (Reporting results)
Is there a procedure place for telephoning results?	Sop exist	Yes	Compliant
Is there procedure for authorizing results before release?	SOP exist	Yes	Compliant
Is there evidence of monitoring of turnaround times?	Turnaround time log examined	Yes	Compliant

VERTICAL AUDITS FINDINGS FROM THE PRE EXAMINATION, EXAMINATION AND POST EXAMINATION PHASES

Pre-examination phase:

*   SOP for dealing with management of accidental exposure to body fluid is not available. Staff did not seem to know what the procedure is for dealing with accidental exposure to body fluids. This constitutes non-compliance to standard C (Premises and environment) Sub standard C5 (Health and safety).
*   Recorded temperature on fridge used for storage of temperature dependent reagents (QC) used on analyzer is higher on several occasions than manufacturer's defined storage temperature. This constitutes non-compliance to Standard D (equipment information systems and materials) sub standard D3 (Management of reagents, calibrations and quality control).

Examination phase:

*   No SOP exists for decontamination of the OLA sample sorter following spillage of samples. Non-compliance to CPA standard C (Premises and environment) Sub standard C5 (Health and safety).

Post Analytical phase:

*   Verbal instruction said to exist on need for a second staff to check result transcribed from worksheet onto the LIMS before validation. No standard work is available for performing this task. This constitutes a Non-compliance to standard G (Post examination processes) and sub section G1 (Reporting results)

Conclusion:

Regular audits are essential to sustain or improve a quality system. Non-compliance notes raised against identified short falls are being addressed and will be reviewed in subsequent audits.

VERTICAL AND HORIZONTAL AUDIT ASSESSMENT FORM

Appendix 1:Non-compliance note

Item	Description	Sensitivity
RBH 01	Recorded temperature on fridge used for storage of temperature dependent reagent (QC) used on analyzer is higher on several occasions than manufacturer's defined storage temperature. This constitutes non-compliance to Standard D (equipment information systems and materials) sub standard D3 (Management of reagents, calibrations and quality control).	High
RBH 02	No SOP exists for decontamination of the OLA following spillage of samples. Non-compliance to standard C (Premises and environment) Sub standard C5 (Health and safety).	High
RBH 03	Verbal instruction said to exist on need for a second staff to check result transcribed from worksheet onto the LIMS before validation. No standard work is available for performing this task. This constitutes a Non-compliance to standard G (Post examination processes) and sub section G1 (Reporting results)	High
RBH 04	SOP for dealing with management of accidental exposure to body fluid is not available. Staff did not seem to know what the procedure is for dealing with accidental exposure to body fluids. This constitutes non-compliance to standard C (Premises and environment) Sub standard C5 (Health and safety).	High

NON-COMPLIANCE NOTE

Date: 25/5/09

Non-Compliance Details:

Recorded temperature on fridge used for storage of temperature sensitive reagents (QC) used on analyzer is higher on several occasions than manufacturer's defined storage temperature. This constitutes non-compliance to Standard D (equipment information systems and materials) sub standard D3 (Management of reagents, calibrations and quality control).

Auditor: OSARO   Fix by:25/8/09   Responsible Manager: COLE SMITH

Remedial Action-Evidence seen:

Replace fridge and effectively monitor fridge temperature to ensure that manufacturers defined storage conditions for temperature sensitive reagents are met.

Action Satisfactory/Effective: Date: 25/5/09
Satisfactory

Investigation details and further corrective action taken to eliminate root causes: A new fridge has been procured for the storage of temperature dependent reagents used on analyzer. A temperature logger has been connected to the fridge to ensure that daily temperature log is collected to ensure effective temperature management.

Root-Cause corrective action: Follow up audit on the storage condition of temperature-dependent reagents used on analyzer is scheduled for November 2009.

NON-COMPLIANCE NOTE

Date: 22/05/09/ RBH. 02

Non-Compliance Details:

No SOP exists for decontamination of the OLA following spillage of samples. Non-compliance to standard C (Premises and environment) Sub standard C5 (Health and safety).

Auditor: Dr Osaro   Fix by: 25/5/09   Responsible Manager: Dr Adias Teddy
Erhabor   Charles

Remedial Action-Evidence seen: Draw up standard work of the decontamination of the OLA sample sorter and train all staff performing task.

Action Satisfactory/Effective: Date: 25/5/09
Satisfactory

Investigation details and further corrective action taken to eliminate root causes: Standard work of the decontamination of the OLA sample sorter has been drawn and all staff performing task has been effectively trained.

Root Causes corrective action: Follow up audits of the operation of the OLA is scheduled for November 2009.

NON-COMPLIANCE NOTE

Non-Compliance Details:

Verbal instruction said to exist on need for a second staff to check result transcribed from worksheet onto the LIMS before validation. No standard work is available for performing this task. This constitutes a Non-compliance to CPA standard G (Post examination processes) and sub section G1 (Reporting results).

Auditor: Osaro Erhabor	Fix by: 25/5/09	Responsible Manager Dr Adias Teddy Charles

Remedial Action-Evidence seen: Draw up a standard operating procedure for transcription of results from work sheet into the LMIS and train staff undertaking task on SOP.

Action Satisfactory/Effective: Date: 25/5/09
Satisfactory

Root-Cause corrective action: Standard operating procedure for transcription of results from work sheet into the LMIS and training of staff undertaking task has been carried out. Progress on this issue to be reviewed at next audit scheduled for November 2009.

NON-COMPLIANCE NOTE

Non-Compliance Details: SOP for dealing with management of accidental exposure to body fluid is not available. Staff did not seem to know what the procedure is for dealing with accidental exposure to body fluids. This constitutes non-compliance to standard C (Premises and environment) Sub standard C5 (Health and safety).

Auditor: Dr Osaro Erhabor   Fix by: 25/5/09   Responsible Manager: Dr Adias Teddy Charles

Remedial Action: Draw up a standard operating procedure for management of accidental exposure to body fluids and train staff on remedial actions to take following accidental exposure to body fluid and other infective agents.

Action Satisfactory/Effective: Satisfactory   Date: 15/5/09

Root-Cause corrective action: Standard operating procedure for management of accidental exposure to body fluids and training of staff on remedial actions to take following accidental exposure to body fluid and other infective agents has been drawn up. The issue has been effectively handled by the laboratory manager. Progress on this issue to be reviewed at next audit scheduled for November 2009.

CHAPTER 5

INTRODUCTION TO LEAN AND SIX SIGMA PRINCIPLES AND APPLICATIONS IN THE LABORATORY

Lean is based on Toyota's philosophy that when you make lead time short and focus on keeping production line flexible, you get better quality, responsiveness, productivity, maximize utilization of staff, equipments and space. Lean is about speed and continuous removal of waste (muda).It is about sorting out, setting apart, shinning, standardizing, sustaining level of quality improvement and being safety conscious. It is the relationship between step and process. It is about eliminating non-value added elements from the process. It is not batching but shrinking sizes down to *create a one piece flow.* The ideal batch size in a leaned process is one. It also include a decreased distance that staff needs to travel to complete task. Lean can potentially improve turnaround times for laboratory results. About 70% of patient management decision is dependent on laboratory results. Improvements in the process in the laboratory can have a significant effect on patient waiting time in critical departments (Accident and Emergency, Intensive Care Unit and High Dependency Unit) and patient discharge. Lean principle implementation can potentially detect the bottlenecks and waste in the system enabling the process to run more efficiently.

WHAT CONSTITUTES WASTE FROM LEAN PERSPECTIVE?

*   Injuries (including damage to people like stress).
*   Inventory (stuff waiting to be worked, waiting list, and samples waiting to be analyzed).
*   Defects (Stuff that need fixing, samples that needs repeating)
*   Overproduction (unnecessary request and excess inventory).
*   Waiting (waiting for materials to arrive).
*   Motion (unnecessary human movement, having to walk up and down to obtain appropriate supplies and materials to achieve a given task).

- Transportation (moving stuff).
- Processing waste (task that does not add value to process e.g. continuing to care for patient in hospital when they could be discharged home)

KEY PRINCIPLES OF LEAN

- Value (what the customer perceives as value).For example what do you value when you have a hair cut (cost, time, surrounding, quality).
- Value stream (How we deliver value-centred service to our customers from start to finish).Three categories exist in our work; value added (activity that contribute directly to satisfying the needs of customers e.g. having an operation; non value added (activity that uses time or resources but does not contribute directly to satisfying customer need e.g. Waiting for the operation; essential but non value added (activity that does not add value but required in service delivery e.g. cleaning the theatre.

POSSIBLE BENEFITS OF LEAN IMPLEMENTATION IN THE LABORATORY

- Improved turnaround time
- Decreased patient waiting times
- Decreased distance travelled to achieve task
- Removal of non-value added work (removal of steps from the process that does not add value to the process from the customer's perspectives).
- Increased touch time
- Identification and removal of waste from the process

NON-VALUE ADDED TIME AND WORK

Non-value added work is work which is part of the process but which the customer feels does not add any value to the process. Non value added work include:

- Unnecessary movement (long distance travelled to achieve task)
- Defects in product or service (repeat testing)
- Excess inventory (risk of inventory such as reagents going out of date).
- Un-utilized staff creativity.
- Waiting time (idle time)
- Over-processing and incorrect processing (doing test not indicated or requested as well as re-run of samples).
- Overproduction produces inventory that will need to be stored until needed (extra cost).

CORE VALUES OF LEAN

- Having the right process guarantee the right results
- Build a culture of continuous quality improvement by root causing every problem, errors, near misses and negative outcome can help facilitate organization learning (mistakes and errors should be seen as learning opportunities).
- Investment in employee has value adding potential
- Value added work is work carried out transforming raw materials into products and services that meet the customer requirements.
- One piece flow rather than batching increases efficiency, productivity, profitability and quality.

THE SIX S LEAN TOOLS

- Sort out (keep only items that are needed).
- Straighten out (making sure things are where they should be).
- Shine (cleanliness and uncluttered working environment).
- Standardize the process (Use standard operating procedures to remove variation in work done).
- Sustain the level of improvement.
- Safety (ensure a safe and healthy environment for the carrying out of task).

FLOW AND PULL

- Flow (smooth, process, removal of all barriers and interruptions to deliver value.
- Pull (production triggered by demand from the customer).
- Perfection (Create a culture of proactive and continuous improvement).
- One piece flow (analyzing samples one by one as they come in).
- Developing standard work (to enhance best service and ensure that work is done the same correct way in the standard work always thus preventing variation in service delivery).
- Implement 6s as a quality improvement measure to ensure defect free products (sort out, set apart, shine, standardize, sustain and safety).
- Pull (production of goods and services on demand).
- Use of visual management

KEY DEFINITIONS

- 1 piece flow (putting all the value-adding steps in a sequence with no piles, no waiting to obtain a continuous flow).
- Standard work (creating a system that do what is needed, when it is needed in the right quantity needed and using best known practices to do the job).
- Pull (not starting a task until you are triggered by demand from the customer. Don't do it before it is needed. E.g. make a cup of tea when thirsty and not making 5 cups in advance in case you get thirsty.
- 6S (a systematic way to create a safe, clean and orderly workplace and maintaining it that way).
- Visual management (a system that enables anyone to immediately at a glance access the current status of a giving process).
- Perfection (lean is about creating a culture of continuous cycle of improvement.

IMPLEMENTING LEAN IN THE DIAGNOSTIC LABORATORY

- It is not a one-off project but rather, it is all about eliminating waste and making improvements forever and creating a means of measuring such improvements.
- Planning phase (has an understanding of the current situation and plan a value stream analysis, decide on what to focus on and communicate to staff by way of training).
- Plan a one week event (plan a rapid improvement event and plan and implement improvements).
- Follow up phase (consolidate improvements, sustain improvements, communicate improvements to staff and start the process of identifying next improvements).

HINDRANCES TO EFFECTIVE LEAN IMPLEMENTATION IN THE LABORATORY

- Conventional fixed ideas (should be discarded)
- Concentrate on how to do it and not why it cannot be done.
- Flexibility and not idealistic
- No room for excuses (start by genuinely questioning the current practices).
- No time wasting (do it right away even if only 50% of initial quality improvement targets are achieved initially).
- If you make mistake correct it straight away, find out the root causes, determine and implement corrective action.
- Wisdom is brought to bear when we face challenges.
- When mistake are made ask Why 5 times to get to the root causes and to put in place immediate remedial and corrective action to prevent root causes.
- Lean is not necessarily money but more of creativity.
- Lean is people driven (involve everybody that is involved in the process).
- Create an atmosphere that encourages staff suggestion (use wisdom of all rather than of one).
- Communicate improvement regularly to all involve in the process.
- Lean related improvements are forever.

CORE BELIEFS OF LEAN

- The right process will produce the right results.
- Developing staff and partners adds value.
- Continually solving root problems drives organizational leaning (using the 5 Why's approach).
- One piece flow increases profitability, productivity and quality.
- Products don't like to wait in the line (they are impatient).
- Value added processes are those that transform information/raw materials to what customers want.
- Errors are opportunity for leaning (doing a root cause analysis and improving the process thereby).
- Problem solving is 20% tools and 80% thinking.

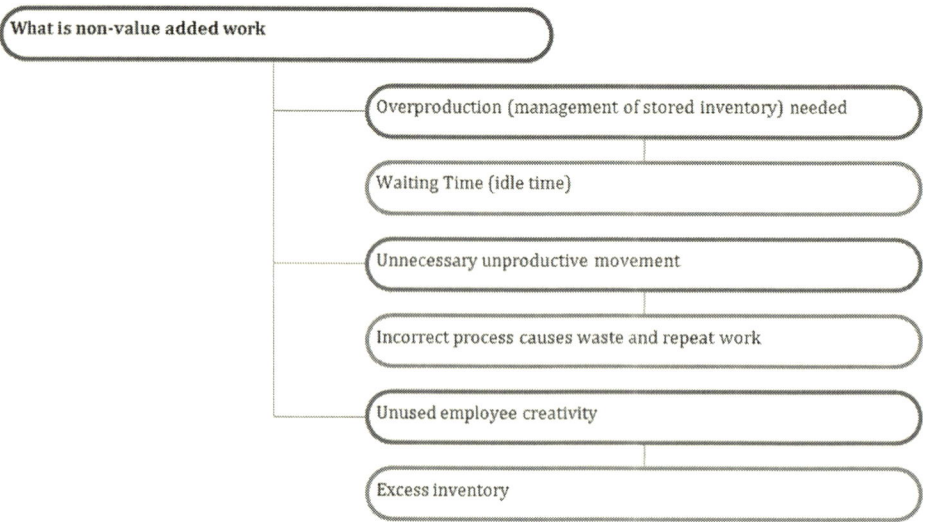

What is non-value added work

Overproduction (management of stored inventory) needed

Waiting Time (idle time)

Unnecessary unproductive movement

Incorrect process causes waste and repeat work

Unused employee creativity

Excess inventory

Figure: Non-value added work (waste)

THINGS TO CONSIDER IN LEAN IMPLEMENTATION IN THE LABORATORY

- Who are our customers? What do they want (The laboratory of the future is one that is constantly modifying their process to enable them meet the changing requirements of the customers).
- What is out current state?
- Develop a future state (what type of laboratory and what kind of service do we want to render to our customers).
- Level and sequence the work load.
- Standardise the task and eliminate waste and redundancy (remove all non-value added element from the process).
- Implement change.
- Measure performance (Lead time, percentage on time delivery, user satisfaction surveys).
- Monitor and sustain level of improvement already attained.
- Set new targets and repeat the process.
- The Toyota suggestion system by Yuzo Yasuda defined "Kaizen" (Continuous Improvement) as the key element of the lean methodology.
- Getting all staff members involved is the key to sustained lean success.
- The fact remains that whether Kaizen lives or dies depend on the interaction between staff and front line supervisors and managers.
- Supervisors should avoid statements (verbally and through body language) that turn off employees from making suggestion to improve workplace. The transformation observed in Toyota in the past 40 years was based on the implementation of more than 20 million quality improvement ideas and suggestion made by the staffs.
- Staff should be proactive and seek better ways of improving their task.
- Toyota's Creative idea Suggestion System started in 1951. By the 1988, the cumulative number of suggestions it had elicited reached 20 million.
- Staff welfare and morale is focal if any meaningful improvement in the process and service delivered is to be achieved.

Six Sigma Principles

Six Sigma is a <u>business management strategy</u> originally developed by <u>Motorola</u>, USA in 1986. Six Sigma is used to improve the quality of a process by the continual identification and removal of defects (waste or errors) and by so doing significantly reduce <u>variability</u> in the process as well as maximize profit. The term "six sigma process" comes from the notion that if one has six <u>standard deviations</u> between the process <u>mean</u> and the nearest specification limit, practically no items will fail to meet specifications. This is based on the calculation method employed in <u>process capability studies</u>. Six sigma seeks to improve the quality of process outputs by identifying and removing the causes of defects (errors) and minimizing <u>variability</u> in <u>manufacturing</u> and <u>business processes</u>. Sigma rating is the percentage of defect-free products it creates. A six Sigma process is one in which 99.99966% of the products manufactured are statistically expected to be free of defects (3.4 defects per million). Six Sigma principles can be combined with lean manufacturing to create a (Lean Six Sigma).

Principles of 6 Sigma

- Continuous efforts to achieve stable and predictable process results (reduce process variation) are of vital importance to business success.
- Manufacturing and business processes have characteristics that can be measured, analyzed, improved and controlled.
- Achieving sustained quality improvement requires commitment from the entire organization, particularly from top-level management.

What makes Six Sigma different from other quality improvement initiatives?

- Six sigma has a clear focus on achieving measurable and quantifiable financial returns from its implementation.
- An increased emphasis on strong and passionate management leadership and support.
- A clear commitment to making decisions on the basis of verifiable evidenced-based data (no assumptions and guesswork).

SIX SIGMA ASSOCIATED QUALITY-MANAGEMENT TOOLS

- Use of root cause analysis (5 why's and cause and effect analysis)
- Analysis of variance
- Critical quality tree (CTQ)
- SIPOC (Suppliers, Inputs, Process, Output and Customers)
- Chi-squared test of independence and fits
- Use of Control chart
- Correlation analysis
- Use of cost-benefit analysis
- Histograms
- Pareto analysis and charts
- Pick charts
- Regression analysis
- Scatter diagram
- Cause and effect diagram (fish bone analysis or Ishikawa diagrams)
- Business process mapping

AIMS OF SIX SIGMA

- Improve manufacturing processes
- Objective collection and analysis of evidenced-based data used to improve the current state to produce a future state.
- Eliminate defects (A defect is any process output that does not meet customer specifications/requirement).

SIX SIGMA DOCTRINES

- There is an objective continuous efforts to achieve stable and predictable process results (reduce process variation) is paramount in the success of a business.
- All processes involved in manufacturing must be measured, analyzed, improved and controlled.
- Achieving quality improvement requires commitment from the staff involved in the manufacturing process including top-level managers.

The Lean Six Sigma principles

- Process flow (having a process oriented service delivery)
- Waste reduction
- Continuous quality improvement
- Carry out root causes of errors, mistakes and unfavorable outcomes with the hope of arriving at the root causes and implementing the corrective actions.
- Collection of evidenced-based data that can be used to improve the quality of goods and services delivered.
- Deliberate approach to continually identify and remove waste from the process as a way of optimizing the quality of the goods or service rendered and maximizing profit.
- Seeking to know what the changing customer requirements are to enable the tailoring of the process to meet these requirements.

Six Sigma project methodologies

Six Sigma projects follow two project methodologies composed of five phases each; bear the acronyms DMAIC and DMADV. Six Sigma methodologies used to drive defects to less than 3.4 per million opportunities. It is based on intensive collection of relevant data (no gimmicks just only cold, hard facts).It is aimed at improved service delivery and improving profit. It is Implemented with the support of a everybody from those directly involved in the every day process to top management with a responsible person as (process owner) having the responsibility of driving the process to ensure that goals are achieved.

- DMAIC is used for projects aimed at improving an existing business process.
- DMADV is used for projects aimed at creating new product or process designs.

DMAIC

DMAIC project methodology phases	
Define the problem	Definition of the problem lies on first of all identifying who our customers are, knowing what the customer requirements and determining what future state we want to achieve (project goals) specifically.
Measure key aspects of process	Measurement of key aspect on the current process is vital to enable the collection of relevant evidenced based data. Data collection must be done objectively.
Analyze the data	Effective analysis of collected data must be done without any pre-conceived ideas to investigate and verify cause-and-effect relationships. Determine what the relationships are, and attempt to ensure that all factors have been considered. Seek out root cause of the defect under investigation and note the corrective measure to be implemented to eliminate root causes.
Improve or optimize the current process	Improvement or optimization of the current process must be based upon effective data analysis using techniques such as design of experiments and mistake proofing. Corrective measures arrived at are used to improve the current process helping to create a new future state process. Produce standard work for the future state process and set up pilot runs to establish process capability and efficiency.
Control **the future state**	Put a process in place to monitor and control the future state ensuring that any deviations from target are corrected before they result in defects. Implement control systems such as statistical process control, production boards, visual workplaces, and continuously monitor the process.

DMADV OR **DFSS**

The aim of DMADV is to align improvement or design efforts (process) with customer requirements. Customers have a requirement they expect a product to meet. DMADV is all about knowing what the customer requirements are and finding ways implementing measurable terms in the process aimed at meeting the customer requirements. The DMADV project methodology, also known as DFSS (Design for Six Sigma) features five phases:

DMADV or DFSS project methodology phases	
Define design goals	Goals must be consistent with customer requirements or demands and the organizations strategy.
Measure and identify CTQs	Determine what constitutes quality from the customer's perspectives (characteristics that are Critical To Quality). Determine the key measurable characteristics of a product, service or process whose performance standards or specification limits must be met in order to satisfy the customer (determine ways to measure product capabilities, production process capability and risks).
Analyze	Analyze collected data and use it to create a high-level design and alternatives of the process that is aimed at producing this product or service that meet the requirements of the customer, evaluate the design capability to select the best design.
Design	Optimize the design, and plan for design verification. This phase may require simulations to determine the workability and practicality of the design.
Verify	Verification of the design involves setting up pilot runs, implementing the production process and handing it over to the process owner for implementation.

CHAPTER 6

USE OF A3 AS A QUALITY IMPROVEMENT TOOL IN THE LABORATORY

A3 is a quality improvement tool. It is a logical problem-solving approach that uses a tool called the A3 Problem-Solving Report. It is a critical review of the current state, future state (target state) and identifying the things and process to be put in place to facilitate movement from the current state to achieve the future state.

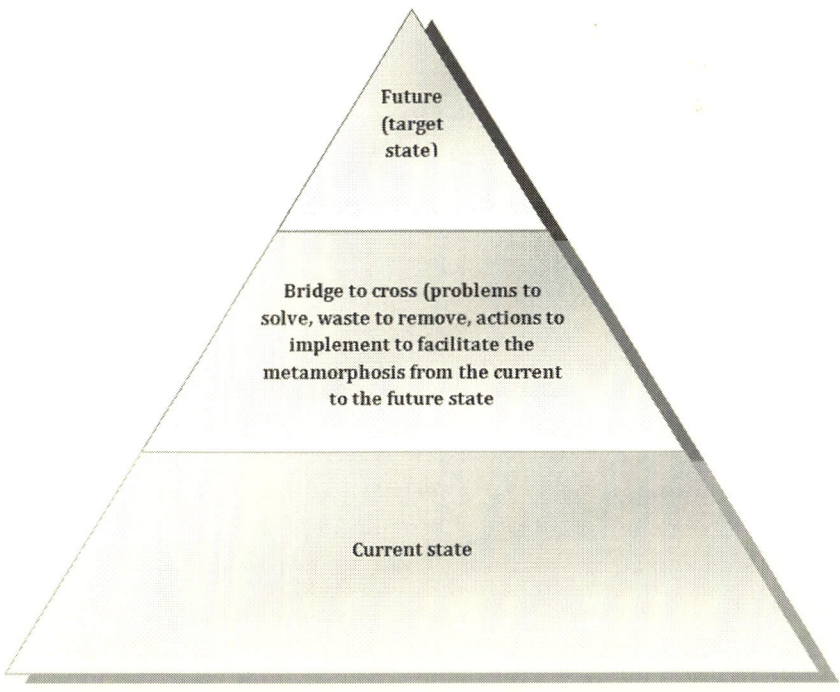

Figure: A3 approach to solving organization problems

Most problems that arise in organizations are addressed in superficial ways (first-order problem-solving). Rather than carrying out an objective root cause analysis, they work around (circle round) the problem but do not address the root causes of the problem. By not addressing the root cause, the organization continues to encounter the same problem or same type of problem again and again without any improvement in operational performance or service delivery. By carrying out root cause analysis objectively, an organization is able to:

- Identifying the root causes of the problem
- Arriving at immediate remedial actions (quick fix to obviate root causes)
- Determine corrective actions to be implemented to eliminate the root causes and prevent the problem from re-occurring in future
- Finally the process should be audited after an agreed period to ensure that the root causes has indeed been eliminated.

A3 problem solving is a standard method used by Toyota to define and address problems at all levels of the organization.

- The A3 approach is effective because it forces teams to keep things simple and provides a means of communicating both the problem and proposed solutions.
- The A3 process helps people engage in collaborative brainstorming and in-depth problem-solving.
- It drives problem-solvers to address the root causes of problems and facilitates improvement in service delivered and can help grow the profit accruable to the laboratory as a business.
- The A3 Process can be used for almost any situation strictly and objectively following all the steps.
- A method to help teams identify the best solution for solving problems and eliminating waste is the A3 process.
- Ability of an organization to continually improve her process and performance.
- Problem solving using the root cause analysis approach can potentially fosters learning, collaboration and sharing of evidenced-based best practices.

The A3 process is so named because all the actions (quality improvement changes to the process, waste to be identified and removed, corrective actions and policies to implemented) to move an organization from the current state to the future state) is captured on an A3-sized paper.

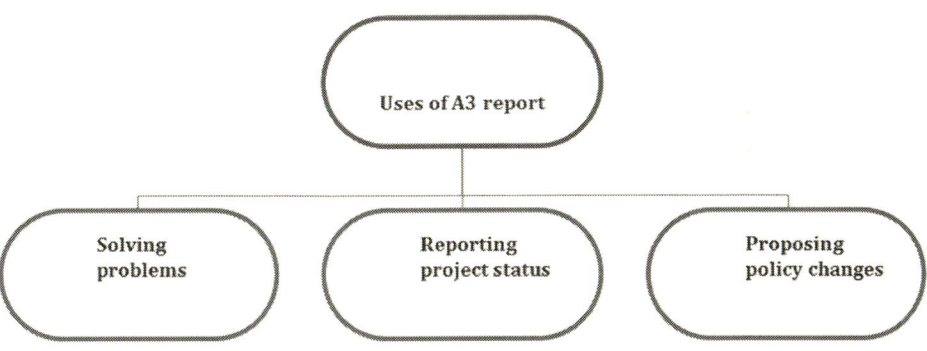

Figure: Uses of A3 report

THE BASIC FORMAT OF AN A3 PROBLEM SOLVING PLAN

Title: Describes the problem or issue to be solved or dealt it.

Owner/Date: Identifies the person who is pioneering the problem solving and the date of the latest A3 revision. As analysis continues, frequent amendments will need to be made and dated.

Background to the quality improvement drive: Deals with the history behind the problem/issues and a description of the reason why the issue is being addressed.

An objective description or picture of the current state: Describes what the problem really is, what is currently known about the problem (displayed using charts, maps or drawings).

Goals for future state: Identification of goals; analysis; proposed counter measures; plan and follow-up that needs to be implemented (bridge to cross) to facilitate the metamorphosis to the future state (desired situation) or the specific outcomes required (maps or charts and descriptive text).

Analysis: Contains the method used to define the root cause(s) of the problem. The appropriate problem analysis tool should be used and documented. Examples of problem analysis tool include:

- 5 Why's: In problem solving, by objectively asking "Why?" five times, successively, you can delve into a problem deeply enough to understand the ultimate root cause. By the time you get to the 4th or 5th why, you will have the correction action that needs to be implemented to eliminate the *problem or* root causes. The purpose behind a 5-why analysis is to get the right people in the room discussing all of the possible root causes of a given defect in a process. Often times, teams will stop once a reason for a defect, error or unfavorable outcome has been identified. These conclusions often do not get to the root cause. A disciplined 5-why approach will push teams to think outside the box and reach a root cause where the team can actually make a positive difference in the problem, instead of treating symptoms.

- **Cause and Effect Analysis (Ishikawa Diagrams or Fishbone Diagrams:** Cause and effect analysis (fish bone diagram because a completed diagram can look like the skeleton of a fish) can be used to solve a serious problem in an organization. It is however vital to explore all of the possible causes (brainstorm) before you start to think about a solution. That way you can solve the problem completely, first time round, rather than just addressing part of it and having the problem re-occur over and over again. Effective cause and effect analysis pushes teams to consider all possible causes of a problem rather than just the ones that are most obvious. Cause and effect analysis can be used to:

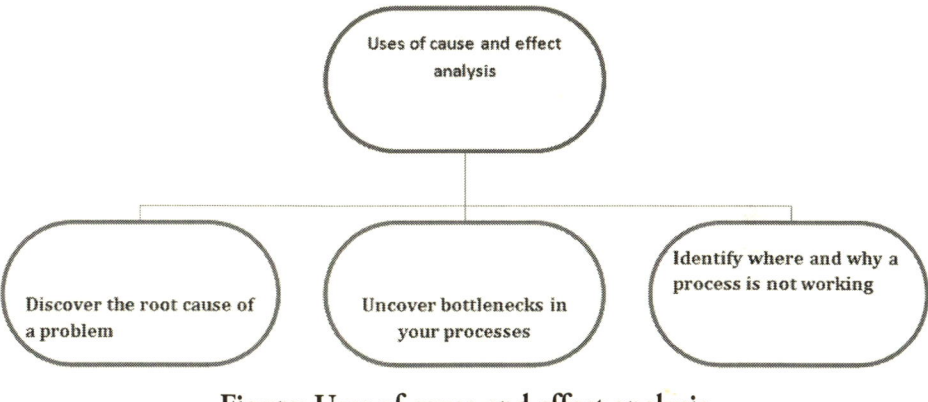

Figure: Uses of cause and effect analysis
(Ishikawa or fish bone analysis)

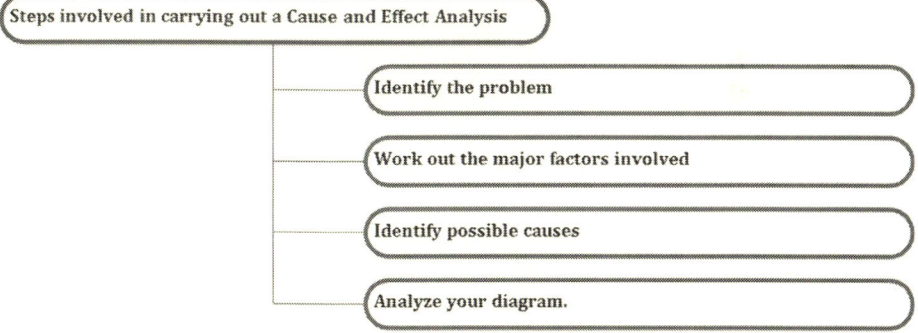

Figure: Steps involved in carrying out a Cause and Effect Analysis

Proposed Countermeasures: Defines the solution identified which if implemented can cause the metamorphosis from the current to the target state. This should define how the proposed solution will help remove the root causes. The word countermeasure is used to describe the corrective measures that can be put in place to counter the identified problems. This corrective action will continue to be implemented until the system is audited.

Action plan: Defines the activities (corrective action) that will need to be implemented to achieve the future state. These activities should state the following:

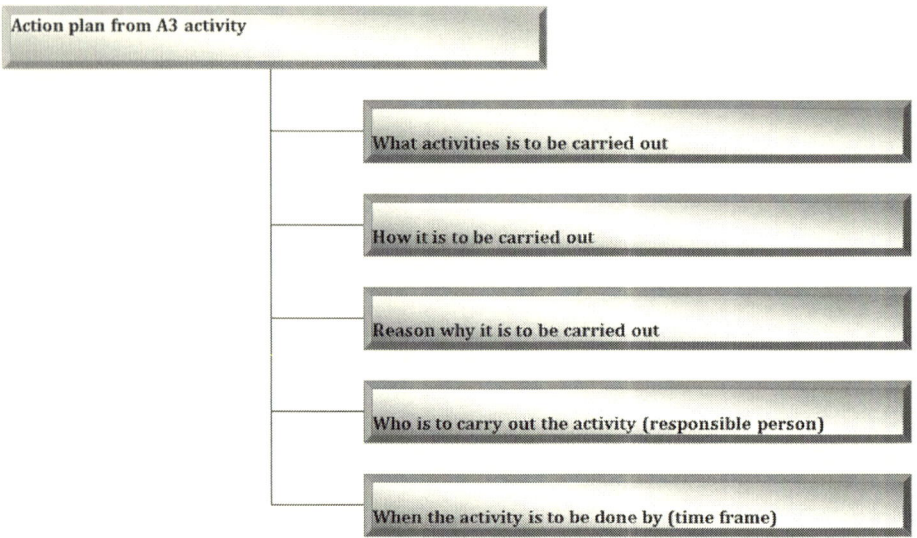

Figure: Action plan arrived at from A3 activity

Follow-up: The system should ideally be audited with a period of implementation (after 2-3 months).The aim of the audit is confirm that the new system is actually improving the situation, that the root causes of the initial problems have been eliminated as well as confirm that the new system being implemented has not created any bottlenecks in the system. The follow-up plan indicates how and when the improvement of the system will be audited.

Beneficial effects: The A3 problem solving method is effective and can be used to potentially improve service delivery and improved customer satisfaction. It can be used to identify problems (waste and bureaucracy) in the process. The A3 is an effective communication tool and improvement efforts are made visible.

Conclusion: A3 can be a powerful tool available to a continuous improvement conscious organization for solving problems and it is often an avenue for organization to continually improve their service delivery, customer satisfaction and profitability. Adequate and quality time must be put in to understand the current situation, identify all the potential problems and waste that is causing unexpected negative outcomes, analyze the root causes and develop effective corrective measures to eliminate the root causes. Findings from an A3 should be shared with members of the team to facilitate a hitch free implementation.

CASE STUDY 1 ON USE OF A3 IS A QUALITY IMPROVEMENT TOOL

Title: Use of A3 quality improvement tool to optimize the inventory control and effective management of reagents in Nelson Biomedical Limited.

Current state: Nelson Biomedical limited is a diagnostic services company. The company in the last one year has had problem with meeting turnaround times for laboratory investigations. Stock of reagents has continually run out. Stock out of reagents has significantly affected the laboratory's turnaround times. Samples have had to be batched for days until the suppliers supply the required reagents. The requesting clinicians are often calling the laboratory to enquire about the availability of test results for their patients. Patients booked for surgery have had their surgery cancelled severally because of the unavailability of important pre-operative laboratory test. In the laboratory annual customer satisfaction survey, most customers have complained about the delay caused by these perennial reagent stock out.

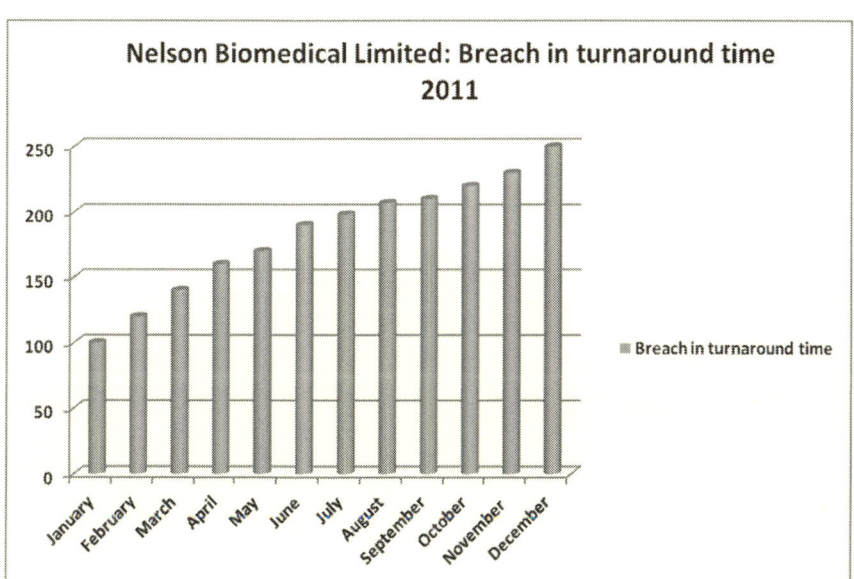

Goals for future state (Target state): The department is determined to investigate the challenges associated with the optimum stocking of reagents to enable them offer an uninterrupted quality service to their customers. The desire of the laboratory is to put in place a system that enables the laboratory to meet the set turnaround times for laboratory test.

Analysis: We intend to use root cause analysis tool (5 Why's) and cause and effect analysis (Hishikawa or fish bone analysis). The major problem of the laboratory is not meeting the turnaround times for laboratory test. The plan is to carry out a root cause analysis why turnaround times are not being met.

Table: Root cause analysis for breach in turnaround time in Nelson Biomedical Limited

S/N0	Problem	Root cause (Why)
1.	Why do we have problems meeting our set turnaround time	Because of regular stock out of reagents
2.	Why do we experience stock out of reagents	Because of the absence of an effective inventory control of reagents
3.	Why is there absence of an effective inventory control of reagents	Forecasting for reagents and stock levels are often suboptimal.
4.	Why do we have problems with forecasting and maintenance of optimum stock levels of reagents	There is no dedicated person responsible for inventory control management of reagents. The workload has increased significantly in the last one year. The fridge compartment for storage of reagent has become inadequate.

5.	Why is there no person responsible for inventory control management and fridge compartment inadequate	Why is there no person responsible for inventory control management because the previous inventory control officer retired a year ago and has not been replaced? Work load has increased in the past year and there is no inventory control officer to justify to the laboratory manager the need to procure more reagent refrigerators or cold room for reagent storage.
Major root causes		• The lack of a dedicated inventory officer has affected the forecasting and optimum stocking of reagents. • This lack of an inventory officer has also prevented the presentation of justification of the need for bigger storage space for reagents to the laboratory manager.

Proposed Countermeasures (corrective action): The corrective action that need to be implemented to obviate the root causes include:

• Advertise the job for inventory control officer
• Organise interview to hire an inventory control officer
• Provide new staff after induction and training with records on workload over the last few years to allow for the effective forecasting as well as determination of minimum and maximum stock levels as well as emergency order level.
• Draw up a standard operating procedure on inventory control management of reagents
• Determine the size and type of refrigerator that can store a little above the maximum reagent requirement to be held at any material time.
• Request quotes from registered contractor for cold room that meet the reagent storage requirement of the department.
• Receive, open bid and award contract for the supply of new cold room.
• Delivery, installation and validation of new cold room
• Commissioning of new cold room

Title: A3 Analysis of root cause analysis for breach in turnaround time in Nelson Biomedical

Owner/Date: Dr Osaro Erhabor (Laboratory Manager)/25/01/2012

Action Plan

S/No	What needs doing	How will it be done	Why it need doing	Who is responsible	When task is to be performed
1.	Advertise the job for inventory control officer	In 2 a national dailies	To appoint a new inventory control officer	Dr Osaro the Biomedical manager	25/01/2012
2.	Organise interview to hire an inventory control officer	Oral interview for shortlisted applicants	To hire a motivated inventory control officer	Dr Osaro and Dr Teddy	25/02/2012
3.	Carry out new staff induction and training for inventory control officer	Department induction and staff training	To intimate staff on the process control in the department and the role of the inventory control officer in service delivery in the department	Dr Osaro	25/3/2012

4.	Draw up a standard operating procedure on inventory control management of reagents.	To be drawn by the new inventory control officer according to department's document control policy	To ensure that the process of inventory control is standardized to enable other staff to be trained on the SOP	New inventory control officer	2/4/2012
5.	Determine the size and type of refrigerator that can store the optimum level of reagents required by the department	Inventory control officer to determine size based on maximum stock levels to be maintained	To allow for optimum storage of adequate level of reagent stock	New inventory control officer	2/4/2012
6.	Request quotes from registered contractor for cold room	Place advert in the company notice board	To enable contractor to bid to supply new cold room	Dr Osaro	5/4/2012
7.	Receive, open bid and award contract for supply of cold room	Managers to open bids and award to most competitive bidder	To enable the award of contract to supply new cold room.	Dr Osaro and, Dr Teddy	12/4/2012
8.	Delivery, installation, mapping and validation of new cold room	Successful contractor to deliver new cold room to the corporate office	To enable the operation of the new cold room	Successful contractor	26/4/2012
9.	Commissioning of new cold room	Laboratory manager, other managers and staffs	To enable use of new cold room	Managers and staffs	2/5/2012

Follow-up: Post implementation audit is to be carried out on the 2/8/2012 to investigate the number of turnaround breaches that result from stock out of reagent to determine if the root causes have been eliminated and that the process if working optimally.

Case study 2 on use of A3 is a quality improvement tool using the cause and effect (Hishikawa or fish bone) approach to improve staff morale productivity and turnaround time in the laboratory.

Title: Use of A3 quality improvement tool to investigate the problem the laboratory manager is having with un-cooperative biomedical staff in Nelon Biomedical Limited

Current state: Nelon Biomedical limited is a diagnostic services company. The laboratory manager has been having problems with uncooperative biomedical staff in the department. The workload has increased significantly in the last one year because of a new contract the company got to analyse all sample from a general hospital in the region. However staff levels have declined because 4 staff have left and had not been replaced. Secondly the retention of staff is poor, down time of analyzes has increased in the department because analyzer is unable to cope with the increased workload. Turnaround time breaches have increased significantly. Supervision of biomedical staff during the day and out of hours is suboptimal. Staffs are reluctant to put themselves forward to cover sickness absences. Error rate and near misses has increased in the last one year. Staff morale has declined significantly. Reagent stock out is a re-occurring decimal and space is suboptimal. Benches are often cluttered.

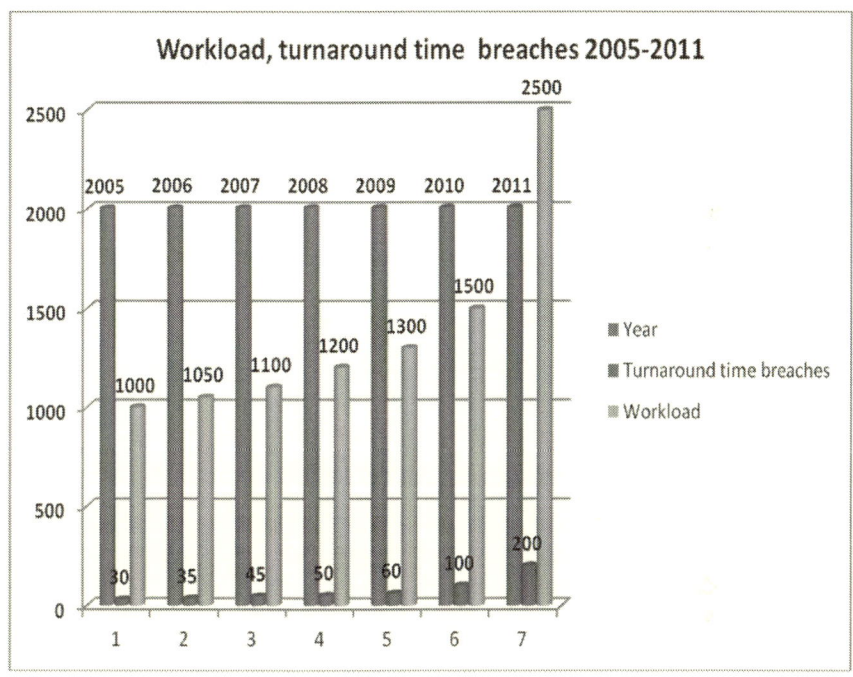

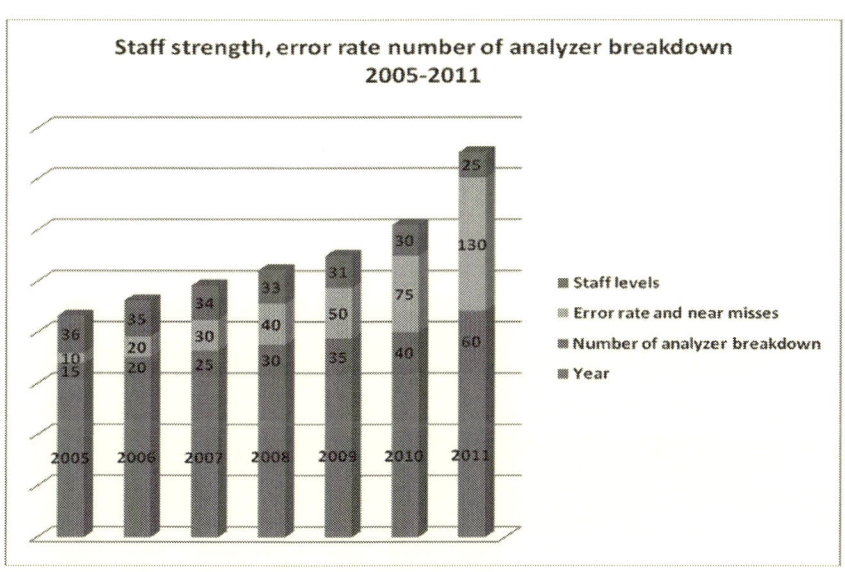

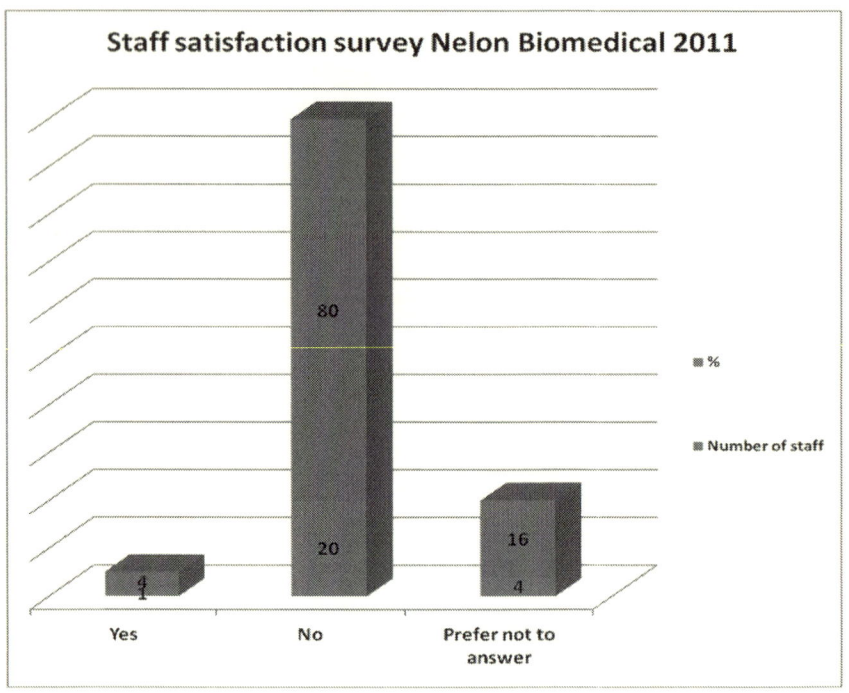

Goals for future state (Target state): It is the desire of the management to increase the morale, productivity, joy and pride at work among biomedical staff. They intend to improve on the turnaround time and service delivery to their customers.

Analysis: Cause and effect analysis identified the following problems:

- Lack of high throughput analyzers
- Inadequate staffing levels resulting from increased workload and non-replacement of staff who have left
- Poor inventory control due to lack of dedicated inventory control staff
- Cluttered benches due to inadequate bench space
- Poor supervision due to suboptimal supervisory staff

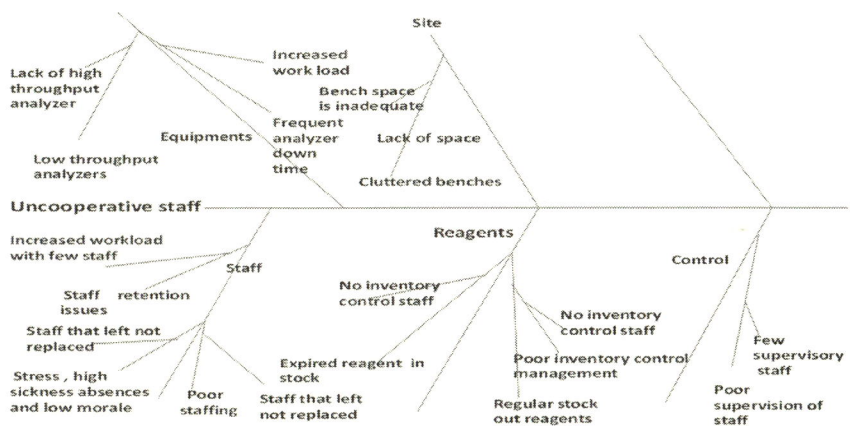

Figure: Cause and effect or fish Bone analysis (Hishikawa) of challenges experienced in Nelon Biomedical

PROPOSED COUNTERMEASURES (CORRECTIVE ACTION)

- Procure a high throughput analyzer that can cope with current and envisaged future increases in workload.
- Advertise and employ 2 new medical laboratory scientists, a senior medical laboratory scientist and an inventory control officer to obviate the effect of negative workload and staff low morale due to stress resulting from inadequate staffing levels, supervisory challenges and inventory control challenges.
- Organise a health and safety training for all staff to re-affirm the need to work in a safety and tidy work environment.

ACTION PLAN

S/No	What needs doing	How will it be done	Why it need doing	Who is responsible	When task is to be performed
1.	Decide on a high throughput analyzer to be procured based on current and future envisaged increase in workload.	Managers to meet and decide	To facilitate replacement of main departmental analyzer	Managers	1st June 2012
2.	Invite contractors to bid for supply of new analyzer	Advertise on hospital contractors notice board	To facilitate award of contract to replace analyzer	Business manager	7th June 2012
3.	Receive bids, open bids and award contract to supply new analyzer	Tenders board meeting	To facilitate award of contract to replace analyzer	Department's tenders board	21st June 2012
4.	Inform successful contractor of contract award and receipt of supply of new analyzer	Business manager	To facilitate supply of new analyzer	Business manager	21st July 2012
5.	Installation and training of staff on use and proactive maintenance	Laboratory Manager	To facilitate effective use of new equipment	Laboratory Manager	1st August 2012

6.	Advertisement in 2 national dailies and the profession's job website for 2 laboratory scientist, one senior laboratory scientist and 1 inventory control officer	Laboratory manager	To facilitate the employment of new staff	Laboratory Manager	3rd June 2012
7.	Receipt of applications and selection of applicants for interview	Laboratory managers and unit heads	To facilitate the employment of new staff	Laboratory manager	**3rd July**
8.	Interview of shortlisted applicants and appointment of new staff	Laboratory managers and unit heads	To facilitate the employment of new staff	Laboratory manager	3rd of August 2012
9.	Induction and training of new staff	Laboratory managers and unit heads	To enhance service delivery in the department	Laboratory managers and unit heads	17th August 2012
10.	Organise a health and safety training for all staff	Departmental health and safety officer	To enhance health and safety conscious as well as good laboratory practices	Laboratory manager	20 August 2012

CHAPTER 7

ETHICAL AND MEDICO-LEGAL ASPECT OF LABORATORY SCIENCE PRACTICE

PROFESSION ETHICS

Medical ethics is a system of moral principles that apply values and judgments to the practice of laboratory medicine. There are six general principles on which judgements bordering on professional ethics-related ligations are based. They are six of the values that commonly apply to medical ethics as it relates to medical laboratory science practice:

Autonomy: Autonomy relates to a patient right to refuse or accept treatment after counseling (*Voluntas aegroti suprema lex.*). The laboratory must respect the decision-making capacities of a person that is conscious and in the right frame of mind (self determination) enabling individuals to make informed decisions after counseling. An autonomous decision does not necessarily have to be a correct decision from objective viewpoint. It must however be an autonomous decision that is informed. Respect for patient's autonomy is the basis for informed consent. Persons with a psychiatric condition such as dementia or clinical depression as well as patient who are in their right frame of mind but unconscious may not have the capacity to make life and death decisions. For these classes of persons, a request to refuse laboratory testing or treatment may be sought from their next of kin. If the next of kin is unavailable then the laboratory scientist or healthcare professional owes the patient the duty to offer the best quality of professional care available. However there are situations when public interest may over ride a patient right to autonomy (if a patient is an offender and a laboratory test is required in the interest of the state to determine if an individual is guilty of a crime (rape and terrorism for example).

Beneficence: It is a general expectation of law that medical treatment will be beneficial. It is expected that the laboratory scientist and other health professionals will act in the best interest of the patient. (*Salus aegroti suprema lex.*). The biomedical scientist is expected by law to act to benefit the patient. However there are situation when a competent patient makes an informed decision which the laboratory scientist or health professional feel is not in their best interest. In such case there is a clash between the principle of medical ethics and the principle of respect for autonomy. However from a legal point of view the autonomy right of a competent patient cannot be overridden by the decision of the health professional even if they feel the diagnostic test or procedure being anticipated is supposedly in the best interest of the patient. However healthcare professional owe a patient who is incompetent and unable to give an informed consent (unconscious patient) the best possible and available standard of care. Under the principle of beneficence, healthcare professionals are expected to take decisions that is beneficial and in the best interests of patients.

Non-Maleficence *(Primum non nocere)*:

It is a general expectation by law that medical treatment will not cause harm. Medical laboratory scientist are expected to promote their patient's best interests and strive to achieve optimal outcomes without any harm. *Medical laboratory scientists are expected to maintain a safe, effective* and competent practice to avoid causing injury to vulnerable patients. The principle of non-maleficence also covers reporting suspected abuse from healthcare professionals. Although most treatments potentially involve some risk even if minimal but the general expectation however is that the potential benefit of treatment must outweigh potential risk and harm. In some circumstances, a risk benefit analysis may need to be carried out. There are situations where the outcome without treatment can be grave. In such cases, a risky treatments (can cause harm) but can potentially benefit a patient may be justified. Violation of non-maleficence right of a patient if not protected can become subject of <u>medical malpractice</u> litigation. Sometimes under situational ethics a medical laboratory scientist can take a decision that can possibly cause minimal harm but can potentially save a patient's life (for example a blood scientist can decide to give a woman without child bearing potential who is bleeding to death and who is Rhesus negative for which all the rhesus negative blood bank has been used some Rhesus positive units even if they know that such transfusion can potentially sensitize such patient to produce immune anti-D but possible safe her life). The benefit of such decision (prevention of exsanguinations and death) possibly outweigh the risk of alloantibody production.

TRUTHFULNESS AND HONESTY

This principle involves the concept of informed consent. Under the principle of truthfulness and honesty it is vital in most cases to note that some single actions or decision can produce a double effect (combined effect of beneficence and non-maleficence). An example is the use of morphine in a dying patient can both be beneficial (ease the pain and suffering of the patient) but can also have a maleficent effect of hastening the demise of the patient through suppression of the respiratory system. Conflicts between autonomy and beneficence/non-maleficence can also arise. Autonomy can sometimes conflict with the principle of beneficence particularly when a patient does not consent to having a treatment that health care professionals believe are in their best interest. When the patient's interests conflict with their welfare, the wishes of a mentally competent patient takes precedence irrespective of whether the health professionals believes that patient may not be acting in his own best interests. Examples include when a patient does not want a treatment because of religious views (for example a Jehovah's Witness refusal to accept a transfusion even when they run the risk of bleeding to death).Other examples include risky potentially harmful cosmetic surgery which is not medically indicated and seen as un-necessary by the health professionals but which a patient has given an informed autonomy (example is a breast enhancement surgery).

EUTHANASIA

This refers to the practice of intentionally ending a life in order to relieve pain and suffering. In most countries, the law that treatment should potentially benefit a patient and will not cause arm still outweighs euthanasia even if the intention by health professionals is to help the patient in the intentional and active relief of suffering particularly in cases where there is no cure. However in countries such as the Netherlands, Belgium and states like Oregon in the USA, principle of euthanasia may in some cases outweigh the principle of non-maleficence are always hinged on the argument that:

- People have a right to <u>self-determination</u>, and thus should be allowed to choose their own fate
- That assisting a subject to die might be a better choice than requiring that they continue to suffer
- That there is need to distinguish between passive euthanasia (passive euthanasia entails the withholding of common treatments, such as antibiotics, necessary for the continuance of life) which is often permitted, and active euthanasia (entails the use of lethal substances or forces, such as administering a lethal injection to kill) which is not is not acceptable.
- That permitting euthanasia will not necessarily lead to unacceptable consequences.

JUSTICE

The principle of justice concerns the distribution of scarce health resources, and the decision of who gets what treatment (fairness and equality).It involves fairness in the distribution of benefits, risk and cost. This principle supports the notion that patients in similar positions should be treated in a similar manner. It is relevant to often consider cost effectiveness of treatment options for a patient and thwe impact the decision to offer a particular treatment has on the availability of treatment for other patients awaiting a similar procedure. The principle of justice also takes into consideration the role the treatment plays in improving the quality of health of patient. It may be justified to offer a young 25 years old man who although is lower on the donor's waiting list who requires a heart transplant in preference to a terminally ill elderly cancer patient who has been given 2 weeks to live who requires a heart transplant. The principle of justice is critical particularly in resource-limited settings where the health budget is slim. Treatment are often given based on the justification that expensive treatment required will be beneficial, improve the quality of life of patients and produce a prolongation of life.

DIGNITY

This principle states that the patient has the right to dignity. Dignity is a state, quality or manner worthy of esteem or respect. The principle of dignity expects that every patient irrespective of race, colour gender, religious affiliations is treated fairly and with respect. Dignity in care is defined as care offered in any setting which supports and promotes, and does not undermine a person's self respect regardless of any difference. Every patient deserves a dignified care (treated with respect and worth). Lack of it can have a profound effect on patient/client well-being. Dignity is concerned with how people feel, think and behave in relation to the worth or value of themselves and others. Making sure you get an informed consent from them before carrying out any procedure on them (the only exception includes patients in coma, in emergency situations and those who are demented or those with history of mental health problems and unable to make an informed decision on their own).

Treating people with respect is all about:

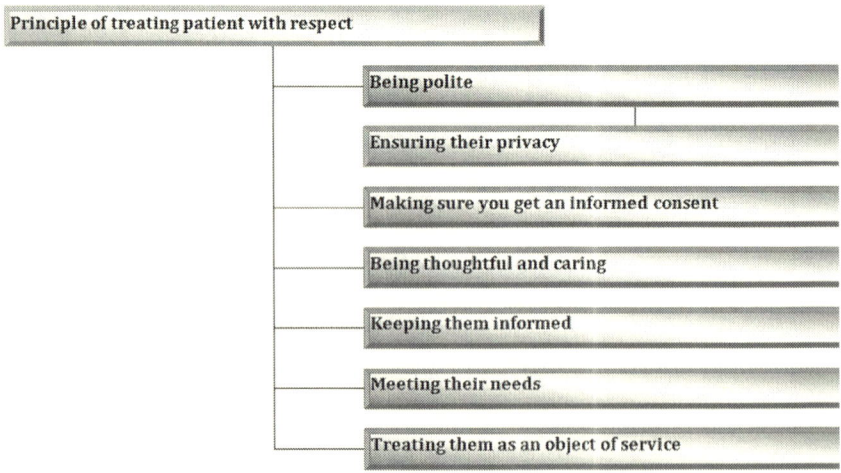

Figure: Treating patients with respect

Dignity is the result of being treated with respect. It is internal and often associated with a sense of:

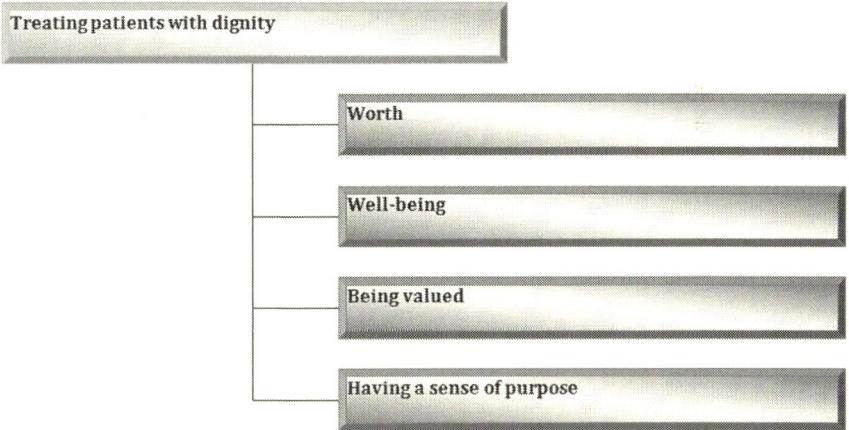

Figure: Core principles of dignity

Dignity is maintained by the little things done to reassure patients when they are unwell and in an unfamiliar environment. Dignity and Respect are key principles of the Human Rights Act. When a person's dignity is compromised and no respect is afforded them, it is an abuse of their human rights. To ensure that the rights of individuals are upheld the following key principles must be in place:

Human right act (key principles)

- Fairness
- Respect
- Equality
- Dignity
- Accountability

Figure: Key principle of the human right act

INFORMED CONSENT PRINCIPLES

Informed consent in ethics usually refers to the idea that a person must be fully informed about and understand the potential benefits and risks of their choice of treatment. An uninformed person is at risk of mistakenly making a choice not reflective of his or her values or wishes. It does not specifically mean the process of obtaining consent, nor the specific legal requirements, which vary from place to place, for capacity to consent. Patients can elect to make their own medical decisions, or can delegate decision-making authority to another party. If the patient is incapacitated, laws around the world designate different processes for obtaining informed consent, typically by having a person appointed by the patient or their next of kin make decisions for them. The value of informed consent is closely related to the values of autonomy and truth telling.

ENSURE YOU GAIN CONSENT

- You must ensure that you gain consent before you begin any treatment or care.
- You must respect and support people's rights to accept or decline treatment and care.
- You must uphold people's rights to be fully involved in decisions about their care.
- You must be aware of the legislation regarding mental capacity and treatment of patient in coma ensuring that such people who lack capacity remain at the centre of decision making and are fully safeguarded.
- You must be able to demonstrate that you have acted in someone's best interests if you have provided care in an emergency.

WHAT IS INFORMED CONSENT?

- A process of obtaining a patient's permission before disclosing specific information on the patient.
- A process of obtaining a patient's permission for a procedure after the patient and doctor have discussed the risks, benefits, and alternatives of the procedure and the patient understands them.

- A process by which a patient/client confirms his or her willingness to participate in a particular trial, after having been informed of all aspects of the trial that are relevant to the subject's decision to participate voluntarily in an experiment after understanding the risks involved.

WHAT ARE THE PRINCIPLES OF INFORMED CONSENT?

- To trust another person with private and personal information about oneself is a significant matter. The patient or client has a right to believe that this information given in confidence will only be used for the purposes for which it was intended and will not be released to others without their permission (consent).
- It is impractical to obtain the consent of a patient every time you need to share information with other health professionals or staff involved in the health care of the patient or client. What is important is that the patient understands that some information may be made available to others involved in the delivery of their care.
- We need to obtain the explicit consent of a patient or client before we disclose specific information and it is important that the client or patient can make an informed consent as to whether the information should be disclosed.

HOW CAN DISCLOSURE OF PATIENT INFORMATION OCCUR?

- With the consent (written or verbal) of a client or patient.
- Without the consent of the patient or client when disclosure is required by the law or by the order of a court.
- Without the consent of the patient when the disclosure is in the interest of public interest.
- The public interest means the interest of an individual, or groups of individuals or of society as a whole and would cover issues such as; serious crime, child abuse, drug trafficking or other activities which places others at serious risk.
- It is our responsibility as health professional (part of our duty of care) and we are accountable for the release of information on

a client or patient. The deliberate release of patient information without their consent even in the interest of the public must be justified.

- The organization that employs the health professions who make records are the legal owners of the records, but this does not give anyone in the organization the legal right to access or release this information to a third party without the consent of the client.

- If patients or clients record need to be used to help student gain the knowledge and skills which they require, the same principle of informed consent applies. The person providing the training will be responsible for making sure the student understand the need for confidentiality and informed consent and the need to follow local procedures for handling and storing of records.

- Informed consent includes being informed and giving consent, two closely related elements. Being informed requires offering information to potential human subjects. In any research on human beings, each potential subject must be adequately informed of the aims, methods, sources of funding, any possible conflicts of interest, institutional affiliations of the researcher, the anticipated benefits and potential risks of the study and the discomfort it may entail. Information provided by researcher should be simple and clear enough for the potential subject to understand and it is the duty of researcher to answer their questions. The subject should also be informed of the right to abstain from participation in the study or withdraw consent to participate at any time without reprisal.

BRIEFLY GIVE AN OVERVIEW OF YOUR UNDERSTANDING OF THE IMPORTANCE OF INFORMED CONSENT IN BIOMEDICAL SCIENCE PRACTICE.

The principle of informed consent, aimed at the lawfulness of health assistance, tends to reflect the concept of autonomy and of decisional auto determination of the person requiring and requesting medical and/or surgical interventions. It is the right and responsibility of every competent individual to advance his or her own welfare. This right and responsibility is exercised by freely and voluntarily consenting or refusing consent to recommended medical procedures, based on a sufficient knowledge of the benefits, burdens, and risks involved. The ability to give informed consent depends on;

- Adequate disclosure of information.
- Patient freedom of choice
- Patient comprehension of information given
- Patient capacity for decision-making

Three necessary conditions that must be satisfied in obtaining informed consent are;

- That the individual's decision is voluntary.
- That this decision is made with an appropriate understanding of the circumstances.
- That the patient's choice is deliberate insofar as the patient has carefully considered all of the expected benefits, burdens, risk and reasonable alternatives.

Legally, adequate disclosure includes information concerning the following;

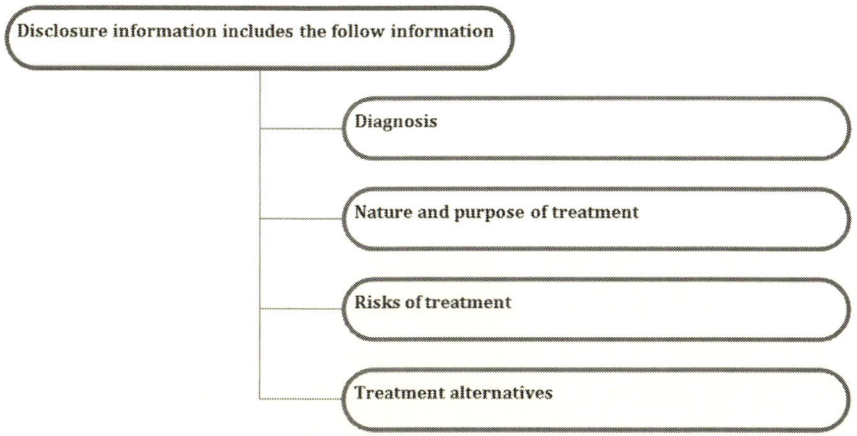

Informed Consent-Related Questions and Answers

1. Mrs Ford came to the laboratory to have her blood taken for HIV screening. Later that morning her husband Mr Ford who is on warfarin also attends the clinic to have his blood taken for INR investigation. He enquires about whether his wife had attended clinic that morning and what the report of her HIV test was. How will you manage this situation?

    Answer: We need to obtain the explicit consent from a patient or client before we disclose specific information and it is important that the client or patient can make an informed consent as to whether the information should be disclosed.

2. A staff nurse in Eye clinic that has no duty of care for a patient refereed from GUM clinic has called the laboratory to enquire about the urine microscopy, culture and sensitivity result of her ex-partner who is suspected to have a sexually transmitted infection. How will you handle this enquiry?

    Answer: The organization that employs the health professions who make records are the legal owners of the records, but this does not give anyone in the organization the legal right to access or release this information to a third party without the consent of the client particularly when the information accessed is not for the purpose of patient care.

3. Mrs A goes to her family GP in Bolton to submit her early morning urine for pregnancy test. Later that afternoon a doctor based in Wigan who has no duty of care to the patient but who introduces himself as a doctor and partner of Mrs A rings to enquire about her pregnancy test result. How will you deal with such situation?

    Answer: It is against the principles of patient confidentiality and informed consent to give confidential information on a patient to a relative clinician or healthcare worker who has no duty of care whatsoever to the patient and does not require the information for the management of the patient.

4. Your brother's partner has just returned from holidays in the Caribbean. She presented to her doctor with an episode of vomiting and abdominal pain. Her doctor promptly referred her to the laboratory for pregnancy test. Your brother knowing you work in the laboratory in Hospital rings you to enquire about his partners laboratory results. How will you deal with this situation?

   Answer: As healthcare workers, we are ethical bound not to disclose confidential information on patients or clients to third parties without their consent.

5. A man has just been told that his son's blood group is O positive by his doctor. The man however knows that his own blood group is AB positive and that his wife's blood group is O positive. He has read from the internet that a blood group AB parent cannot give birth to an O child. He rings you in the Laboratory to confirm the wife's blood group and enquire about the possibility of the child being his. How will you deal with this issue?

   Answer: It is against the principles of patient confidentiality and informed consent to give confidential information on a patient or client to a third party without the consent of the patient. By giving such information without the consent of the wife, the husband will know that he is most likely not the putative father of the child.

EXAMPLE OF AN INFORMED CONSENT FORM

PARTICIPATION CONSENT FORM

Study Title:

Name . . . .

Address . . . .

- I give consent for myself / child to be a participant in this study. I have been fully informed what participation will involve and had all my questions answered. I understand that I can withdraw from this study at any time without giving reason and without penalty.
- I also give consent for recordings to be made relating to my participation.
- I also give consent for my personal data to be used by the research workers in any way they wish and passed to anyone they wish.

Date . . . .

Signed . . . .

Participant

This study is approved by the hospital Research Ethics Committee

Note:

- Participant address should only be obtained if necessary.
- Separate consent should be obtained for electronic recordings to be taken of participants.
- Separate cwonsent may also be required for research workers to distribute participant personal data.

PRINCIPLE OF CONFIDENTIALITY

Confidentiality is commonly applied to conversations between doctors and patients. This concept is commonly known as patient-physician privilege. Legal protections prevent physicians and health care workers from revealing their discussions with patients, even under oath in court. Confidentiality is mandated by the laws in most developed countries.

However, numerous exceptions to the rules have existed. Examples of exceptions to the rule of confidentiality include:

- In most countries physicians are required to report gunshot wounds to the police as well as impaired drivers to the Department of Motor Vehicles.
- Confidentiality is also challenged in cases involving the diagnosis of a sexually transmitted disease (HIV infection) in a patient who refuses to reveal the diagnosis to a spouse.
- Confidentiality is also challenged in cases requiring the termination of a pregnancy in an underage patient, without the knowledge of the patient's parents.

The principle of confidentiality is a key principle in medical ethics. It is often seen as a relatively non-negotiable tenet of medical practice. As medical personnel, we are duty bound to respect people's confidentiality:

- You must respect people's right to confidentiality
- You must ensure people are informed about how and why information is shared by those who will be providing their care.
- You must disclose information if you believe someone may be at risk of harm, in line with the law of the country (rape and other serious crime that put the larger society at risk).

MAINTENANCE OF ETHICAL VALUES IN A HEALTHCARE SETTING

It is critical for every hospital to ensure that appropriate ethical values are upheld. Management must ensure that ethical considerations are taken into account in the following circumstances:

- With respect to maintenance of professional integrity among healthcare workers
- Resolution of conflicts of interest issues
- Dealing with issues concerning medical research ethics (informed consent and ethical approval to carryout research using patients data)
- Organ transplantation ethics

Ethical guidelines for carrying out research involving humans (Helsinki declaration).

The World Medical Association (WMA) has developed the Declaration of Helsinki as a statement of ethical principles for medical research involving human subjects, including research on identifiable human material and data. Based on Helsinki declaration, the well-being of the individual research subject must take precedence over all other interests in medical research involving human subjects. Medical research is subject to ethical standards that promote respect for all human subjects and protect their health and rights. Some research populations are particularly vulnerable and need special protection. These include those who cannot give or refuse consent for themselves and those who may be vulnerable to coercion or undue influence.

Core principles of the Helsinki declaration

- The Declaration of Geneva of the WMA binds the physician, scientist and others involved with the words, "The health of my patient will be my first consideration," and the International Code of Medical Ethics declares that, "A physician shall act in the patient's best interest when providing medical care."
- Populations that are underrepresented in medical research should be provided appropriate access to participation in research.
- In medical research involving human subjects, the well-being of the individual research subjects must take precedence over all other interests.
- The primary purpose of medical research involving human subjects is to understand the causes, development and effects of diseases and improve preventive, diagnostic and therapeutic interventions. Even the best current interventions must be evaluated continually through research for their safety, effectiveness, efficiency, accessibility and quality.
- Medical research must be subject to ethical standards that promote respect for all human subjects and protect their health and rights.
- Physicians should consider the ethical, legal and regulatory norms and standards for research involving human subjects in

their own countries as well as applicable international norms and standards.

- Medical research must protect the life, health, dignity, integrity, right to self-determination, privacy, and confidentiality of personal information of research subjects.
- Medical research involving human subjects must conform to generally accepted scientific principles
- That the welfare of animals used for research must be respected.
- Appropriate caution must be exercised in the conduct of medical research that may harm the environment.
- The design and performance of each research study involving human subjects must be clearly described in a research protocol. The protocol should contain a statement of the ethical considerations involved and should indicate how the principles in this Declaration have been addressed.
- The research protocol must be submitted for consideration, comment, guidance and approval to a research ethics committee before the study begins.
- Medical research involving human subjects must be conducted only by individuals with the appropriate scientific training and qualifications.
- Medical research involving a disadvantaged or vulnerable population or community is only justified if the research is responsive and beneficial to the health needs and priorities of this population or community.
- Every medical research study involving human subjects must be preceded by careful assessment of predictable risks and burdens to the individuals and communities involved in the research.
- Every clinical trial must be registered in a publicly accessible database before recruitment of the first subject.
- Physicians may not participate in a research study involving human subjects unless they are confident that the risks involved have been adequately assessed and can be satisfactorily managed. Physicians must immediately stop a study when the risks are found to outweigh the potential benefits.
- Participation by competent individuals as subjects in medical research must be voluntary.

- Every precaution must be taken to protect the privacy of research subjects and the confidentiality of their personal information and to minimize the impact of the study on their physical, mental and social integrity.

- In medical research involving competent human subjects, each potential subject must be adequately informed of the aims, methods, sources of funding, any possible conflicts of interest, institutional affiliations of the researcher, the anticipated benefits and potential risks of the study and the discomfort it may entail, and any other relevant aspects of the study. The potential subject must be informed of the right to refuse to participate in the study or to withdraw consent to participate at any time without reprisal.

- After ensuring that the potential subject has understood the information, the physician or another appropriately qualified individual must then seek the potential subject's freely-given informed consent, preferably in writing. If the consent cannot be expressed in writing, the non-written consent must be formally documented and witnessed.

- For medical research using identifiable human material or data, physicians must normally seek consent for the collection, analysis, storage and/or reuse. There may be situations where consent would be impossible or impractical to obtain for such research or would pose a threat to the validity of the research. In such situations the research may be done only after consideration and approval of a research ethics committee.

- For a potential research subject who is incompetent, the physician must seek informed consent from the legally authorized representative. These individuals must not be included in a research study that has no likelihood of benefit for them unless it is intended to promote the health of the population represented by the potential subject.

- Research involving subjects who are physically or mentally incapable of giving consent, for example, unconscious patients, may be done only if the physical or mental condition that prevents giving informed consent is a necessary characteristic of the research population. In such circumstances the physician should seek informed consent from the legally authorized representative.

If no such representative is available and if the research cannot be delayed, the study may proceed without informed consent provided that the specific reasons for involving subjects with a condition that renders them unable to give informed consent have been stated in the research protocol and the study has been approved by a research ethics committee.

- Authors, editors and publishers all have ethical obligations with regard to the publication of the results of research. Authors have a duty to make publicly available the results of their research on human subjects and are accountable for the completeness and accuracy of their reports.

- Sources of funding, institutional affiliations and conflicts of interest should be declared in the publication. Reports of research not in accordance with the principles of this Declaration should not be accepted for publication.

- The physician may combine medical research with medical care only to the extent that the research is justified by its potential preventive, diagnostic or therapeutic value and if there is good reason to believe that participation in the research study will not adversely affect the health of the patients who serve as research subjects.

- The benefits, risks, burdens and effectiveness of a new intervention must be tested against those of the best current proven intervention, except in the following circumstances:

- The use of placebo, or no treatment, is acceptable in studies where no current proven intervention exists; or

- Where for compelling and scientifically sound methodological reasons the use of placebo is necessary to determine the efficacy or safety of an intervention and the patients who receive placebo or no treatment will not be subject to any risk of serious or irreversible harm. Extreme care must be taken to avoid abuse of this option.

- At the conclusion of the study, patients entered into the study are entitled to be informed about the outcome of the study and to share any benefits that result from it (access to interventions identified as beneficial in the study or to other appropriate care or benefits).

- The physician must fully inform the patient which aspects of the care are related to the research. The refusal of a patient to participate in a study or the patient's decision to withdraw from the study must never interfere with the patient-physician relationship.
- In the treatment of a patient, where proven interventions do not exist or have been ineffective, the physician, after seeking expert advice, with informed consent from the patient or a legally authorized representative, may use an unproven intervention if in the physician's judgement it offers hope of saving life, re-establishing health or alleviating suffering.

RESEARCH AND ETHICS BOARDS (REBs)

It is a requirement based on the Helsinki declaration that every hospital or research center must have an ethical committee. This committee composed primarily of health care professionals, but may also include philosophers, lay people, and clergy and legal personnel in order to provide balance. Research and Ethical Boards (REBs) should have five or more members, including:

- One clinician with interest in biomedical research
- At least one scientist
- One non-scientist
- One person not affiliated with the institution, an individual knowledgeable in the law and standards of practice and professional conduct
- Special memberships are advocated for lay people to protect the interest and concerns of the general public.

The European Forum for Good Clinical Practice (EFGCP) recommend that in setting up REBs, a quorum must include both sexes from a wide age range and reflect the cultural make-up of the local community. They suggest that the composition should include: Two practicing physicians who share experience in biomedical research and are independent from the institution where the research is conducted, one paramedical professional (medical laboratory scientist, nurse or pharmacist), one lay person and one lawyer.

ETHICAL ISSUES IN MEDICAL PRACTICE

A conflict of interest (COI): Conflict of interest occurs when an individual or organization is involved in multiple interests, one of which could *possibly* corrupt the motivation for an act in the other. A conflict of interest can be discovered and voluntarily defused before any corruption occurs. A conflict of interest can, however, become a legal matter for example when an individual tries to influencing the outcome of a decision. Situations in which an individual or corporation is in a position to exploit a professional or official capacity in some way for their personal or corporate benefit. The influence of the pharmaceutical industry on medical research has been a major cause for concern. A medical laboratory scientist should not allow a conflict of interest to influence their medical judgment. It is unethical and against the principle of conflict of interest for healthcare professionals to:

- Accept company gifts of various kinds, including meals and drug samples to enable favours to be done to the company.
- Act as promotional speakers or writers on behalf of companies for financial gratification.
- Have a financial interest in a medical product company whose products (drugs, reagents or equipments) they prescribe, use, or recommend.
- Refer patients to a facility in which they have a vested interest for medical-related services.
- Accept money from client to render a service that he or she is expected to render by lay without receiving any gratification.
- Bias a community-based research in which they are involved in that are being carried out by an organization in which they he has vested interest or in return for gratification

Giving a patient a negative pre-employment or pre-marital HIV test result when they are suppose to be positive for financial gratification or giving a patient whose haemoglobin genotype is AS an AA result for financial gratification to enable them marry a lady who is AS (to enable the church and girls parent give consent for their wedding).

Many health professionals treat their family members. Healthcare workers who do so must be vigilant not to create conflicts of interest or treat inappropriately. Most health professional groups strongly discourages against health professionals treating members of their own family, but does not prohibit, physicians from treating family members, limiting such situations to those of necessity and cautioning that the patient be transferred to the care of another physician as soon as practical. There are situations in which family members can provide routine care for short-term, "minor" problems. Most professional groups insist that treatment of family members should be limited to minor or emergency care or instances when another physician is not available. The reason why treatment of family members is frown at is because they likely to be informal and may result in compromised care (history taking, physical examination, diagnosis, treatment and follow-up). Treating family members and other intimates is an unwise decision because emotional involvement can potentially interfere with the medical laboratory scientist ability to be objective. Loss of objectivity can affect diagnostic laboratory test to exclude all possibility of disease that may be indicated (including HIV screening), are less likely to recommend an invasive and painful procedures even when they are indicated. Diagnostic reasoning (such as test for diagnosis of cancer in spouses) can potentially be compromised. They may fail to record their encounters, so there may be no documentation to consult for follow up purposes. These omissions and informalities can compromise care and can potentially harm patients.

Sexual Relationships: Sexual relationships between a health profession and patients over whom they have a duty of care are clearly unethical and can create ethical conflicts. Medical laboratory scientist who enter into sexual relationships with their patients can face the threats of de-registration and prosecution. Sexual relationships between health professionals and patients relatives may also be prohibited in some jurisdictions. This prohibition is highly controversial. All codes of ethics set up by medical professional bodies prohibit sexual relationships between a health professional and a current patient. Most medical professional groups adopt a zero tolerance policy towards sexual relationships between their members and patients.

Referrals: It is unethical for a health professional to receive financial gratification for referring patients for medical tests. There is the tendency for such professionals to refer more patients for medical tests even when it is not indicated and not required for the management of the patients' condition. Fee splitting and the payments of commissions to attract referrals of patients are considered unethical and unacceptable in most parts of the world. There is tendency for quality to be compromised. Health professional may be compelled to refer patients for a laboratory test in a center where they have vested interest even when they are apparently aware that there are other better more endowed centers of excellence for the test required. Diversion of patients by medical laboratory scientist from a government facility to their private laboratory is unethical.

ERRORS AND IMPLICATIONS IN MEDICAL LABORATORY SCIENCE PRACTICE

Reducing errors in diagnostic practice is important to prevent medico legal issues and litigation. Such litigations can results in settlement verdicts. Diagnostic laboratories must continuously improve their services and reduce diagnostic error. These strategies must be shared among health care professionals, Laboratories must have a record and track all diagnostic errors and show evidence of root cause analysis done and corrective action put in place to prevent re-occurrence of error and improve patient safety. Laboratories can be potentially liable for errors made in diagnosis that causes patient harm. Such claimant may be awarded a significant compensation by the law court. This can affect the funds available to the laboratory that could have been used to:

- Improve service delivery
- Procure new high throughput and modern laboratory equipment
- To introduce new assay
- Train laboratory personnel
- Diversify the business
- Provide motivation for staff

Most common causes of diagnostic errors

There are a diverse group of factors that cause diagnostic errors and litigation. The factors can generally be group into eight categories and how these factors contribute to medical errors is described below:

- **Communication problems:** Communication-related challenges represent the most common cause of medical errors. Communication problems can cause many different types of medical errors and can involve all members of a health care team. Communication problems can result in poorly documented or lost information on laboratory results and diagnostic testing.
- **Inadequate information.** Poor flow of information can potentially cause problems in laboratory diagnosis. The unavailability of critical information needed to influence prescribing decisions, blood product requisition and absence of a timely and reliable communication of critical test results that can potentially influence a change in treatment being offered can cause challenges in the care and management of patients.
- **Poor information during inter-hospital transfer**: Often, necessary information does not follow the patient when he or she is transferred from another hospital (patient retroviral status to enable the decision to offer CMV negative blood products, patients on purine analogues (fludarabine) and those who have had bone marrow transplant who will need gamma irradiated blood products, patient that require HLA matched platelets), patients on certain medication (such as patients on warfarin) that may affect the treatment they receive.
- **Human error or negligence**: Human problems relate to how standards operating procedures are followed. Errors can often occur when staff refused to follow policies, guidelines, protocols, and processes. Such failures also include none or suboptimal documentation of activities and poor labelling of specimens. There are also knowledge-based errors resulting from inadequate training to provide the care and services required from staff.
- **Patient-related issues** can include improper patient identification, incomplete patient assessment, failure to obtain consent, and inadequate patient education to allow for an informed choice to

be made can potentially results in litigation when things go wrong or errors are made.

- **Sub-optimal training of staff:** Deficiencies in staff orientation or training, and lack of, or inconsistent, education and training for those providing diagnostic care. Laboratories with staff retention problems and those who are under staffed are prone to errors due to stress and inadequate training. Often when new staff is employed there is the rush to get them up to speed as quickly as possible. Sometimes staffs that have not been optimally trained and certified competent are placed on bench to carry out diagnosis on patients' sample. This can predispose to diagnostic error with implication for litigation and payout of claims.

- **Suboptimal staffing levels stressful shift patterns.** Sub-optimal staff levels can cause errors particularly when staffing levels are not commensurate with workloads. Laboratory staffs can become too busy because of inadequate staffing. Error rate, near misses and sickness absence in such laboratories are likely to be high. In such laboratories supervisory function particularly out of hours is likely to be inadequate or not available. Inadequate staffing can potentially put health care workers in situations where they are stressed and under pressure and thus more likely make an error.

Technical failures. Technical failure including equipment and reagent failures is a common cause of error in the diagnostic laboratory. Analyzers and devices used for laboratory analysis can fail (sub-optimal sampling of sample and reagent) and can lead to generation of wrong result which can potentially cause harm to patients. In many instances it is often assumed that the analyst made an error. A complete root cause analysis often reveals that technical failures rather than analyst error was responsible. Sample integrity can also affect diagnostic results. Use of inappropriately stored sample, haemolysed, clotted, under filled and overfilled sample can potentially result in diagnostic errors. To avoid potential equipment and reagent failure, the following must be put in place:

- Equipment must be proactively maintained. They should be calibrated and quality-controlled regularly.

- Analyzer should never be used to analyze patient sample if there quality control (QC) failure. All QC failures must be investigated and corrective action put in place. Analyzer must be calibrated and the quality controlled after every major maintenance. It should only be used to run patient sample unless the QC passes.

- Reagents must be appropriately stored as prescribed by the manufacturers.
- Reagents that are outdated must never be used for testing of patients samples.
- Critical results must be investigated (check for clots, that sample is not overfilled, under filled, signs of haemolysis, lipaemia, cold agglutinins). If there is no justification for such results, a repeat sample can be requested.
- **Absence or inadequate policies and standard operating procedures (SOPS).** All laboratory investigations carried out in the diagnostic laboratory must have standard operating procedures detailing how to carry out test, the principle, sample and reagent requirements, factors that can affect results, calculations and result interpretation. SOPS often guides the delivery of excellent diagnostic service and help prevent inter-analyst variation in testing. New staff should be trained and certified competent based on the SOPS. Absence of SOPS is a significant contributing factor in many diagnostic errors.
- **Poor documentation.** Often failures in the process of carrying out diagnostic services can be traced to poor documentation, non-existent, or clinically inadequate procedures. It is a common policy that if an action has not been documented, then it is imperative that the task has not been done. Also request forms are often inadequately completed. Clinical details, gender, age, time sample was collected and other vital information that can affect diagnostic results are often missing on the request form.
- **Delay in transfer of results.** Delay in transfer of diagnostic result can potentially affect decision making and patient management. An urgent prothrombin time result on a patient on warfarin who require urgent surgery will help clinician determine if patient need to be administer Vitamin K or prothrombin complex concentrate (PCC) prior to surgery to prevent the chances of intra-operative haemorrhage. The results are of no value if they are made available to the requesting surgeon after the patient has come out of theatre. Every laboratory must have in place a procedure for dealing with

urgent samples and critical results. A fibrinogen request of a patient bleeding in theatre will need to be tested urgently and results make available to enable the clinician decide whether to transfuse cryoprecipitate (cryoprecipitate is indicated in major haemorrhages when fibrinogen level is < 1g/L). All genuine critical results (haemoglobin < 8g/dl, international normalized ratio (INR) > 5.0, activated partial thromboplastin time (APTT) > 90 seconds, fibrinogen level <1 g/L, diagnosis of leukaemia, positive haemoglobin S test in a patient going to theatre, positive blood culture, positive malaria result amongst other must be phoned to the requested clinician as soon as possible after testing. A log of the call (name of person to which result was phoned, time results was phoned and the name of the laboratory staff that phoned results through) should be documented in the laboratory Information Management System (LIMS).This may be required to carry out an audit trail in case of litigation, complaint, near miss or an unexpected negative outcome requiring an investigation.

- **Sample collection from wrong patient:** Samples miss-matches are a potential source of error in the diagnostic laboratory. Samples should ideally be labelled once collected by patient's bedside after patient has adequately identified themselves. Transfusion sample should be hand labelled. The use of addressograph labels on a transfusion sample is not acceptable. Phlebotomy staff must be effectively trained and made aware of the devastating effect sample mismatches can have on patient management. Laboratory scientist should often query the result or possibly ask for a repeat sample if critical results obtained is significantly different from previous results without any possible cause (haemolysed sample, clotted sample, lipaemic sample, effect of cold agglutinins, sample taking from a drip arm, EDTA contamination in case of electrolyte analysis resulting in a raised potassium level).

- **Poor quality control culture.** Poor culture with internal quality control and external quality assurance can cause errors in the laboratory results. Internal QC materials are materials of known content. Analyzers must be quality controlled before patients samples are tested on them. Patients sample must only be analysed if the QC passes. Internal QC is a test of precision of laboratory results. Enrolment in external quality assurance is a measure of the accuracy of a laboratory's results. The diagnostic accuracy of a laboratory is often compared with their peers using the same analyzers and reagents. Performance of internal quality control and enrolment an active participation in external quality assurance is often a way to ensure the precision and accuracy of laboratory results and can help a laboratory prove that that they quality conscious in cases of litigation arising from results obtained in the laboratory.

- **Poor storage of reagents:** Diagnostic reagents will only perform optimally if they are adequately stored at the manufacturer's stipulated storage temperature. Most temperature sensitive laboratory reagents are stored optimally at $2\text{-}8^0C$. Refrigerators used for the storage of temperature sensitive reagents must have their temperature monitored round the clock to ensure that the optimum storage temperature is maintained. Poor storage of reagents can result in loss in potewncy and stability of the reagents which can potentially produce wrong results when used for analysis of patients' sample.

MEDICAL NEGLIGENCE

Prior to the nineteenth century, what is described as negligence (writ of tort) today was often treated as writ of trespass. Trespass was initially concerned only with *direct* acts of intentional wrongs (trespass).However, during the nineteenth century the focus shifted to include even act of unintentional wrongs (negligence). As we have seen, negligence was originally described in terms of a duty imposed by law and thus it will be seen that duty is one of the three key elements of negligence today. Negligence as a tort is a breach of a legal duty to take care which results in damage to the claimant. Contained within this definition are the three key elements which must always be established for a successful action in negligence. For a claimant to be able to effectively prove negligence and demand compensation successfully the claimant must be able to provide a substantive evidence of these 3 principles.

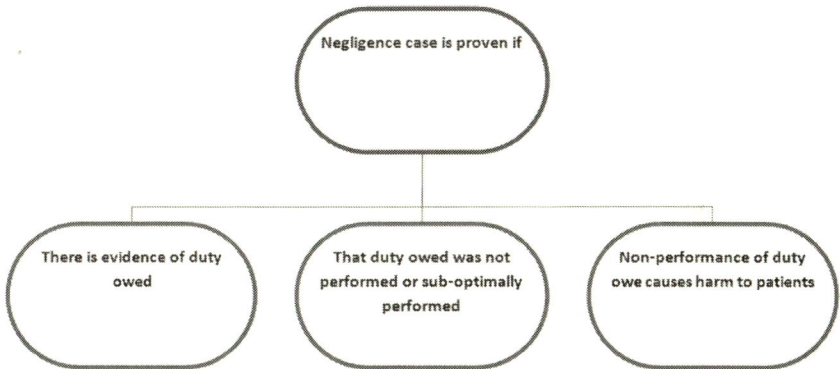

Figure: Principles of negligence claim

PROOF OF NEGLIGENCE

- Duty of care: Does the defendant indeed owe the claimant a duty of care?
- Breach: Has the defendant really broken that duty of care owed?
- Damage: Had that breach of the duty of care owed caused damage of a legally recognised kind to the claimant?

NEGLIGENCE CASE REPORT 1

Case: Mrs James and a friend went to a fast food restaurant in California where the friend Mr Obi purchased a bottle of Banco ginger drink for her. Mrs James drank some of the Banco ginger drink from the opaque bottle but when more Banco ginger drink was poured into her glass, she observed that part of a decomposed cockroach poured into her glass and part was stuck to the bottom of the Banco ginger drink bottle. She claimed that she had suffered shock and sickness as a result and sought compensation. She could not claim in contract from the sellers because their contractual relationship was with her friend who had made the purchase. Instead she sued the manufacturers of the bottled Banco ginger drink for negligence.

Duty owed: The general principle of negligence claim involving a product or service is that; a manufacturer of products does so with the intention that the product will reach the ultimate consumer in the form in which it was produced with no reasonable possibility of intermediate examination. Secondly, that the manufacturer will exercise reasonable care in the preparation of her product so that the product does not cause an injury or harm to the consumer's life or property.

Breach of duty owed: Although a third party, the manufacturer owes Mrs James value for the money paid for the bottle of coke. It is expected that manufacturer would have taken reasonable steps to ensure that the drink reach their customer in a state that does not put their lives potentially at risk.

Harm caused by the breach: There was a breach in the duty owed Mrs James by Banco Ginger bottling company which resulted to harm is not performed and the consumer suffers arm from the negligence of the manufacturers, then the manufacturer is liable.

Liability: In ruling in the plaintiff's favour on a preliminary point of law that it was evident that the existence of a contract between the defendant and the purchaser would not bar a claim in tort by Mrs James, despite the fact that she was effectively a third party. Coca cola was found liable and paid the claimant one hundred thousand dollars.

Negligence case report 2

Case: Mr John has gone to a hospital in Lagos as a result of ill health. He obtained a card and paid for consultation. He was diagnosed of having an enlarged prostate and required surgery for which he was billed N50, 000 which he paid promptly. Patients will normally be discharged home one week after this kind of surgery. He however developed post operative anaemia and had to be transfused two units of blood. Mr John is blood group O positive confirmed during his several session to donate blood on voluntary basis. The laboratory made an error in typing his blood group and grouped him as A positive. Two units of A positive blood was said to have been crossmatched and confirmed compatible. While being transfused with the first unit Mr John suffered a severe haemolytic blood transfusion reaction and his condition deteriorated and he had to be moved to ICU having developed renal failure. Laboratory investigation carried out on Mr John post transfusion sample proved that he was actually O positive and that the hospital laboratory had made an error in his blood group which resulted in Mr John receiving the wrong blood product. Mr John had had prolonged hospitalization of 6 weeks.

Duty owed: The hospital owed Mr John the best possible standard of care from the moment he walked into the hospital and obtained a card and paid for his consultation and surgery. A contractual agreement had inadvertently been gone into between both parties.

Breach in duty owed: The hospital laboratory is expected by law to have a validated process and standard work to follow in the provision of blood and blood products for transfusion. The laboratory should ideally be enrolled in an external quality assurance programme as a way of protecting the interest of the vulnerable public. The laboratory should have evidence to prove that staff performing task are trained, certified and has been found competent. The blood group (forward and back group) of Mr John should have been determined by 2 different methods to ensure that there were no discrepancies. There was no evidence that the process of provision of transfusion had ever been audited. The laboratory did not seem to have been accredited by the Medical Laboratory Science Council of Nigeria (MLSCN). The hospital is suppose to have a laboratory management information system to allow the checking of Mr John previous blood group results from his previous several visits to the hospital. The hospital did not have a significant checks and procedures in place to avert the error.

Harm caused: My John had severe haemolytic transfusion reaction and developed renal failure, had prolonged hospitalization and lost a month income due to this breach. Medical encyclopaedia has shown that acute haemolytic reactions occur with transfusion of red blood cells, and occur in about 0.016 percent of transfusions, with about 0.003 percent being fatal. This is usually due to ABO incompatibility between donor and recipients (for example a group O donor red cells given in error to non group O recipient) resulting in the destruction of donor red cells by the group specific antibodies in the recipient. Usually this type of reaction occurs as a result of clerical error resulting from a sample mismatch at venepuncture or patient misidentification during the bed side check. The anti A and /or anti B in the recipient plasma often react with A or B antigens on the donors red cells resulting in intravascular haemolysis. Signs and symptoms usually occur after 5-10 mls of donor red cells have been transfused. Patients may feel agitated, flushed, feel pain in the venepuncture site, show pain in the abdomen. Other symptoms include fever, hypotension chills, chest pain, back pain, bleeding from wound, increased heart rate and shortness of breath, haemglobinuria, disseminated intravascular coagulation and acute renal failure.

Liability: The hospital was found liable. The hospital owed John a duty to provide him with the best possible care. There was breach on the part of the hospital for not providing the duty owed satisfactorily which resulted in harm and loss of income to the claimant. The hospital was found liable and paid the claimant Five hundred thousand naira.

NEGLIGENCE CASE REPORT NUMBER 3

Case : Mrs Kennedy was referred the cytology laboratory of Ayetero laboratories in Ibadan for a routine Pap smear by Dr X of Stage hospital Ibadan. She was charged twenty thousand naira which she appropriately paid. Pap test is used to detect potentially pre-cancerous and cancerous processes in the endocervical canal of the female reproductive system. Changes can be treated, thus preventing cervical cancer. Since the introduction of the Pap test, deaths caused by carcinoma of the cervix have been reduced by up to 99% in some populations wherein women are screened regularly.

Duty owed: Ayetero laboratories had a contract with Mrs Kennedy the moment she paid for the Pap test. Mrs Kennedy expects that the hospital will have the appropriate equipment, reagents and trained staff to carry out and interpret the test result and that her referring doctor was suppose to have confirmed that Ayetero hospital had all it takes to effective carry out the Pap test.

Breach caused: The laboratory made a sample identification error which resulted in Mrs Kennedy's being given a negative result while infarct she was positive and had carcinoma of the cervix. Mrs Kennedy became sick 6 months later and was diagnosed with carcinoma of the cervix at a specialist hospital in Lagos and later died.

Liability: The Court ordered judgment for the plaintiff (claimant) to the tune of five million naira with liability to be shared between the pathology provider (Ayetoro laboratories) who provided the incorrect result and Stage hospital that relied on the incorrect results.

Professional indemnity insurance scheme

Medical scientists work in healthcare to diagnose disease and evaluate the effectiveness of treatment through the analysis of blood, body fluids and tissue samples from patients. They provide the "engine room" of modern medicine with 70% of diagnoses based on the laboratory results provided by laboratory scientist. Medical laboratory scientist are at the heart of the medical team providing clinical staff with vital scientific information that allows them to make effective medical judgements needed for the effective management of the patient medical condition. When a major incident occurs it is medical laboratory scientists that ensure the right amount of blood reaches the right patient at the right time. We measure vital blood chemicals to monitor patient conditions and detect signs of internal bleeding, we determine coagulation analysis to determine if patients are prone to thrombosis and require anticoagulation, we screen blood and blood product for transfusion to patients to ensure they are free from transfusion transmissible diseases, we carry out blood cultures to determine patients with septicaemia and require antibiotics treatment, we determine the specific antibiotics that is required to treat infective processes in patients, we study biopsies to determine if patients have cancers or are predisposed to cancers and we study Pap smear to determine if a patient is predisposed to having cervical cancers or if they infarct have cervical carcinoma.

Medical laboratory scientist strives to provide their clients with continually improving quality diagnostic services. In the process of rendering these lives saving task, things can sometimes go wrong that may or may not necessarily be our fault as laboratory scientists. However if things go wrong, it pays to be properly insured. Most professional organizations or regulatory authorities (IBMS, Royal College of Pathology, MLSCN, MDCN, and PSN) should provide some level of professional indemnity insurance for their members. They could charge members a minimal fee for this service and could engage a reputable insurance company to provide this service for her members. Professional indemnity insurance serves several purposes:

It can be used to cover legal costs and expenses in defending a claim, and any compensation or costs that may subsequently be awarded to the plaintiff following:

- Professional negligence, such as making a mistake in a piece of work for a client or giving them poor advice.
- For duty owed that was not performed or sub-optimally performed and resulted in harm to a patient.
- Unintentional breach of confidentiality and/or copyright
- Defamation and libel
- Loss of documents or data
- Loss of money or goods (your own or for which you are responsible).

Professional indemnity insurance protects the healthcare professional against claims made by dissatisfied clients. In the course of rendering our professional duties and responsibilities as a medical laboratory scientist or as a medical or allied medical professional; we may find ourselves in dispute with a client. When this does occur, our professional indemnity policy should cover the cost of defending any allegations or claims made against us so we won't have to be personally responsible for meeting the legal fees and any other liability that may be awarded to the plaintiff by the law court.

If the laboratory scientist is found to have made wrong judgment, the insurer will either pay the cost of putting the mistake right or pay compensation on your behalf to the complainant (plaintiff). Professional indemnity insurance will:

• Protect your financial interests
• Minimize disruption to your business
• Cover the cost of defending you even if the claim against you isn't valid.

Your policy will also protect you against claims resulting from:

• The dishonesty of your employees, partners or directors
• Defamation of character
• Infringement of intellectual property rights
• Negligent misstatement or misrepresentation
• Loss of documents or data

CHAPTER 8

LABORATORY QUALITY POLICY AND MANAGEMENT REVIEW MEETING REQUIREMENTS

QUALITY FEATURES OF LABORATORY PRODUCTS AND SERVICES

In a pathology laboratory, a quality product or service can be defined as: the right result from the right specimen collected from the right patient, efficient and effectively communicated to the requesting clinician in a timely fashion to enable them render the best possible care to their patients.

CHARACTERISTICS OF A GOOD QUALITY DIAGNOSTIC SERVICE

- Accurate
- Reproducible
- Timely
- Properly interpreted
- Cost effective

LABORATORY QUALITY POLICY

Our customers receive product (laboratory result) and service (advice) from us. The important quality features of the service rendered from the perspective of the customers are-

- Response time for medical laboratory test is very critical to the quality of care received by patients. Laboratory results should not be received later than expected for the intended purpose.
- Customers expect a continuing improvement in laboratory processes which they believe can have a ripple effect on patient waiting time and positively affect service delivery. Customers want to be informed about the turnaround times of laboratory test.

- Customers expect that laboratory results are reliable and that laboratories meet external and internal quality assessment programs.
- Customers expect a simple and easy to follow instructions on the collection and handling of samples.
- Customers require that information to support requesting and interpretation of laboratory results are sufficient.
- Customers require a prompt and customer focused and friendly phlebotomy services.
- Customers want a service that is continually improving and fashioned towards customer requirement (customer focussed).
- Customer requires a cost effective quality service that contain inherent safety and environmental systems.
- Customers expect laboratories to be process oriented and to possess a feedback system

LABORATORY QUALITY POLICY

Every diagnostic laboratory must have a quality policy. It is a commitment made by the laboratory to provide innovative, high quality and continually improving medical diagnostic services that meet the requirement of her customers, the expectations of the health-care community, and that meet the requirements of regulatory authorities (MLSCN, CPA, MHRA, PSN and ASM) applying the principles of Good Laboratory Practice (GLP) in a health and safety and environmentally conscious laboratory environment implemented by highly motivated professional workforce. The objective of any diagnostic laboratory should be to produce cost effective, accurate, reproducible and timely results which are comparable with the results obtained in a similar laboratory elsewhere which are promptly, effectively and appropriately communicated to the users of the service. The results must be unchallengeable. In this way the quality of the product or service can be guaranteed. Example of the quality policy of a laboratory organization is shown below.

The laboratory management of the Nelson Laboratories UK shall establish a quality policy that includes the following:

a. Nelson Laboratories UK shall provide all the elements of routine haematology service. This shall include blood cell counting and morphology, estimation such as haemoglobin and vitamins, coagulation studies, haematological monitoring of patients with haematological malignancies and other haematological conditions. The Blood transfusion unit of the department shall provide blood transfusion services including; blood grouping, antenatal testing, compatibility testing, processing of blood components and plasma fractions for administration to patients. The department shall refer to other CPA accredited external laboratories specialized immunology and other investigations that are not cost effective for the laboratory to run because of the limited number of request. Haematology and Blood transfusion services shall be provided on 24 hours a day by shift-working.

b. The department of Haematology and blood transfusion is committed to providing the highest quality and timely diagnostic service. We shall strive to provide service that is continually improving and takes into consideration the needs and requirements of its users.

c. The department shall operate a quality management system to integrate the organisation, procedures, processes and resources. Quality management shall be exercised using the lean and six sigma principles in all her processes. It focuses on 4 elements of quality; best possible diagnostic service, no defects, no waste and highest staff morale).

d. We shall use continuous improvement and lean and six sigma tools in delivering services that meets the needs of our patients and other service users. The Department's management team shall provide a framework for setting quality objectives, ensuring that these objectives are reviewed regularly to ensure that quality policy commitment and customer requirements are consistently met. The quality management system shall include a mechanism for continual improvement.

e. We shall develop a culture of pro-active performance management. We shall use analytical tools to show common variances, gather evidenced-based data based on observation as a way of monitoring our processes. Annual reviews of the quality management system by the laboratory management team will allow for a critical evaluation of current quality status to be compared with previous years. The responsibility for quality improvement shall reside with the department Board.

f. The department shall ensure that all personnel are familiar with the contents and work within the context of the quality manuals and all standard operating procedures relevant to their work. We shall ensure that our personnel are adequately trained, certified, maintain a Continuous professional development (CPD) profile, regularly appraised and has a professional development plan (PDP).

g. The department shall ensure that all personnel uphold professional and ethical values and continues to show commitment to good professional practice, good laboratory practice and good manufacturing practice principles and conduct.

h. The department is committed to the health, safety and welfare of its entire staff. Visitors to the department will be treated with courtesy with due consideration given to their safety while on site. We shall implement the principle of appreciative intelligence ensuring that our personnel are motivated and remain our greatest resource. The department is committed to supporting and appreciating our staff ensuring that staff morale is continually enhanced.

i. The department is committed to complying with all relevant environmental legislation. As required by environmental regulators, we shall implement the following best practices by training employees on proper procedures to reduce our facility's impact on the environment. Employee training may include the following; spill response training for personnel who handle hazardous material and hazardous materials management. We shall ensure that all staff has a legal obligation to take reasonable care of your own health and safety and that of others who may be affected by your acts or omissions. All work will be carried out within current Health, Safety and environmental legislation. We will ensure that our employees understand the health, safety and environmental commitment of the department.

j. The department will comply with standards set by the regulatory authorities and is committed to:

- Staff recruitment, training and development and retention of qualified staff at all levels to provide a full and effective service to our users.

- Proper procurement and maintenance of equipments as are needed for the provision of the service.

- The collection, transport and handling of all specimens in such a way as to ensure the correct performance of laboratory examinations.

- The use of examination procedures that will ensure the highest achievable quality of all laboratory tests performed.

- Reporting results of examinations in a ways that are accurate, timely, confidential and clinically useful.

- The assessment of user satisfaction in addition to internal audits and external quality assessment, in order to produce continual quality improvement.

- The quality policy shall be signed dated and issued by the Laboratory Medicine Department manager

- The department is committed to ensuring that the quality policy is communicated in an understandable language and that it is readily available and being implemented throughout the laboratory.

- The department is committed to ensuring that the quality objectives set for the department are reviewed regularly at annual laboratory department management meetings to ensure that policy commitment and customer requirements are being meant.

Signed by the Laboratory Manager Nelson Laboratory UK

_____

Date _____

MANAGEMENT REVIEW MEETINGS IN THE EFFECTIVE RUNNING OF AN ORGANIZATION

Management review meeting is an extremely important part of the success of a quality management system and it is an organization's most significant source for improvements. Management review can be used to tie together all the elements of an organization's program and bring cohesiveness to the quality management system. Management reviews are an integral part of the corrective action / quality improvement process. It should ideally be focused on "trends, objective evidence, and data-based decisions," not on daily operations.

The following topics should be included in the agenda of a typical management review meeting:

- *Follow-up actions: Discuss matters arising* from previous management review meetings.
- Update reports from managerial and supervisory personnel.
- Quality Assurance Report: Discuss changes to the quality assurance standard, external quality assessment reports including non-conformance to standard procedures and regulatory issues.
- Reports of assessment by outside regulatory authorities like the CPA, MLSCN and MHRA
- Equipment/Maintenance: Discuss calibration information, repair & maintenance trending data, trend on equipment maintenance cost and equipment downtime as well as effect of equipment downtime on the laboratory set turnaround time.
- Quality of Subcontractors: Subcontractor/suppliers performance, quality related subcontractor problems and actions, subcontractor trends.
- Customer Complaints: Review results of audits, customer feedback service, summary of user satisfaction surveys, complaints for trending of feedback, issues and resulting actions.
- Corrective and Preventive Actions: Status of previous preventive, corrective and improvement actions. Current type & source of corrective issues, areas most commonly having issues, trends of root causes, reoccurring problems and corrective improvement actions.

- Internal Auditing of Quality management system: Discussion of internal audit results, audit schedule and non-conformances by units.
- Quality Planning: Discussion on upcoming projects, status of ongoing projects, significant changes including staffing and staff morale boosting implementations.
- Resources: Review major changes in organization, management, resource (staff, facility, and equipment) or process.
- *Improvement:* Review of quality policy, quality objectives and overall quality system effectiveness and improvement of system and product.
- Contribution to patient care: Discuss indicators that monitor the laboratory's contributions to patient care.
- Date and Time of Next Meeting. The date and time for the next meeting should be fixed before the end of every management review meeting. The Quality Assurance Manager will produce documentation (including analyses, reviews, proposals, etc.) for circulation to participants before the next meeting. The content of the meetings will be formally documented and recorded by the Quality Assurance Manager. These records will be made available to External Assessors.

Other topics may be added as appropriate depending on the nature and scope of the laboratory. There may be some slight variations between laboratories (equipments or subcontracting used). Although there is no specific requirement for frequency of management review meetings, quarterly meetings are however most often recommended. This allows an organization to stay on top of upwwcoming issues and yet collect data between meetings that are meaningful. The disadvantage of annual meetings is that management may not be able to prevent issues or resolves issues in a timely manner.

It is extremely important for management to try and keep good, detailed records of what was discussed, what conclusions were reached and what actions are needed. If meetings are set around an organization quality objectives, then for each topic at the meeting the following questions should be asked objectively:

- What is our measurement?
- What are our objectives?
- How are we doing?
- Are there any trends?
- Is there any action needed? (people, process, materials, equipment and premises)
- Is there anything else we should consider?
- Have there been any incidents, near misses, complaints from customers or report from customer's satisfaction surveys.
- Updates on audits and accreditation
- Tender for new equipment

These objective actions arrived at during management review meeting can help prompt laboratory management to ensure that actions are discharged within appropriate and agreed timescale. Management Review Meetings are designed to ensure that all quality-related functions are reviewed at the highest possible level so that all levels of management affecting quality are made aware of changes, updates revisions, verification activities and policies. Management review meetings allow for the coordination and Planning of changes in order to provide a continuously improving user requirement focused service and to maximize the productivity of persons involved in the planning, coordinating and implementation of quality changes.

THE VALUE OF MANAGEMENT REVIEWS

- Highlight management's commitment to quality;
- Give them the opportunity to find out what is going on in their laboratory, using a wide range of markers;
- Allow management to instigate changes based on evidence and
- Allow management to allocate resources based on evidence.

MANAGEMENT REVIEWS SHOULD

- Be held at regular, pre-defined periods, usually annually;
- Have a regular agenda, covering all the quality improvements and corrective action areas.

- Yield information that should be summarised to show trends, only giving details of important issues.
- Minutes must be taken during the meeting and all actions followed up should also form part of the minute.

CHAPTER 9

RISK ANALYSIS OF SAMPLE ANALYSIS CYCLE

The accuracy (quality) of laboratory result can be affected by a range of factors, particularly those that occur in the pre-analytical, analytical and post analytical phases of sample analytic process. The figure below shows all the process involved in the sample analysis cycle from test ordering to sample collection to transportation to the laboratory up to result transmittance and availability to the requesting clinician. Risk analysis is an attempt to capture all the steps and risk involved in the process of getting a result on a patient sample. It also shows some of the critical control measures put in place in our laboratory/hospital at each step of the analysis cycle to manage this risk. The process of risk analysis can also potentially detect risk for which the laboratory may need to develop critical control.

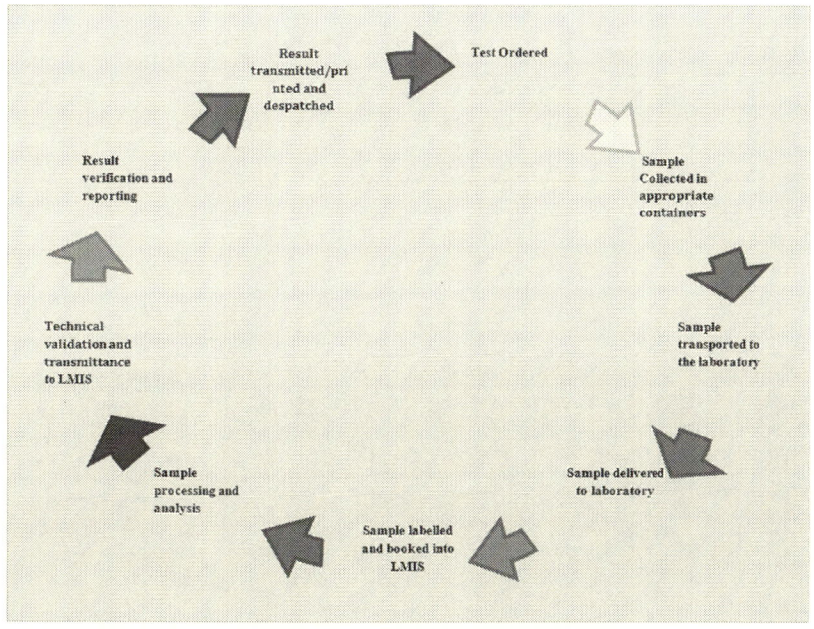

Figure: Sample analysis cycle

PHASE 1: TEST ORDERING

Associated Risks	Control Measures in Place	Control Measures not yet in place
• Incorrect test ordering	• Contact requesting clinician for correction before sample analysis.	• Computerised test ordering.
• Request Form Design	• Encourage requesting clinicians to use the available pathology handbook	
• Verbal orders	in ordering and sample requirement	
	• Educate Clinician on form design	
	• Use separate request form for each category of tests.	
	• Use colour coded forms for different test category.	
	• Use simple form design and avoid overcrowding of test request forms with too many required information.	
	• Get written confirmation for all verbal test orders.	

Phase 2: Specimen Collection

Associated Risks	Control Measures in Place	Control Measures not yet in place
Incorrect syringe/ needle	Use appropriate needle size (e.g. 21G, 23G).	Electronic patient identification and booking system (Bar-coding).
Haemolysis	Allow alcohol solution used for disinfecting phlebotomy site to dry before venepuncture.	
Pre-sampling labelling	Perform venepuncture on 'large' veins. Confirm patient identity before sample collection and label sample by patient bed side.	
Cross contamination	Collect plasma samples before samples that contain clot activator.	
Inadequate sample volume	Collect enough samples to ensure adequate blood to anticoagulant ratio and to ensure sample collected is adequate for requested test.	
Inadequate mixing Intravenous contamination Competence of Phlebotomist	Ensure proper mixture of anticoagulated samples soon after sample collection to prevent clotting. Do not collect sample from an arm with intravenous infusion. Train staff in Phlebotomy skills and educate staff on essential pre-sampling patient preparation.	
Collection of samples into wrong tube containing the wrong anticoagulants for laboratory test intended.	Ensure only appropriately qualified staff collects blood samples. Encourage phlebotomist to use the available pathology handbook in determining sample requirements (volume of blood, sample tube type and other test requirements).	

DR. ERHABOR AND DR. ADIAS

Risk of accidental exposure to infectious blood and body fluids	Ensure phlebotomy staff observe universal precaution during phlebotomy session and ensure that staffs are fully trained on how to deal with sample spill and accidental exposure to infectious blood and body fluids.

STEP 3: SAMPLE TRANSPORTATION

Associated Risks	Control Measures in Place	ControlMeasures not yet in place
• Delay in transportation of samples to laboratory. • Sample lost on transit (for referred samples). • Sample loss/ spill due to inappropriate packaging.	• Transport van available to ensure samples from General Practice surgeries and clinics are sent to laboratory promptly. Phlebotomy staff and porter sends patient samples following phlebotomy rounds in wards and clinics to laboratory promptly. • Availability of adequately validated transport receptacles for transport of temperature dependent samples and blood for transfusion and samples that need to be transported under peculiar conditions. • Maintain a despatch book for all referred samples. Request repeat sample for samples where possible for all lost samples. • Retention of save sample in laboratory for all samples referred out and use only pre-validated packaging for all referred samples.	No protocol in place yet for sample collection and transportation for non-laboratory personnel.

144

Phase 4: Sample Delivered

Associated Risks	Control Measures in Place	Control Measures not yet in place.
• Spillage	• Protocol available for dealing with spillages. Reception staff should be trained on the observance of universal precaution in handling of infectious blood and body fluid. • Ensure that reception staff are up to date with their vaccination against infectious diseases and that there is provision of post exposure prophylaxis for exposed staff	

Step 5: Sample Labelled and booked into Laboratory Information Management System (LIMS)

Associated Risks	Control Measures in Place	Control Measures not yet in place
• Poor attention to details. • Problem of sample integrity.	• Check all samples for correct labelling prior to analysis. • Reject incorrectly labelled samples. • Ensure patient details on sample match details on request form. • Check all samples to ensure they are indicated for requested laboratory test and ensure the integrity of sample is not compromised (sample tube not expired, sample collection date will not compromise result, and sample is collected in appropriate tubes for test requested	• More dedicated and adequately trained staff needed for booking in of samples. • No electronic booking system in place yet at GP surgeries.

STEP 6: SAMPLE PROCESSING AND ANALYSIS

Associated Risks	Control Measures in Place	Control Measures not yet in place
• Insufficient centrifuging • Poor sample separation • Poor sample integrity	• Centrifuge all samples at prescribed speed, time and temperature. Following SOP. • Avoid delay in sample preparation. • Check for clot, haemolysis, haemodilution and under filled, etc before presenting for analysis.	Employment of more trained and dedicated staff for sample processing.
• Taking short cuts in sample analysis.	• Ensure SOPs are strictly followed.	
• Poor pipetting technique.	• Ensure pipettes are regularly cleaned and calibrated following the standard operating procedure.	
• Use of time expired reagents. • Quality Control (QC) and calibration failure • Mix up of patients samples	• Discard all expired reagents and use only reagents whose expiration dates are still current. • Periodically calibrate equipment. • Run QC samples daily and obtain satisfactory results before analysing patient samples strictly following available SOPS.	

- Ensure periodic and proactive maintenance of equipments following available equipment operating procedures.
- Avoid distractions when analysing samples.
- Crosscheck sample labels before analysis.

PHASE 7: TECHNICAL VALIDATION ON ANALYZER AND TRANSMITTANCE TO LMIS

Associated Risks	Control Measures in Place	Control Measures not yet in place
• Investigation of analyzer flags. • • Results from insufficient samples. • Dealing with improbable results from lipaemic samples and samples with cold agglutinin.	• Protocol available for dealing with analyzers generated flags, technical validation criteria and supplementary test requesting. • Protocol available on running short samples through the manual mode of the haematology analyzer. • Protocol available for dealing with lipaemic samples and samples with high MCHC results before technical validation of results on analyzer.	

STEP 8: RESULT VERIFICATION AND REPORTING

Associated Risks	Control Measures in Place	Control Measures not yet in place
• Clerical errors in transcribing results from machine printouts onto patients result sheet. • Abnormal results over looked and use of wrong reference standards to interpret results.	• Protocol available for crosschecking abnormal results and comparing with previous result. • Use correct laboratory set reference standards. • Analyzer preset to flag all confirmed abnormal results for further review.	Need to have a second staff verify results manually imputed before validation of results to prevent transcription error.

STEP 9: RESULT TRANSMITTED/PRINTED AND DISPATCHED TO REQUESTING CLINICIAN

Associated Risks	Control Measures in Place	Control Measures not yet in place
• Results issued without prior authorisation. • Delay in authorised results being issued. • Results issued to the wrong Clinician. • Loss of hard copy result issued • Telephoning urgent results to wrong person	• Ensure all results are duly authorised and by trained designated staff before being issued. Ensure that laboratory turnaround times for laboratory results are met. • Track results and ensure the right requesting clinician get the result. • Retain copies of test results in the laboratory management information system for future reference.	

- Ensure Caldecott principles and confidentiality of patient test results is protected.
- Protocol in place for telephoning laboratory test result to personnel trained to receive such results to ensure confidentiality.

CHAPTER 10

INTERNAL QUALITY ASSESSMENT (IQA) AND EXTERNAL QUALITY ASSESSMENT (EQA)

Quality assurance in clinical laboratories is for the provision of precise and accurate analyses to support optimal healthcare. The importance and value of internal quality control and external quality assessment have gained a higher professional profile particularly with the introduction of the new Clinical Pathology Accreditation standards. Quality assurance improves test reliability through helping to minimise the variability arising from biological or analytical sources inherent in all qualitative and quantitative measurements. An important contribution to the reliability of laboratory results however lies in ensuring correct specimen collection, handling and identification. Although most modern analytical systems are apparently simple to use, the quality of results does not come automatically with the equipment. Appropriate quality assurance measures that include; analytical quality control measures (IQA and EQA) need to be taken, including of course staff motivation, training and assessment. Internal and external quality assessments are vital components of a quality system that offers valuable insights into the effectiveness of the quality system.

Internal quality assessment (IQA): Internal quality assessment assesses in real time whether the performance of an individual laboratory or testing site is sufficiently similar to their previous performance for results to be used. It controls reproducibility or precision and facilitates continuity of patient care overtime. Most IQA procedures employ analysis of a control material and compare the results with pre-determined limits of acceptability. Discrepancies in results are investigated, with major discrepancies requiring repeat testing, possibly with request for another specimen. Larger numbers of samples can be handled in IQA than in EQA schemes. There is also flexibility of sample types to be assessed. External quality assessment (EQA) by contrast looks at differences between sites testing the same analyte, so there can be continuity of testing over geography. This usually involves the analysis of identical specimens at many laboratories and the comparison of results with those of other sites.

While IQA controls the precision of investigations, EQA should be providing an assessment of their accuracy since it lack bias with respect to other test sites. EQA is done periodically and retrospectively. EQA also provides assessment of the overall standard of performance, the relative performance of the analytical procedures (method principle, reagents and instruments) as well as the specimen distributed. EQA is likely to help stimulate needed quality improvement. EQA may also indicate analytical procedures showing excellent performance characteristics and which can be recommended and also identify unsatisfactory procedures which should be discouraged.

CHARACTERISTICS OF INTERNAL QUALITY CONTROL MATERIAL

- Internal quality control (IQC) is the analysis of material of known content.
- Confirms that the procedures are performing within predetermined specifications.
- Day-to-day monitoring of reproducibility or precision but not accuracy.
- Detect errors in any one analytical run.
- Most qualitative assays include internal controls to validate run.
- Use of QC run on analyzers requires control charts (or Shewhart plots) using **Westgard rules.**

REQUIREMENT THAT MATERIAL USED IN CONTROL CHARTS MUST MEET

- Behave like real samples
- Be sufficient for a period of time.
- Be stable over time period of use.
- Be appropriately apportioned for convenient use.
- May vary little in concentration between aliquots.

PRODUCTION OF A SHEWHART CONTROL CHART

Shewhart charts or process-behaviour charts. They are often used to determine whether an analytical measurement is in a state of control. It is use to determine if an analytical measurement is stable and is within variation observed when same analyte is measured repeated on the same equipment. Shewhart control chart has a baseline and upper and lower limits. Results or measurements that are outside the limits are considered to be out of control. Shewhart chat is used in detecting non-random variation.

HOW TO PRODUCE A SHEWHART CHART

A Shewhart control chart uses the arithmetic mean as the centre line. The mean is calculated by taking analytical measurement severally. The several values are then added together and divided by the values and dividing by the number of values. The relative distances of each individual measurement from the mean are taken into consideration, Shewhart charts are a more sensitive way of detecting whether observed variation is due to common or special causes. Shewhart control charts also contain control limits. The control limits define the boundaries of expected common cause (random) variation around the mean. It is commonly used in quantitative analytical assays to determine whether a quality control material of known content tested on a piece of equipment is within the boundaries of expected outcome to enable the analyst decide whether the control has passed and whether the equipment and reagent is fit for use In the analysis of patients sample to allow for diagnosis to be made. All cases of QC failure must be investigated to determine whether it is as a result of the following:

COMMON CAUSES OF QC FAILURE

- Loss of reagent potency
- Poor pipetting skills of the person that reconstituted the reagent
- Equipment related error
- Contamination of reagent by the diluents used
- Suboptimal missing of QC material prior to testing
- Suboptimal thawing for samples that are kept frozen after each testing to preserve the potency

- Failure to allow the QC material to attain ambient temperature prior to testing
- It may also be due to the fact that the equipment may require re-calibration before retesting
- Due to loss of stability resulting from prolonged storage
- Reagent probe-related blockage result in the uptake of suboptimal volume of reagent and sample.
- Suboptimal dissolution of lyophilized control material in the diluents or improper mixing of lyophilized reagent with the diluents.

HOW TO OBVIATE QC FAILURE

- The first step in trying to solve observation of a QC failure is to mix the QC material properly, ensure that it has attained ambient temperature and re-test the sample
- If the test subsequently fail, it may be worthwhile to reconstitute another bottle of the QC material with diluents from a new uncontaminated source and repeat the test.
- If the new reconstituted reagent subsequently fails, it may be necessary to carry out a reagent and sample probe clean and repeat the test.

PREPARATION OF A SHEWHART CHART FROM THE INTERNAL QUALITY CONTROL DATA OBTAINED FOR PROTHROMBIN TIME ESTIMATION.

Mean: 13.5 Seconds

Standard deviation: 0.25

Coefficient of variation %: 1.82

Plus (+)/ minus (-) 1SD limits: 13.75-13.25

Plus (+)/ minus (-) 2SD limits: 14.0-13.0

Plus (+)/ minus (-) 3SD limits: 14.25-12.75

Plus (+)/ minus (-) 4SD limits: 14.5-12.5

TABLE: VALUES OF PROTHROMBIN TIME FOR QC MATERIAL TESTED 20 CONSECUTIVE TIMES

S/No	Date	Analyst	Batch number	Expiration date	Test results (minutes)	Comment/ action
1	1/04/09	O. Erhabor	N0987320	30/09/11	13.7	Acceptable
2	2/4/09	O. Erhabor	N0987320	30/09/11	13.7	Acceptable
3	3/4/09	O. Erhabor	N0987320	30/09/11	13.6	Acceptable
4	4/4/09	O. Erhabor	N0987320	30/09/11	13.7	Acceptable
5	5/4/09	O. Erhabor	N0987320	30/09/11	13.3	Acceptable
6	6/4/09	O. Erhabor	N0987320	30/09/11	13.1	Acceptable
7	7/4/09	O. Erhabor	N0987320	30/09/11	13.4	Acceptable
8	8/4/09	O. Erhabor	N0987320	30/09/11	13.7	Acceptable
9	9/4/09	O. Erhabor	N0987320	30/09/11	13.9	Acceptable
10	10/4/09	O. Erhabor	N0987320	30/09/11	13.2	Acceptable
11	11/4/09	O. Erhabor	N0987320	30/09/11	13.1	Acceptable
12	12/4/09	O. Erhabor	N0987320	30/09/11	13.7	Acceptable
13	13/4/09	O. Erhabor	N0987320	30/09/11	13.4	Acceptable
14	14/4/09	O. Erhabor	N0987320	30/09/11	13.4	Acceptable
15	15/4/09	O. Erhabor	N0987320	30/09/11	13.9	Acceptable
16	16/4/09	O. Erhabor	N0987320	30/09/11	13.8	Acceptable
17	17/4/09	O. Erhabor	N0987320	30/09/11	13.6	Acceptable
18	18/4/09	O. Erhabor	N0987320	30/09/11	13.4	Acceptable
19	19/4/09	O. Erhabor	N0987320	30/09/11	13.6	Acceptable
20	20/4/09	O. Erhabor	N0987320	30/09/11	13.3	Acceptable

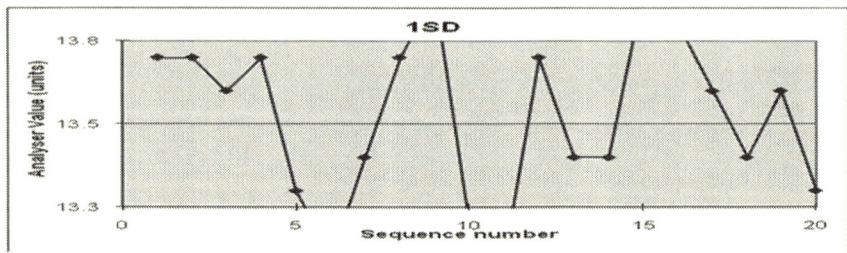

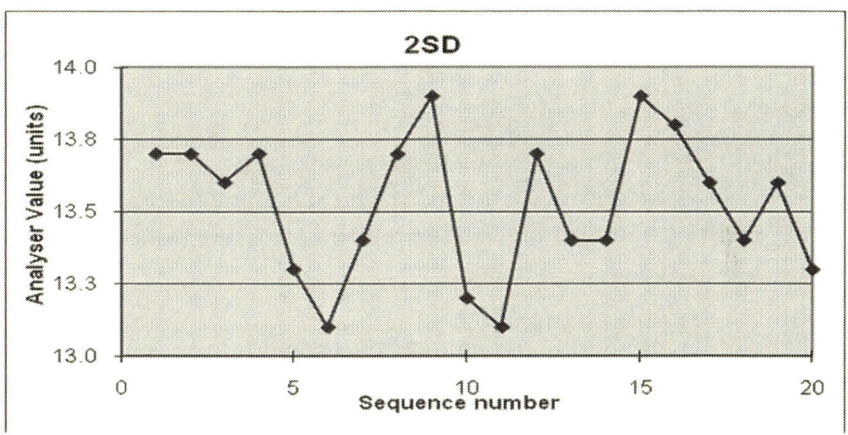

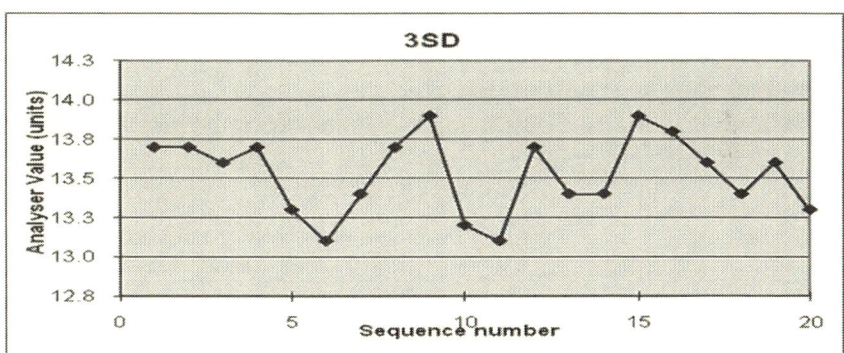

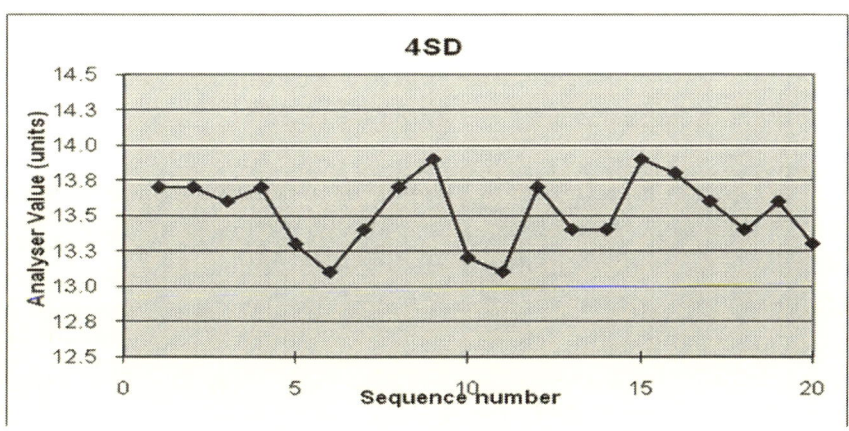

WESTGARD RULES:

1. Rule 1 2S: One internal control is outside the +/-2 standard deviation (SD) limit. This type of result warns of an impending problem. Examine other control results before accepting or rejecting results. From the chart, no value is out of the +/-2SD limits, an indication that the results are reliable and therefore patients results can be accepted and reported with confidence.
2. Rule 1 3S. One internal controls is outside the +/-3SD limits. Violation of this rule may be due to random or systematic error. Results should not be accepted if any one control violates this rule. From the chart this rule was not violated.
3. Rule 2 2S. Two consecutive internal controls are both outside either the +2/-2 SD limits. Violation of this rule may indicate a systematic error. This rule was not violated from the chart.
4. Rule 2 4S: The results of two consecutive internal controls are more than +/-4SD limits. This rule detects random error. This rule was not violated from the chart.
5. Rule 4 1S. This rule is violated when four consecutive controls are outside either +/-1SD limit. This rule detects systematic error and may indicate the urgent need for equipment calibration or maintenance. Rejection of the results is not mandatory. This was not observed in the results charted.
6. Rule 10x. This rule is violated when 10 consecutive internal controls are all on the same (+/-) SD side of the target mean. This rule detects systematic error and may indicate the need for recalibration or instrument maintenance. Rejection of results is not mandatory. This pattern of result was not observed on the chart.

External quality assessment (EQA): EQA is the challenge of the efficacy of laboratory quality assurance procedures by specimens of known but undisclosed content. A central body periodically distributes EQA specimens to different testing sites, and compare individual laboratory results with that of other participating laboratories. It gives participants an insight into their routine performance so that they take appropriate corrective action where necessary. External quality assessment facilitates optimal patient care by providing a comprehensive external quality assessment service in laboratory medicine. Through education and the promotion of best services, it helps ensure that the results of investigations are reliable and comparable wherever they are produced. Assessment of IQA results can be more sensitive to local clinical and technical styles than it is possible with EQA schemes and scoring made more stringent than in EQA.

ADVANTAGES OF EXTERNAL QUALITY ASSESSMENT

- **Comparability**: Participating laboratories are able to assess whether their results are comparable with those of other laboratories. This provides a means of detecting and checking whether such differences are affecting results of investigations of clinical specimens, hence patient care.
- **Educational stimulus**: Participation in EQA can serve as an educational tool for laboratory staff, especially in the area of quality management.
- **Credibility**: Participation in EQA scheme is a demonstration that the laboratory has a responsible attitude to quality issues.
- **Insight into National Performance levels**: EQA results provide laboratory professionals, funding organisations, and health service administrators with an insight into national performance levels for informed decision making on the use of and support for laboratory services.
- **Improvement in national performance levels**: Identification of problem areas enables laboratory professionals to take action to remedy deficiencies, which results in performance improvements over time.
- External quality assessment schemes are standardised and has expert direction.

The EQA process is essentially retrospective and provides an assessment of performance rather than control for each test performed. Participating laboratories may give EQA samples special treatment to improve their chances of getting a high performance score. This practice does not give a fair reflection of the performance of the laboratory and may not give true insight into where there may be genuine problems in the process, therefore hinder improvements in the system. In contrast however, IQA results can be more sensitive to local clinical and technical styles than it is possible with EQA schemes and scoring made more stringent than in EQA.

Internal quality assessment can be used to monitor the whole laboratory, from specimen registration to issue of reports. Performance standards can be derived from the process.

Used together IQA and EQA provide a method of ensuring accuracy and consistency of results and are vital tools in the quality assurance of the clinical laboratory.IQA and EQA results should be reviewed at laboratory meetings and should be readily available information that could stimulate quality improvement in the laboratory.

CHAPTER 11

Performing Root Cause Analysis as a Problem Solving Tool in the Laboratory

Problem Solving Using the Fish Bone Analysis or Cause and Effect Principle (Ishikawa)

The cause and effect or Fish Bone analysis (Ishikawa) is a major problem solving tool that can be used to identify the causes of problems, errors, mistakes and unexpected negative outcomes. They include the Fish Bone Analysis or root cause analysis (RCA) done by asking Why an error or mistake occurred objectively 5 times. Cause and Effect Analysis was first introduced in the 1960s by Professor Kaoru Ishikawa, a pioneer of quality management. RCA if done objectively, can potential lead us to the root cause by the time you ask the 5th why. By using this problem solving tools objectively we can get to the root causes of a problem. Root cause analysis is used to identify all the likely causes of problems. It is a way of critically probing into the potential causes of a problem with the intention of determing all the possible causes of a problem before attempting to proffer corrective measures that needs to be put in place to eliminate the root causes and by so doing prevent the error from happening again in future. An organization can actually build a culture of continuous quality improvement by always finding out the root causes of a problem and implementing corrective actions. Root cause analysis enables an organization to deal with the root causes on long-term basis rather than apply short-term remedial actions which are only quick fixes but does not eliminate the actual root causes of the problem. By implementing short-term remedial action to a problem, we are providing a short-term solution that can only produce a temporary relief to the actual cause of the problem. Root cause analysis requires effective brainstorming that enables staff carrying out the analysis to consider all possible causes of a problem, rather than just the ones that are most obvious. The diagrams created by doing a Cause and Effect Analysis are often referred to as

Fishbone Diagrams primarily because a completed diagram can look like the skeleton of a fish. Potential uses of RCA include;

- Discover the root cause of an error, a mistake, a problem or an unexpected negative outcome.
- It can be used to identify the bureaucracies and bottlenecks that prevent the free flow in a process.
- It can be used to identify the factors that are having a negative effect on the process.
- It can be used to find lasting solution to a re-occurring problem

Root cause analysis (RCA) is a class of <u>problem solving</u> methods aimed at identifying the <u>root causes</u> of problems, errors, mistakes, near misses and unexpected negative outcomes or events. The principle is based on the fact that problems are best solved by attempting to identify, address, correct or eliminate root causes rather than attempting to solve the symptoms of the problem by implementing immediate remedial actions. By directing corrective action to root causes, it is less likely that the problem will re-occur in the near future. RCA is often considered to be an important aspect of building a culture of continuous improvement. Steps involved in carrying out a root cause analysis:

PRINCIPLES

- The primary aim of RCA is to identify the root cause(s) of a problem in order to create effective corrective actions that will prevent that problem from re-occurring in future
- There may be more than one root cause for an event, error, mistake or a problem. It is vital that the factor that is persistently responsible is identified.
- The purpose of identifying all solutions to a problem is to prevent recurrence at lowest cost in the simplest way.
- Root cause analysis can help build a change in perspective from being reactive to problems into a forward-looking proactive culture that solves problems before they occur or escalate. More importantly, it reduces the frequency of problems occurring over time within the environment where the RCA process is used.

- RCA as an element of change can be a threat to many old cultures and traditional beliefs. Threats to cultures can often be met with resistance. For the implementation of corrective action to root causes of problems to be implemented effectively and efficiently, it must have the backing of top management.

General process for performing and documenting an RCA-based Corrective Action

- Define or identify the problem or event
- Gather all the relevant data and evidence
- Objectively ask "why" and identify the causes associated with each step in the sequence towards the defined problem or event.
- Classify the root causes
- Most times there may be multiple root causes to a problem.
- Identify corrective action that will eliminate the root causes and prevent future recurrence of the problem or error.
- Implement the recommended corrective actions.
- Ensure effectiveness by monitoring the implementation of the corrective actions.
- Audit the process again in the near future to confirm that the root causes has been eliminated.

Basic elements of root cause

Element	Root causes
Materials	• Defective raw material • Wrong type of material or tool for a job • Lack or stock out of raw material
Man Power	• Inadequate capability • Lack of Knowledge • Lack of skill • Stress • Improper motivation • Lack of appreciation, praise and recognition (appreciative intelligence)

₁. .chine / Equipment	• Incorrect tool selection • Poor maintenance or design • Poor equipment or tool placement • Defective equipment or tool
Environment	• Disordered workplace • Poor job design and/or layout of work • Surfaces poorly maintained • Inability to meet physical demands of the task • Forces of nature • Poor health and safety compliance • Poor aeration, lightening of laboratory • Problem of posture • Lack of manual handling aids • Lack of optimum storage facility for chemicals
Management	• Lack of management involvement • Inattention to task • Task that are hazardous not dealt with properly
Methods	• No standard operating procedures or poor procedures • Practices are not the same as written procedures • Poor communication • Poor quality reagent
Management system Safety-related	• Training or education lacking • Poor employee involvement • Poor recognition of hazard • Previously identified hazards were not eliminated. • Lack of protective equipment • Suboptimal safety training • Absence of protective vaccine and other occupational health related issues • Absence of post exposure prophylaxis
Other	• Stress demands • Lack of Process • Lack of Communication

162

There are four steps to using Cause and Effect Analysis.

- Identify the problem.
- Work out the major factors involved.
- Identify possible causes.
- Analyze your diagram.

Identify of the actual or specific problem: Identification of the problem includes the determination of what the specific problem really is, identification of staff group, process or equipment that is associated with the problem, identification of when the problem normally occurs as well as where the problem normally occur. Write the problem in the box on the left hand comer of a plain white sheet of paper and draw a line horizontally touching the box (primary fish bone). This allows you to attach side bones (identification of the specific factors associated with the main problem). For example a laboratory manager recently observed that the morale of his staff was low and that they were becoming un-co-operative. The management staff decided to carry out a root cause analysis of the problem.

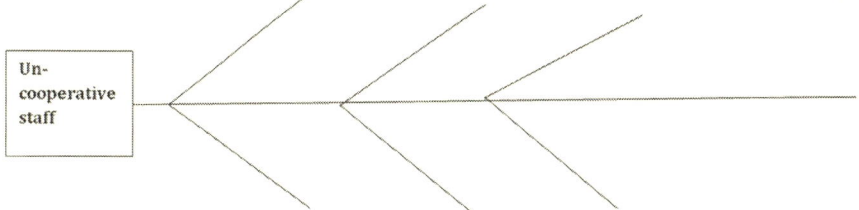

Figure 1—Cause and Effect Analysis Example Step 1

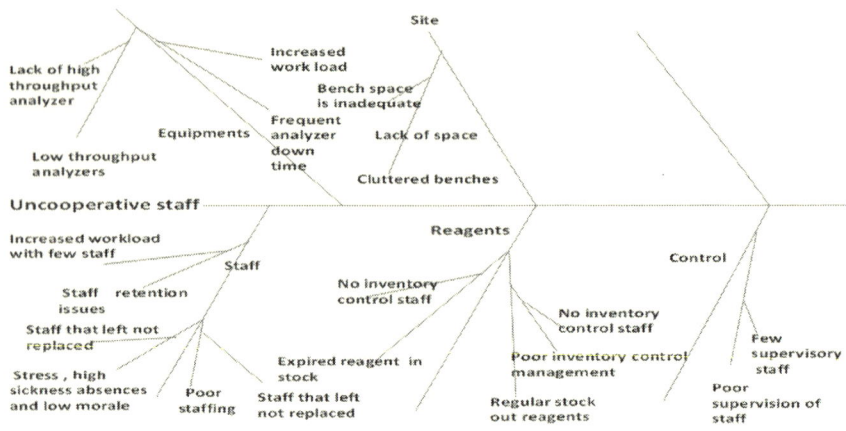

Identify Possible Causes of the problem: Now: For each of the factors you considered in step 2, brainstorm on their possible causes of the problem to which the factor is related. Show these possible causes as shorter secondary bones branching off the primary bones bones. Brainstorming carried out by the laboratory management indicated that staffs were un-cooperative because of; staffing, equipment, reagents, site and control related factors.

Cause and Effect Analysis: Brainstorming carried out on the factors identified from step 2 indicated that staffs were highly stressed because of poor staff levels, poor retention levels. Equipment wise they were dissatisfied with the fact that the main laboratory analyzer was always breaking down due to its inability to cope with the increased work-load that the laboratory has experienced in over the last 6 months. Brainstorming on the reagent-related factor indicated that that staff were unhappy that the set turnaround time targets were not being achieved due to regular stock out of reagent result from holding of suboptimal stocking levels and failure to replenish stock due to the absence of a dedicated inventory control officer. Brainstorming of the control-related factors indicated that staffs are requiring supervisory advice out of hours but that they are not getting the help they deserve due to suboptimal numbers of supervisory staff present in the laboratory. Site related factor investigated indicated that benches are often cluttered due to suboptimal work benches

Analyze Your Diagram: Step 4 involves the analysis of the diagram to show all of the possible causes of the problem. Further investigation identified the following root causes responsible for the lack of co-operation the laboratory manager has experience from his staff.

CAUSE AND EFFECT ANALYSIS IDENTIFIED THE FOLLOWING PROBLEMS

- Lack of high throughput analyzers to manage increased work load was causing stress among staffs.
- Inadequate staffing levels resulting in the midst of increasing workload due to non-replacement of staffs who have left.
- Poor inventory control due to lack of dedicated inventory control staff.
- Cluttered benches due to inadequate bench space.
- Poor supervision due to suboptimal supervisory staffs.

PROPOSED CORRECTIVE ACTION

- Procure a high throughput analyzer that can cope with current and envisaged future increases in workload.
- Advertise and employ 2 new medical laboratory scientists, a senior medical laboratory scientist and an inventory control officer to obviate the effect of negative workload and staff low morale due to stress resulting from inadequate staffing levels, supervisory challenges and inventory control challenges.
- Expand the number of working benches and organise a health and safety training for all staff to re-affirm the need to work in a safety and tidy work environment.

CHAPTER 12

LABORATORY ACCREDITATION PROCESS AND REQUIREMENT

LABORATORY ACCREDITATION

The goal of Laboratory Accreditation Program is to improve patient safety by advancing the quality of laboratory services through education, standard setting, and ensuring laboratories meet or exceed regulatory requirements. The laboratory is the backbone and the most important aspects of modern medicine. Laboratory services contribute to 60-70% of clinical diagnosis enabling clinicians make life saving clinical decision on their patients. There are several processes put in place to ensure that laboratories produce reliable (accuracy and precision) results. These processes have been instituted by regulatory agencies and laboratory professional organizations; Clinical Pathology Accreditation (CPA), Medicine and Healthcare Products Regulatory Agency (MHRA), United Kingdom Accreditation Service (UKAS), American Association of Laboratory Accreditation (A2LA) and the Medical Laboratory Science Council of Nigeria (MLSCN) to protect the interest of the vulnerable public. Laboratory accreditation is a formal recognition by these third-party organizations of a laboratory's capability to carry out accurate high quality diagnostic testing. Individual laboratories themselves must ensure that there are processes in place to ensure that these quality standards are being met. Accreditation is a way of building the confidence of service users and the laboratory that the quality requirements are being maintained.

ACCREDITATION STANDARDS

The standard under which a laboratory is accredited includes 8 standards A-H. Section A describes the organization of the laboratory with it quality management system which uses human and material resources B, C and D (personnel, premises and equipments) to carry out the processing of patients samples during the pre-examination, examination and post examination phases (E, F and G) to produce a diagnostic service that is continually evaluated and quality assured to ensure that the ever changing customer requirement (H) are met.

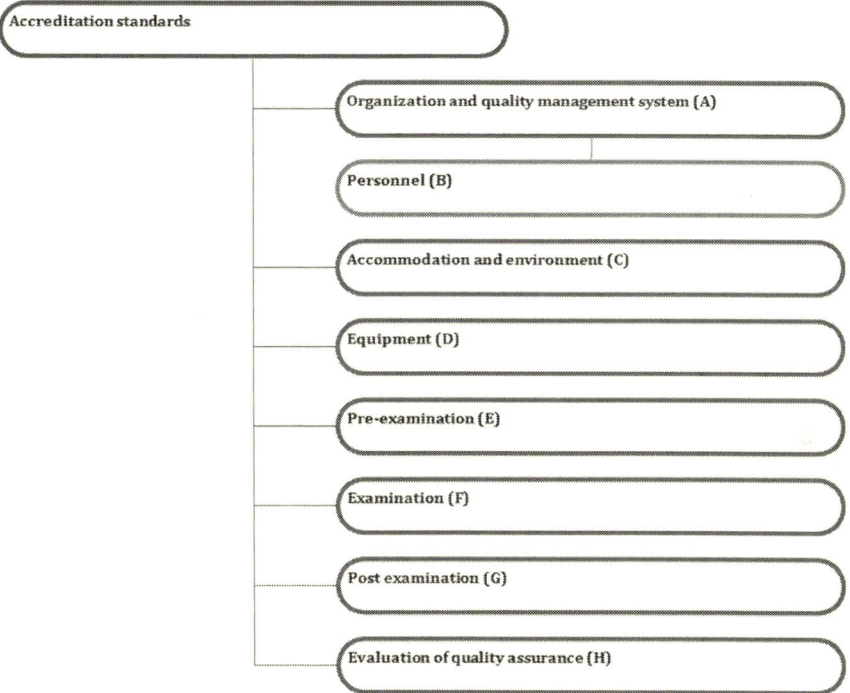

ORGANIZATION AND QUALITY MANAGEMENT SYSTEM

Organization and quality management system

- Organization and management
- Needs and requirements of customers
- Quality policy
- Quality management system
- Quality objectives and plans
- Quality manual
- Quality manager
- Document control
- Control of process and quality records
- Control of clinical materials
- Management reviews

ORGANIZATION AND MANAGEMENT (STANDARD A)

It is expected that laboratories have a clearly defined way the organization is managed and organized. The must commit themselves to meeting the requirements of their service users (customers). The requirements expected from laboratories under standard A includes:

- The laboratory or the parent organization must realize that they are a legal entity and that they can sue and by sued.
- The operation of the process in the laboratory must meet regulatory requirements (CPA, UKAS, MHRA, A2LA and MLSCN).
- Laboratories must create an enabling environment (human and material endowment) to carry out its operation. Laboratories must be adequately staffed (right mix of staff) with highly motivated, qualified, trained, certified, competent and continual professional development compliant personnel. The materials required to effectively carry out required task must be provided by the laboratory management. Other requirements include that:

- Process must be in place to ensure the protection of confidential information on service users and ensure the integrity and impartiality of the laboratory.
- Every laboratory must have an organogram which clearly defines the organization and its relationship with organization to which it is affiliated. It must specify the responsibilities, authority and interrelationships of all personnel (chain of command).
- The laboratory is expected to have regular meetings. Meetings should be have a minute of actions agreed and time scales for implementation. The agreed actions should be implemented with despatch appropriately in a timely fashion.

Director of Laboratory Services

Assistant director of Laboratory Services

Chief Medical Laboratory Scientist

Assistant Chief Medical Laboratory Scientist

Principal Medical Laboratory Scientist

Senior Medical Laboratory Scientist

Laboratory Scientist 1

Laboratory Scientist 2

Laboratory Technician

Laboratory Assistant

Phlebotomist, Clerical and Secretariat Staff

Figure; Example of an organogram showing the chain of command in the diagnostic laboratory

NEEDS AND REQUIREMENTS OF CUSTOMERS

It is expected that the laboratory as an organization must meet the requirements of their service users. All agreements between the service providers (diagnostic laboratory) and service users must be clearly documented and complied with. Other requirements include that:

- The laboratory must identify their service user's requirements and include them as their key objectives.

- Should regularly review their service user's requirements (customer satisfaction surveys) as a way of tailoring their service towards meeting the requirements.
- Laboratories must demonstrate their commitments to their service users. They must have among other things:

  - Have in place a laboratory quality policy
  - Operate a quality management system
  - Have in place quality objectives and plans
  - Have a regular management review meetings at least once a year
  - Ensure that there is adequate human (with the right professional mix) and materials resources for laboratory to meet the requirements of standards B (personnel), C (equipment) and D (environment).

All agreement entered into by a laboratory with her service users must be:

- Documented and include procedure for review of such agreements.
- The user requirement and the examination procedures must be well defined.
- There must be adequate and materials resources on ground to enable laboratory meet her user requirements.
- Procedures must be in place to inform users of service of any deviation from agreement.
- The agreement must contain information of test referred to other 3rd party laboratories

QUALITY POLICY

A laboratory quality policy is a document that defines the operations of the laboratory to fulfil the customer requirements. Every laboratory must establish a quality policy that includes:

- The scope of service delivery it intends to provide
- A commitment by laboratory to meeting her service user's requirements.

- A statement of purpose of the quality management system
- A commitment to meeting set quality objectives as well as offer a continually improving quality service.
- A statement that staffs are familiar with the contents of the quality policy relevant to their work and are committed to meeting its requirements.
- A commitment to good laboratory practice, good manufacturing practice, good housekeeping ethics, health and safety and welfare of staff and visitors.
- A commitment to complying with environmental regulations and other regulatory requirements (CPA, UKAS, MHRA, A2LA and MLSCN).

Laboratory must ensure that the quality policy meets the following requirements:

- Signed and issued by an appropriate authority
- Communicated in a clear, unambiguous and understandable language, freely available and implemented universally throughout the laboratory.
- Must be reviewed in the annual management review meeting to ascertain it continued suitability and effectiveness.

QUALITY MANAGEMENT SYSTEM

A quality management system that that provides an integration of organizational structure, process, procedures and resources must be in place to fulfil the commitment in place in the quality policy to meet the requirements of customers. Other accreditation requirements include:

- Laboratory must have a quality management system in place.
- Roles, responsibilities and authorities of all personnel required to implement the quality system must clearly defined to allow for effective implementation.

Laboratory management must be responsible for:

- Setting up quality objectives and quality planning, preparation of the quality manual.
- Appointment of a quality manager.
- Establishment of a document control procedure
- Establish a procedure for the control of clinical materials
- Conduct a regular management review.

QUALITY OBJECTIVES AND PLANS

It is a requirements that laboratory establish their quality objectives and plans based on the service users requirements. Other requirements include:

- The objectives and plans must be consistent to the contents of the quality policy
- There must be a plan in place to achieve and maintain quality objectives.

QUALITY MANUAL

A quality manual is a description of the quality management system including policies and arrangements in place for its implementation. Every laboratory is expected to have a quality manual. The content of the quality manual shall include:

- The quality policy, description of the quality management system, organogram of the organization with clearly spelt out roles and responsibilities of laboratory management to ensure compliance to standards.
- An outline of the documentation used in the quality management system.
- Laboratory personnel must be familiar and work to current version of quality manual and all referenced documents.
- Review and update quality manual regularly and promptly communicate changes to all staff involved in the process.

QUALITY MANAGER

A quality manager is an officer who acts on behalf of management to ensure the correct implementation of the quality management system. The following must be in place: Laboratory management must appoint a quality manager. The quality manager's reporting procedure must be agreed by the laboratory management. The quality manager must ensure the following:

- The effective implementation and maintenance of the quality management system.
- Report functioning and effectiveness of quality management system to laboratory management.
- Communicate the needs and requirements of service users to staff.

DOCUMENT CONTROL

Document control involves ensuring that documents in use are up-to-date and that there is the confidential use of personal data of service users. Other requirements include:

- Laboratory management to put in place a procedure to control all documents both internally and externally generated and documents in use must be approved by authorized staff prior to use. Other requirements include:
- All documents should contain the following: title, unique identifier, review date, date of issue or revision, number of pages and name of authoriser.
- Document must be legible, readily available, retrievable, in an understandable language without any ambiguity and should be regularly reviewed and updated.
- Only current version of documents shall be available and in appropriate location to ensure accessibility.
- Laboratory management is expected to decide appropriate retention times of relevant documentation based on local legislation, regulation and guidelines available.

- Control of processes and quality records is an essential part of quality management system.

Good document control practice expects that procedures must be in place to control quality records. Such procedure must include:

- Identification and indexing of documents
- Security and retention of relevant documentation
- Storage, retrieval and effective and confidential disposal
- Laboratory management should ideally determine the process and quality records for retention and for how long it is retained.
- Quality records must be readily available to ensure compliance with requirements of the quality management system.
- Process records should be available in order to facilitate the reconstruction of the process of any examination in case of an audit. This is to ensure that an audit trail can be carried out in the case of litigation or incident investigation to identify who did what and when.

CONTROL OF CLINICAL MATERIAL

Control of clinical materials is an essential part of the quality management system including what clinical material to retain and for how long as well as method of disposal. Procedure must be in place to control clinical material (identification and indexing), security, retention, storage, retrieval and disposal. Laboratory management is required to determine what is to be retained and for how long based on prevailing legislation. Laboratory management to put in place a means of effective storage to facilitate validity in case there is need for repeat testing.

MANAGEMENT REVIEWS

Laboratory management must have regular annual management review to identify changes required to the process to ensure that the laboratory continues to meet the changing user requirements. Laboratory should conduct an annual review of quality policy and objectives of all services. Review to include:

- Reports from management and supervisors
- Report of user satisfaction surveys and complaints
- Internal audit of quality management system
- Report of external quality assessments
- Report of any assessment from external organization
- Report of errors, near misses, unfavourable outcomes, status of preventive and corrective actions and improvements required.
- Evaluation of quality indicators required to monitor the laboratory's contribution to patient care.
- Recent changes to organizational structure, management, resources (human and material)
- Report on follow up on previous review.
- Findings from management reviews as well as all agreed actions must be recorded. Management to ensure that agreed actions are dispatched within set times scales.
- Management reviews should contain an executive summary that must be sent to accreditation and regulatory agencies.

PERSONNEL (STANDARD B)

Personnel are an organization's most valuable assets. Their training, certification, competency, appraisal and continuing professional development is important to enable them meet the quality objectives of the laboratory. Laboratory management is to ensure that appropriate number of staff with the requisite education, qualification, training and competence required meeting the demand of the service and appropriate legislation and regulations. Staffing shall include a focal person for the following roles:

- Quality management
- Training and education
- Health and safety

PERSONNEL MANAGEMENT

Personnel management ensures that staffs contribute fully and effectively to the service while receiving fair treatment from the laboratory management. Laboratory management must ensure that procedures for personnel management including the following are in place:

- Staff recruitment and retention
- Staff orientation and induction
- Job description and contract
- Staff records
- Staff annual joint review
- Staff meeting and communication
- Staff training and education
- Grievance procedures and staff disciplinary action.

STAFF ORIENTATION AND INDUCTION

A comprehensive orientation and induction programme is an important element in the introduction of new staff. Laboratory management are expected to ensure that all new staffs participate in staff induction programme that include information on:

- Information about the laboratory or if applicable its parent organization.
- Terms and conditions of employment
- Patient confidentiality and data protection
- Health and safety
- Occupational health service
- Job description including organizational chart
- Salaries and wages
- Staff facilities
- A record shall be kept of participation in the induction programme.

JOB DESCRIPTION AND CONTRACTS

Written job description and contract enables staff to know their duties, responsibilities, right and limitations. All staff shall have contracts of employment which are in compliance with current legislation and provide clear terms and conditions of service. Laboratory management shall ensure that all staff has their job description that includes the following information:

176

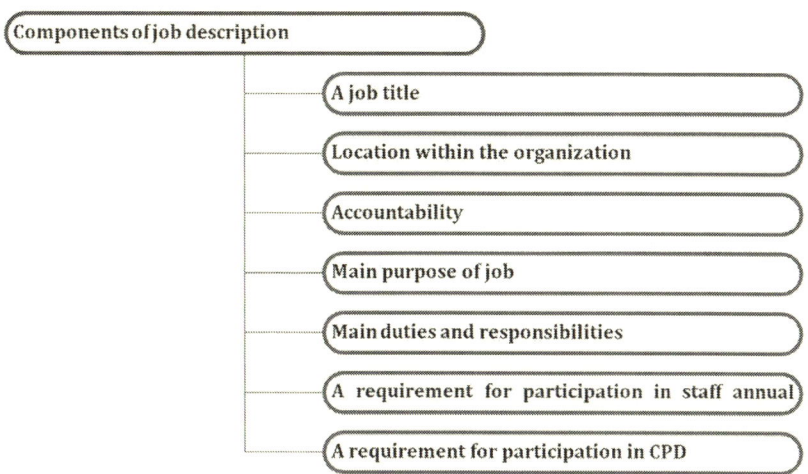

STAFF RECORDS

Maintenance of an accurate staff records is an essential part of personnel management. Laboratory management shall ensure confidentiality of staff records in accordance with local guidelines and national legislation. Staff record shall include:

- Personal details
- Employment details
- Job description
- Terms and condition of employment
- Records on staff induction and orientation
- Record of attendance to mandatory fire, health and safety, manual handling and infection control lectures.
- Record of education and training including CPD
- Record of competency assessments
- Relevant educational and professional qualifications
- Certificate of registration with regulatory agencies (MLSCN and HPC)
- Absence and sickness records
- Accident records
- Records of staff annual joint review
- Record of any disciplinary action
- Occupational health records

Staff annual joint review

Achievement of laboratory and personal objectives is facilitated by regular staff appraisal. Laboratory management shall ensure that staffs participate in an annual joint review (appraisal). All staff performing annual joint reviews shall have received training and those participating shall have received full explanation of the process. Records shall be kept of all staff joint reviews. Personal Development Plan (PDP) must be agreed at such review. PDP is a plan of professional development tasks and activities that staffs are required to meet between their immediate appraisal and next appraisal. It is ways that management can potentially develop their staff professionally to enable them remain relevant to helping the organization meet the changing requirements of their customers and to ensure that staff are also meeting the continuous professional development (CPD) requirement of regulatory professional and licensing authority. Staffs should ideally be appraised yearly.

Staff meeting

Regular staffs meeting are important to keeping staff up-to-date, maintaining good communication and disseminating information on all aspects of the laboratory service. It also facilitates the offering of suggestions by staff on ways to improve the service delivery. There shall be regular meetings open to all staff to provide an opportunity for exchange of information. Records shall be kept and made available to staff.

Staff training and education

Access to continuing education and training is important for all grades of staff and participation in continuing professional development (CPD) is a method to achieving this. There should be a training and education programme for all members of staff governed by the following:

- Training and education shall be in accordance with the policies of the parent organization and guidelines from relevant professional and registration bodies.

- Staff shall be given the opportunity to further their education and training in relation to the need of the service and their professional development.
- Records shall be kept of training and education.
- Laboratory management shall appoint a training officer.

The training programme should be appropriate and include the following:

- Assigned work process and procedures.
- Quality management system.
- Applicable LMIS and computer system.
- Health and safety, prevention or containment of effect of adverse incidents.
- Ethics and confidentiality of information.
- Competency to perform assigned task shall be assessed following training and periodically thereafter. Retraining and re-assessment shall occur when necessary. Records of competence shall be kept.
- There shall be the resources for training and education that includes:
  - Access to reference material and information services.
  - Access to conveniently situated quite room for private study and training with possibly internet facility.
  - Staff attendance at meeting and conference.
  - Offering of financial support to sponsor attendance to relevant conferences and workshops.
  - Access to the premises shall be restricted to authorized personnel.

ACCOMMODATION AND ENVIRONMENT (STANDARD C)

A department requires adequate space and uncluttered benches to ensure that work is performed safely, effectively and efficiently to avoid accident, injury and damage to the environment. The premises shall provide a conducive working environment in which staff can perform required functions in accordance with national legislation and guidelines. The premises shall have space for the following:

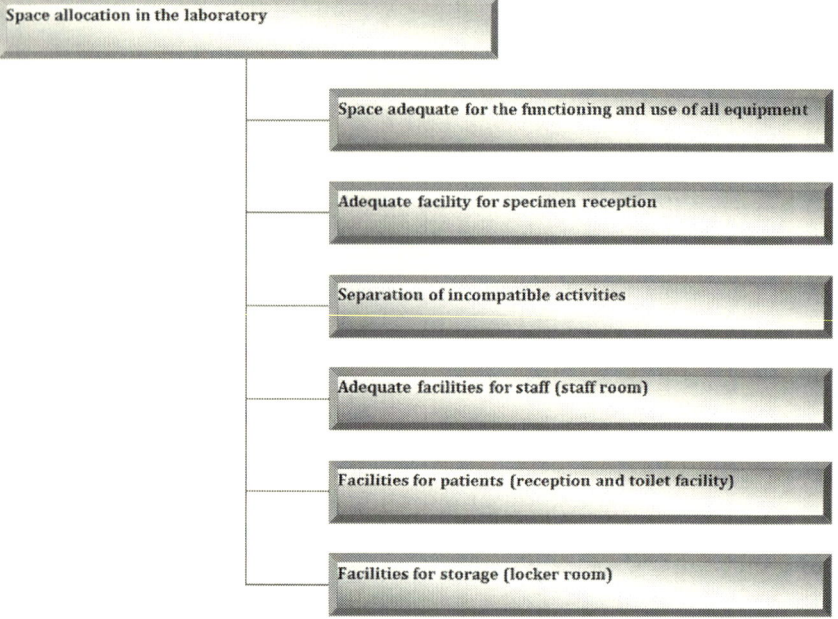

Figure: Creating an enabling environment in the diagnostic laboratory

FACILITIES FOR STAFF

All staff needs facilities within the department to ensure personnel safety, comfort and hygiene. There shall be overnight accommodation when necessary that is conveniently sited and secure particular for out of hours and on call staff. The premises shall have staff facilities that are readily accessible and include:

- Sufficient toilet facility
- Shower facility when required
- A rest area for staff relaxation and breaks
- Basic catering facility and access to supply of drinking water
- A changing area and secure storage for staff personal effects.
- Storage for protective clothing (laboratory coat, aprons, goggles and hand gloves).
- Safe and secure working arrangements

FACILITIES FOR PATIENTS

The facilities available for patient should provide for privacy during reception and sampling and be suitable for examination being performed. There shall be notices advising patients and visitors of health and safety precautions. Facilities for specimen collection and examination should include:

- A waiting reception area with suitable facilities and access for disabled persons.
- A phlebotomy area which offers privacy and recovery facilities.
- Toilet facilities for patients separate from those of staff.

FACILITIES FOR STORAGE

The provision of sufficient storage space, under the correct conditions is vital in maintaining the integrity of samples, reagents and records. The storage facilities shall be in accordance with national legislation, regulations and guidelines prevalent in the country. There shall be separate storage facility for:

- Process and quality records.
- Clinical material
- Blood and blood products
- Hazardous substances
- Drugs, vaccines and other therapeutics
- Reagents
- Waste material including sharps and disposal

HEALTH AND SAFETY

A health and safety statement and procedures to implement it are required to ensure a safe environment in the laboratory for staff, patients and visitors. Laboratory containment facilities shall conform to appropriate requirements and guidelines. There shall be sufficient safety notices and labelling of the laboratory environment such that staffs are aware of the risks and safe practice required. Work area shall be clean, uncluttered and well maintained and there shall be evidence of good housekeeping procedures. Laboratories management shall be responsible for:

- Defining and implementing health and safety procedures
- Ensure that there is safe working environment in accordance with current safety guidelines.
- Providing personal protective equipment.
- Delegating day to day management for health and safety officer
- Providing model rules for staff and visitors to the laboratory.
- Where applicable nominating a microbiologist responsible for infection control and regular reporting to the communicable disease surveillance centre.

All staff shall be aware of their responsibilities relating to health and safety. Laboratory management shall establish a health and safety procedures that include:

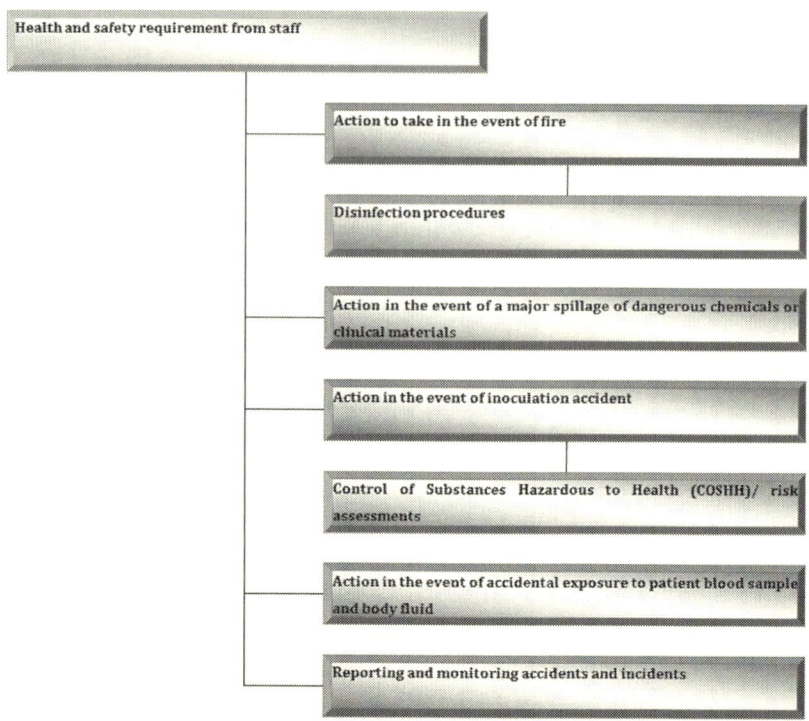

Figure: Health and safety requirement from staff

EQUIPMENT, INFORMATION SYSTEMS AND MATERIALS (STANDARD D).

Procurement and management equipment: The proper procurement and management of equipment ensures that the laboratory can fulfil the needs and requirements and users. Laboratory management shall ensure that equipment is sufficient and appropriate to provide the service. Laboratory management shall establish a procedure for the procurement and management of equipment that includes:

- Assessment and justification
- Selection, acceptance and training
- Preventive maintenance, service and repair
- Calibration and monitoring of the equipment, reagent and the analytical systems
- Decontamination
- Record of instrument failure and downtime as well as subsequent corrective action.
- Planned replacement and disposal
- Adverse incident and vigilance reporting

There should be a programme for preventive maintenance, calibration and monitoring of function shall be documented following manufacturer's recommendations. Every laboratory should have an inventory of equipment that includes:

- Name of manufacturers
- Serial number
- Date of purchase and acquisition
- Current location of the equipment
- Records of contracted maintenance
- Records of equipment breakdowns

MANAGEMENT OF DATA AND INFORMATION

The proper management of data and information in the laboratory is essential for the provision of the service. Laboratory management shall ensure the availability of data and information required to provide a service that meet the need and requirement of service users. Laboratory management shall establish a procedure for the management of data and information that includes:

- Security access
- Confidentiality
- Data protection
- Backup systems
- Storage
- Archive and retrieval
- Secure disposal

MANAGEMENT OF MATERIALS

It is essential to have a proper inventory control management of materials used in the provision of service. Laboratory management shall ensure availability of reagents, calibration, quality control (QC) material required to provide a service that meets the requirements of service users. Laboratory management shall establish a procedure for the management of reagents, calibration and QC including:

- Selection, purchase and ordering
- Assessment of suppliers
- Receipt and verification of identity and condition
- Issue and inventory management
- Risk assessment through classification of hazard and exposure potential and assignment of handling precautions when appropriate.
- Safe disposal
- Materials in use shall be correctly identified with date of receipt, lot numbers, first use and expiry.

PRE EXAMINATION PROCESS (STANDARD E)

To facilitate excellent service delivery to customers, departmental policies and procedures should be made available to service users in an unambiguous, readable and manageable form. Service users require information about availability of clinical advice as well as scope and limitation of service.

Laboratory shall provide up-to-date information to their service users. This information should ideally be in consultation with the users of the service. The up-to-date information for service users can be drawn in conjunction with patient's representative groups (diabetic association, HIV association, Heart foundation and others). The information for users must include:

- Contact details of key members of laboratory staff
- Services offered by the laboratory
- Opening times of the laboratory
- The location of the laboratory
- Information of out of hour's service offered
- Instruction and information required in completing a request form
- Information on sample transport and special handling requirements
- Availability of clinical advice and interpretation of results
- Name and address of laboratory to which test s referred
- Test menu, sample requirement, reference ranges & turnaround times
- List of factors that can affect test performance & interpretation
- Information on time limits for requesting additional test
- An explanation of clinical procedure to be performed as well as instruction regarding preparation for the procedure (For example bone marrow aspiration).

REQUEST FORM

Correctly filled form with all the required information is focal for test performance to the benefit, satisfaction of requesting physicians and by extension the patient. The laboratory shall advocate and ensure the proper completion of laboratory request form). Laboratory shall discuss with service users how they can communicate request including verbal request such as to add on extra test to the laboratory).

The design of the request form which can be paper or electronic form shall include the following important information:

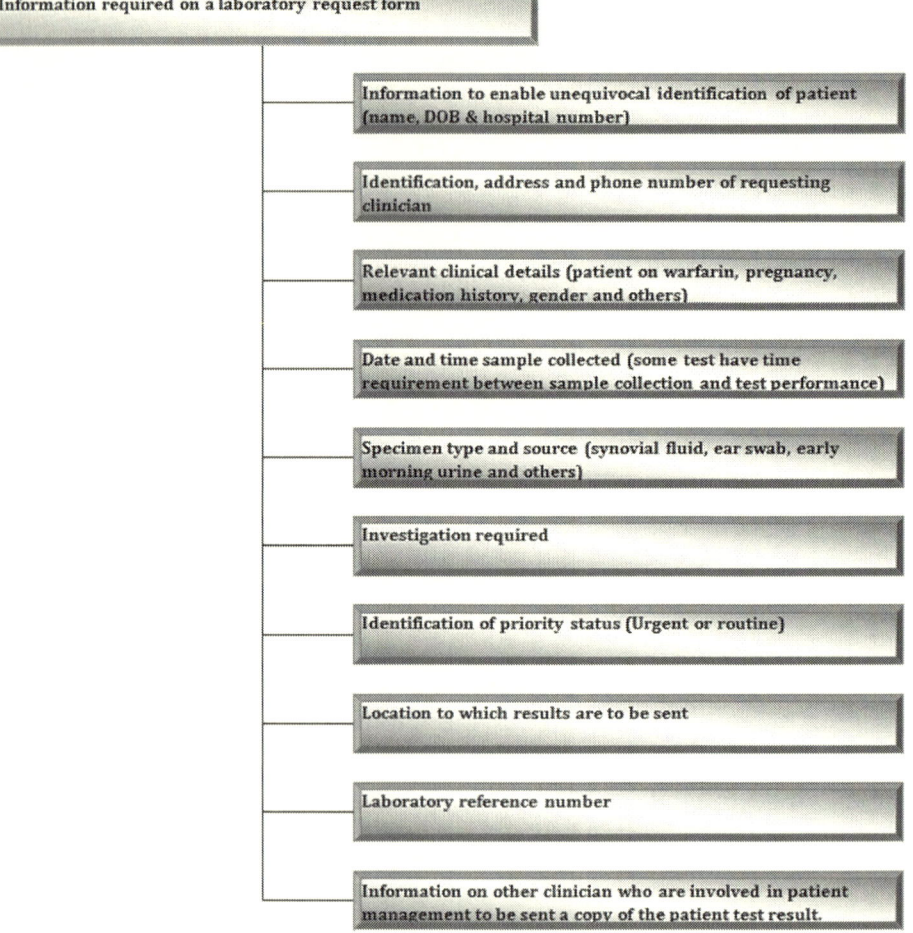

Information required on a laboratory request form

Information to enable unequivocal identification of patient (name, DOB & hospital number)

Identification, address and phone number of requesting clinician

Relevant clinical details (patient on warfarin, pregnancy, medication history, gender and others)

Date and time sample collected (some test have time requirement between sample collection and test performance)

Specimen type and source (synovial fluid, ear swab, early morning urine and others)

Investigation required

Identification of priority status (Urgent or routine)

Location to which results are to be sent

Laboratory reference number

Information on other clinician who are involved in patient management to be sent a copy of the patient test result.

SPECIMEN COLLECTION AND HANDLING

Sample integrity (preparation of patient, collection, transportation and handling) are critical factors that can affect the validity of laboratory results. Laboratory shall establish a procedure for specimen collection and handling which include the following below:

- Useful information shall be available to service users and staff responsible for sample collection and handling (Phlebotomy, porters and sample reception staff).

- Laboratory shall periodical review the sample volume requirement for phlebotomy to ensure that only the desired volume (not excessive or insufficient) are collected particularly for samples like CSF as well as samples from neonates.

SPECIMEN TRANSPORT

Optimum transport and handling facilities is critical to ensure the following: Timely arrival of samples in the right condition and to the right destination is vital. This is to ensure there is minimal risk to courier staff, the environment, members of the public and laboratory staff. Laboratory should establish a procedure for effective transport of samples that include:

- Ensure the safety of couriers, general public, environment and receiving laboratory.
- Packaging, labelling and dispatch
- Ensuring that the specimens arrive within time frame appropriate for the required investigation (to maintain sample integrity).
- Reporting of incident during transport that may affect the specimen or safety of laboratory staff.
- The procedures for the transportation of specimen shall meet regulatory requirements inherent in the country of practice.

SPECIMEN RECEPTION

For laboratory investigation to be correctly performed, samples must be received promptly, efficiently and safely with the sample integrity not compromised. Laboratory management shall establish procedures for specimen reception that includes:

- Put a procedure in place to ensure the linking of request and specimen (use of barcode during booking in).Such link can either be electronically or use of reception note book.
- Recording of the request form and specimen information
- Recording of date and time of receipt of samples
- Procedures for handling urgent samples
- Procedure for ensuring staff safety

Authorised personnel shall review request and samples and decide which are clinically indicated and decide which examinations are performed and the method to be used for their performance. Every laboratory should have a mechanism of linking the primary sample to all further aliquots prepared from the primary sample. This information can be captured electronically by the LIMS or in a paper format. There shall be a procedure for specimen rejection that includes:

- Criteria for rejection of samples (samples with less than 3 identifiers; name, date of birth and hospital number)
- Ways of recording of rejected samples
- Notification of service users concerning the rejected sample and the reason for rejection and advice on the requirement for sample collection for the specific investigation.

Critical factors in sample collection and handling

Request form should allow for unequivocal identification of patient

Ensuring that sample is adequate & collected in the right sample tube

Ensure that patient is adequately prepared prior to sampling (Fasting, not on certain red meat & no prior exercises as the case may be)

Ensure that sample is properly and correctly collected (no anticoagulant contamination for electrolyte determination)

Minimize risk of interchange of samples and subsamples (aliquots)

Ensure that environmental and storage condition optimum to maintain sample integrity is in place

Ensure the safe disposal of clinical waste generated during sample collection (needles, syringes, lancet, swab and hand gloves)

Ensure that high risk samples are properly identified and correctly and safely tested (use of danger of infection yellow sticker)

Ensure that materials required to deal with leaks, breakages and spillage that does not put staff at risk are available.

Minimise the risk to ensure the safety of staff collecting, transporting, the general public and the receiving laboratory

Ensure that medium (cold box, ice box, sample warmers) required for the effective transport of sample from point of collection to the laboratory is optima

REFERRAL TO OTHER LABORATORIES

It is sometimes practically impossible (cost implications, equipment and trained manpower-related challenges) for a laboratory to carry out all diagnostic requests in house. It is expedient, however, to ensure the specimens /data sent to referral laboratories and to consultants for second opinions are documented and efficiently and confidentially handled. Laboratories in consultation with their service users should put in place a procedure for sample referrals to other laboratories and consultants for second opinion. Such procedures should include the following:

- Evaluation of referral laboratories and consultants to determine competence to provide required examination and to ensure that there is no conflict of interest.
- Maintaining a record of all referral laboratories to which samples are sent
- Ensure that referral laboratories should be accredited by regulatory agencies (MLSCN, CPA, MHRA and others) and are enrolled in the relevant EQA scheme for the referred investigation.
- Maintaining a record of all referred specimens
- Recording of despatch date
- Monitoring of returns of results from referral laboratories
- Defining the respective responsibilities for interpretation and reporting of referred test.
- Periodic review of arrangement with referral laboratories to ensure that turnaround times and EQA requirements are being met

EXAMINATION PROCESS (STANDARD F)

Selection and validation of examination procedures: The selection of examination procedures must be clear, clinically appropriate and subject to regular evaluation with the users. Examination procedures including sampling shall meet the need of service users. Examination procedures needs to be validated for the intended use prior to introduction and the methods used, results obtained should be recorded. When examination procedures are changed, results, normal values and interpretation may be significantly different, the implication of this change should be explained to service users prior to introduction. Strict compliance to examination procedures is essential to ensure a quality diagnostic laboratory service. Laboratory must have procedures in place for the conduct of all examination that include the following:

- Purpose and clinical relevance of test
- Scientific principle upon which the investigation is based
- Specimen requirements and means of sample identification (minimum data set; name hospital number and date of birth).
- Equipment and consumables required to carry out investigation
- Reagents, standards, calibrators and internal quality control materials.
- Calibration
- Instruction on performance of investigation
- Limitations of investigation including cause of possible interferences cross reactions and reportable intervals.
- Recording and calculations of results
- Internal quality control procedures and criteria upon which patients samples are judged.
- Reporting reference limits
- Alert and critical values where appropriate and means of dissemination of critical results to requesting clinician.
- Responsibilities of personnel in authorising, reporting and monitoring reports.
- Hazard and safety precautions (risk assessments)
- Performance criteria

ASSURING THE QUALITY OF EXAMINATIONS

A comprehensive programme of internal quality control is required to ensure the quality of all laboratory examinations. The laboratory shall ensure that all examinations are performed under controlled conditions that include the following:

- Implementation of appropriate pre-examination procedures
- Provision of trained and competent staff, appropriate premises and environmental condition, appropriate equipment and materials, information management systems and use of documented procedures (SOP).

191

- Use of internal quality control
- Determination of uncertainty
- Calibration of measuring system
- Verifying the comparability of results
- Participation in external quality assessment programs.

There shall be procedures for internal quality control (IQC) of all examination which confirms that intended quality is achieved. These shall include:

- Records of date, source and storage requirements of IQC material.
- The process of validation of IQC material prior to use
- Appropriate statistical procedures
- Acceptance criteria for results obtained on IQC material (within ± 2SD OR 3SD).
- Ensuring that all IQC results are recorded, regularly evaluated and subsequent remedial and corrective action taken recorded.

Laboratories should determine the uncertainty of results, where relevant and possible. There should a programme of calibration of measuring system and verification of trueness to ensure that results are traceable, where possible, to SI units or to a stated reference material. The laboratory shall have a mechanism of ensuring that all examinations performed using different procedures or equipment give comparable results particularly throughout the clinically appropriate intervals.

THE POST EXAMINATION PHASE (STANDARD G)

The aim and objectives of the laboratory is to produce clinically useful results of examination that is unambiguous and timely communicated to the requesting clinician to allow for the effective management of patients. The laboratory in conjunction with service users shall establish turnaround times for each examination that is reflective of the clinical needs as well as have a mechanism of monitoring non-conformances and recording remedial action. Laboratory in conjunction with users of service shall establish a procedure for reporting diagnostic results which include the following:

- The diagnostic report
- Telephone report
- Amended report
- Clinical advice and interpretation
- Mechanism of informing service users when examination is delayed (particularly in situations where a delay could possibly compromise patient care).

THE LABORATORY REPORT

The main method of communicating the report of laboratory test is through the production of a report. Report can be written (paper) or electronic. The report should be clear, unambiguous, in an understandable language and contain sufficient information to enable the users to interpret the result. The report shall be designed in line with the needs of the service users in accordance with available medical records system. The report shall include the following:

- Laboratory name
- Unequivocal identification of the patient (name, date of birth and hospital number).
- Requester and address of delivery
- Type of specimen, date and time of collection
- Time and date of report
- Results and appropriate comment or reason if examination is not performed.
- Reference ranges as appropriate
- Interpretative comments as appropriate
- Highlighting of abnormal results and inclusion of critical limits
- Status of report (copy, interim or supplementary).
- Identification of persons verifying results and authorising release of the report.

Sometimes secondary reports or letters may need to be issued following receipt of results from referral laboratory. Such report must include the following:

- Include a means of identifying the referral laboratory
- Include the results of referred test
- Include appropriate interpretative comments of the referral laboratory.
- If there is need for results from referral laboratory to be transcribed into the LIMS, there must be a procedure for entering and verification of the correctness of the transcription.
- Laboratory should have a procedure to ensure that laboratory results are transcribed confidentially.

THE TELEPHONED REPORT

Sometimes it may be necessary for the laboratory to telephone critical result to the requesting clinician to allow for timely medical attention. The method for telephoning laboratory results to the requester must be clearly defined to minimise error and to ensure confidentiality. Laboratory management shall establish a procedure for giving laboratory report by telephone or fax which includes:

- The circumstance in which the report may be given
- The nominated individual who can give report
- The nominated individual who can receive the report
- A method of mutual identification of the patient (name, hospital number and date of birth) between the reporter and receiver.
- A confirmation that reported transmitted has been correctly received by the receiver (ask the receiver to repeat the report back to you).
- The mechanism of recording the transmission event
- Mechanism to ensure confidentiality
- The process for sending a follow up report.
- A requirement for a dedicated fax machine that is only accessible to competent staff for the receipt of faxed laboratory results to ensure confidentiality.

THE AMENDED REPORT

The laboratory should have a process in place to ensure that amended reports are issued when necessary. An amended report is a report that is changes in any way after the initial report has been sent out (examples of cases when an amended result may be necessary include; results on a wrong initial sample, sample miss-labelled with a different patients details, results on sample whose integrity is compromised). The laboratory management shall establish a procedure for issuing amended report and shall include:

- The criteria for issuing an amended report
- The authorisation of staff able to issue an amended report
- The identification of the user of the amended reports
- The reason for issuing an amended report
- The instigation of immediate remedial, corrective and or preventive actions
- A process for archiving amended reports

CLINICAL ADVICE AND INTERPRETATION

The provision of interpretative reports is an essential part of service delivery by the laboratory. Laboratory management shall ensure that advice on examination and interpretation of results is available to meet the need and requirements of users of the service. Interpretative comments must be clear, succinct, in an understandable language and unambiguous. Clinical advice and interpretative comments shall only be provided by authorised personnel with appropriate training. There shall be a systematic communication between the laboratory staff and clinical staff to promote effective utilization of laboratory services and to consult on scientific and logistics matter. Appropriate records of such communication shall be kept.

EVALUATION AND QUALITY ASSURANCE (STANDARD H)

Ongoing evaluation and improvement process are essential to ensure that service delivered is continually improving and continues to meet the requirements of service users. System performance involves the quality management system, personnel, premises and equipment while the process performance includes the pre-examination, examination and post examination processes. Laboratory management shall establish a procedure that includes:

- Assessment of user satisfaction surveys and complaints.
- Internal audit of quality management system
- Internal audit of the examination processes
- External quality assessment
- Reports from external bodies (CPA, MHRA, MLSCN)
- Quality improvement measures including corrective and preventive action and the monitoring of quality indicators
- Identification and control of non-conformances.
- The results of these evaluation and improvement processes shall be made available to staff and service users.
- Analysis, recording and interpretation of the evaluation data shall form part of the management reviews.

ASSESSMENT OF USER SATISFACTION AND COMPLAINTS

The main purpose of carrying out user satisfaction surveys and monitoring complaints is to establish that the service provided by the laboratory meets the requirements of service users. Laboratory management shall:

- Establish the process for obtaining and monitoring data on user satisfaction and complaints (it is important that user comments are recorded, reviewed and acted upon).
- Strive to meet performance target in all areas (turnaround times).
- Assess the clinical relevance of investigations carried out as well as the reliability of interpretative reports in conjunction with users of the service.
- Participate in the evaluation of clinical effectiveness, audit, risk management activities of parent organization and external agencies.

INTERNAL AUDIT OF QUALITY MANAGEMENT SYSTEM

Internal audit provides evidence that the quality management system has been effectively established, implemented and monitored. Laboratory management shall establish an internal audit of the quality management system. The internal audit process shall be

- Planned and scheduled
- Conducted against agreed criteria
- Carried out by personnel trained on internal audit who are preferably independent of the work being audited (personnel from one section of the laboratory can help with audits in another section).

Records of all quality audits carried out by the laboratory must be kept. The record of internal audit shall include:

- The activities, areas, individual or item audited (vertical, examination and horizontal audits).
- Any non-conformances or deficiency identified
- Recommendations and time scale for implementation of corrective and preventive actions.
- The results of internal audit shall be regularly evaluated and decisions taken documented, monitored, reviewed and acted upon.

INTERNAL AUDIT OF EXAMINATION PROCESS

Internal audit of pre-examination, examination and post examination process is required to ensure that they are being conducted to agreed procedures. Internal quality control helps to ensure that the examination are being carried out correctly as detailed by the SOP. There shall be internal audit of the pre, examination and post examination processes. The internal audit process shall be:

- Planned and scheduled
- Conducted against agreed criteria
- Carried out by personnel trained on internal audit who are preferably independent of the work being audited (personnel from one section of the laboratory can help with audits in another section).
- Any non-conformances or deficiency identified
- Recommendations and time scale for implementation of corrective and preventive actions.

- The results of internal audit shall be regularly evaluated and the corrective measures and decisions taken documented monitored and communicated.

EXTERNAL QUALITY ASSESSMENT

Participation in external quality assessment (EQA) (proficiency testing) schemes is an essential element in informing both providers and users of the quality of the service provided. Enrolment in the EQA schemes has a major educational component and includes either the analytical service of the laboratory and or the interpretations provided by individual member of staff. EQA schemes provide clinically relevant challenges that mimic patient samples and have the effect of checking the entire examination process. There shall be participation in approved EQA schemes appropriate to the examinations and interpretations provided. A record of result against the agreed performance criteria in approved EQA schemes shall be maintained. The record of the performance in EQA shall be reviewed and communicated to staff and decision taken recorded, monitored and acted upon. When a formal inter-laboratory comparison programme is not available, the laboratory shall develop a mechanism for determining the acceptability of procedures not previously evaluated. Mechanism in such laboratory may involve the exchange of samples and preparation such as slides and digital images between laboratories.

QUALITY IMPROVEMENT

Continual quality improvement is an essential part of maintaining and improving laboratory service delivery. Remedial actions are immediate action taken at the time of detection of non-conformity to mitigate its immediate effects. Corrective action is action taken to eliminate the root cause of the problem responsible for the non-conformance. Preventive action is a pro-active process for identifying opportunities for improvements rather than a reaction to the identification of the problems or complaints. Preventive actions may involve analysis of data, analysis of trends and risk analysis, EQA report and monitoring of quality indicators. Quality indicators to monitor non-examination processes such as customer user survey, worker complaints and satisfaction, laboratory safety and environment and continuing education can provide opportunities for quality improvement.

There shall be a process for continual quality improvement to include remedial action, corrective action, preventive action, monitoring of quality indicators and improvement process. Corrective action shall be taken to eliminate root causes of non-conformances. Corrective action shall be appropriate to eliminate the effect of the non-conformities observed. The process shall include:

- Investigation of the root causes of non-conformities and recording of results.
- Determination of and responsibility for corrective action
- Implementation of corrective within agreed time scale
- Monitoring of corrective action taken

Preventive action shall be taken to eliminate the causes of potential non-conformities. The procedures shall include:

- Investigation of the root causes of non-conformities and recording of results.
- Determination of and responsibility for corrective action
- Implementation of corrective within agreed time scale
- Ensuring that the preventive action taken is effective recorded and submitted for management review.

The laboratory shall establish quality indicators to monitor and evaluate performance throughout the critical aspects of pre-examination, examination and post-examination processes and their relationship to effective patient care. The objectives of quality indicators, their methodology and duration of measurement shall be established prior to implementation. The results of quality improvement programme shall form part of the developmental training and education of all staff.

IDENTIFICATION AND CONTROL OF NON-CONFORMITIES

Procedures are required that ensure that non-conformances in pre-examination, examination and post examination processes are effectively managed to minimize risk to service users. Laboratory management shall establish procedures that are implemented when non-conformances are identified in any aspect of the pre-examination,

examination and post examination processes. Non-conformances can either be; procedural; failure to meet the specified requirements of the quality management system, user or external organization triggered. The procedure shall ensure that:

- The responsibilities and authorities for the management of non-conformances are designated.
- The remedial actions to be taken are defined
- Examinations are halted and reports withheld as necessary
- The medical significance of the non-conforming examination is considered and where appropriate, the service user or requesting clinician is informed.
- The results of non-conforming examinations already released are recalled or appropriately identified.
- The responsibility for authorisation of the resumption of examination is defined.
- Each episode of the non-conformity is documented, recorded, reviewed at regularly intervals by laboratory management to determine trends and to enable the initiation of corrective action.

EXAMPLES OF NON-CONFORMING EXAMINATION ACTIVITIES

- Clinician complaint
- Internal quality control failure
- Instrument calibration failure
- Consumables and reagents-related
- Staff comments related issues
- Reporting
- Laboratory management reviews
- Internal and external quality audits
- EQA-related challenges

Example of non-compliances

- Someone is doing a routine test for which they do not have an SOP.
- Equipment temperature monitoring forms are filled in haphazardly.
- Temperature reading has regularly gone out of set limits. There is no evidence of action taken.
- A diagnostic kit in the refrigerator is beyond its expiry date.
- There is a bottle of clear liquid on the bench with no label on. A member of staff says it is only water.
- A diagnostic kit in the refrigerator is beyond its expiry date.
- The training record of a junior member of staff has not been filled in for some time.
- There is no evidence of training of internal auditors.
- The internal quality control used for a test run was out of limits and there is no evidence that any action was taken.
- A reagent is found on the bench with any label to identify what it is.
- Staff is observed doing a laboratory test without following the SOP
- Equipment is being used to analyse patient sample even though the quality control sample has failed
- Failure to maintain and keep a documentary evidence of maintenance done as prescribed by the manufacturers'
- Staff carrying out a hazardous task without relevant personal protective equipment
- Staff observed dealing with a spill without appropriate spill kit
- Staff observed dealing with a danger of infection sample without appropriate warning sign on the sample
- Staff dealing with potentially hazardous samples for which they have no up-to-date vaccination against
- Staff observed transporting a heave laboratory equipment without the required manual handling equipment
- Staff observed using the laboratory computer immediately after handling a potentially infectious agent with hand gloves on.

TABLE: GENERAL QUALITY REQUIREMENTS OF REGULATORY AUTHORITIES

It is the expectation of regulatory agencies that a laboratory organization be committed to providing a diagnostic service delivery of the highest quality that meets the requirements of her customers. Laboratories are expected to operate a quality management system to integrate the organisation, procedures, processes and resources and have a quality policy with quality objectives and plans. They must ensure that all personnel are familiar with *the* laboratory quality policy and are committed to its applications to ensure *c*ustomer and regulatory requirements are being met. Other requirements include:

- Be health and safety conscious as well as ensure that the environment in the laboratory is enabling and does not compromise the health and safety of staff.
- Treat visitors to the laboratory with ensuring that their safety while in the laboratory is not compromised.
- Committed to the principles of good professional practice and conduct and ensure that professional values are maintained.
- Effectively manage and dispose laboratory waste to ensure that they do not compromise the health of the general public and the environment.
- Committed to the recruitment, training, continuing development and retention of high quality and qualified staff to enable the provision of a continually improving and effective quality service to its customers.
- Ensure the proper procurement, calibration and maintenance of laboratory equipment.
- The use of standard operating procedures, instructions and laboratory request forms to ensure the compliance with document control requirements.
- Ensure that laboratory results are carried out in a timely, safe, confidential, accurate and reliable fashion by highly motivated laboratory professionals.
- Committed to carrying out customer satisfaction surveys and implementing suggestions made to ensure that customer requirements are being met and quality of service is continually improving.

EXAMPLES OF ROOT CAUSE ANALYSIS CARRIED OUT ON NON-COMPLIANCES OBSERVED DURING AN ACCREDITATION VISIT

Non compliance detected	**A laboratory scientist is doing a routine test for which there is no SOP**
Standard violated	This observation constitutes a non-compliance to Examination process and sub standard Examination procedures
Identified root causes	• Absence of a standard operating procedure (SOP) for performing said task. An SOP is a written document / instruction detailing all steps and activities of a process or procedure. These should be carried out without any deviation or modification to guarantee the expected outcome. Any modification or deviation from a given SOP should be thoroughly investigated and outcomes of the investigation documented according the internal deviation procedure. All quality impacting processes and procedures should be laid out in Standard Operating Procedures (SOPs). These SOPs should be the basis for the routine training program of each employee. SOPs should be regularly updated to assure compliance to CPA Standard F (Examination process) and sub standard Examination procedures requirements. Changes of SOPs are in general triggered by process or procedural changes / adjustments.
Immediate remedial action	• Draw up a standard operating procedure (instruction detailing all steps and activities of a process or procedure)
Corrective action	• Train all employees carrying out the specific activity on the SOP and get them to attest to the fact that they are aware of the presence of a standard procedure for the task and that they will continue to carry out the task based on the Standard operating procedure.

Non compliance detected	**Temperature has regularly gone out of set limit and no remedial action was taken.**
Standard violated	This observation constitutes a non-compliance to Standard D (Equipment, information system and materials) and (Management of reagents, calibration and quality control).
Root causes	• Absence of SOP for checking daily storage temperature of fridge used for storage of temperature sensitive reagents and remedial action to take if set limits is not met. • Absence of temperature check in the laboratory daily check list of duties performed by the senior medical laboratory scientist.
Immediate remedial action	• Immediately transfer reagents from the non-functioning fridge to another fridge this is appropriately keeping temperature within manufacturers set limits evidenced from finding on daily temperature log of the fridge. • Check all reagents stored in the fridge to ensure that they are performing optimally (potency). Discard if potency is compromised. • Get a temperature logger. Monitor the temperature of the non-functional fridge closely for few days to get a proper justification for maintenance or replacement of the non-functioning fridge. • Draw up an SOP for monitoring fridge temperature to include remedial action to take if temperature goes out of set limits.
Corrective action	• Consider replacing refrigerator if temperature continues to be above set limit for storage of temperature sensitive reagents. • Include the confirmation of temperature check in the over sight function in the daily check list of duties performed by the senior biomedical scientist. • Train all staff performing the task of recording daily fridge temperature on new SOP as well as intimate them on remedial action to take if temperature goes beyond set limits.

Non compliance detected	**Diagnostic kit in the refrigerator has gone beyond expiry date.**
CPA standard violated	This observation constitutes a non-compliance to Standard D (Equipment, information system and materials) and standard Management of reagents, calibration and quality control).
Root causes	• Poor inventory control management • Lack of regular check of inventory to facilitate the preferential usage of reagents closer to expiration date in preference to those with longer expiration date. • Non-removal and disposal of outdated reagents • Staff not checking the expiration dates on reagents before use. • Lack of a Standard procedure for inventory control of reagents to include remedial actions for dealing with reagents that are out of date.
Immediate remedial action	• Repeat all test carried out using the outdated reagent using reagents that are in date. • Delete results obtained from the use of the outdated reagents from the work sheet. • Fill out a critical incident report and investigate the root causes. • Draw up an SOP for inventory control management of reagents to include how to deal with out dated reagents.
Corrective action	• Remove the reagent immediately out of inventory and discard appropriately. • Train staff responsible for inventory control on the Standard operating procedure for the inventory control management of reagents.

Non-compliance detected	**The internal quality control used for a test run was out of limit and there is no evidence that any remedial action was taken.**
Standard violated	This observation constitutes a non-compliance to Standard F (Examination processes) and (Assuring the quality of examination).
Root causes	• Absence of Standard work for running internal quality control sample and remedial action to take if a run is out of limits. Internal quality assessment helps to ensure precision, reproducibility and facilitates continuity of patient care over time. • Absence of a checking measure to ensure that internal quality control run is within limit before patients samples can be run on analyzer.
Immediate remedial action	• Reject the results of all patients samples ran after running the control that was out of limits • Repeat internal quality control run. If it is still out of limit, investigate the root cause (check that reagents are all in date and properly reconstituted, check that temperature for test is optimal and also consider re-calibrating equipment) • Re-run patient samples once internal quality control run falls back within limits.
Corrective action	• Train staff performing the said task on the drawn SOP to include remedial action to take is run is out of set limits. • Re-affirm to all staff that patient samples must not be run on analyzer until control run are within pre-determined limits of acceptability.

REFERENCES

Clinical Pathology Accreditation (UK) Ltd. Standards for Medical Laboratory: PD-LAB-Standards. Version 2.00, September 2007.

CHAPTER 13

CUSTOMER SATISFACTION SURVEYS AND MISSION STATEMENTS

CUSTOMER SATISFACTION SURVEYS

Customer satisfaction survey is a measure of the extent to which a product or service satisfies customer requirements. Section H of the CPA Standard for the Medical Laboratory in the UK requires laboratories us to assess user satisfaction to allow a laboratory work around meeting the need and requirements of patients. Quality is defined as the degree to which a set of inherent characteristics fulfils requirements. In terms of a laboratory report that means the right result on the right specimen from the right patient that is accurate, timely and properly interpreted. Customer satisfaction is the customer's perception of the degree to which their requirements have been fulfilled. The two key phrases in these definitions are

- Fulfils requirements
- Customer perception

Having done all we can in the laboratory to ensure we are meeting our quality objectives, we must find out what our customers think of the service they obtain. Only then do we really know whether we have satisfied our customers or not. Also, we can use the information obtained to drive quality improvements within our own system. The advantages of carrying out a customer satisfaction surveys include:

- To learn of their requirements and of their level of satisfaction with the service provided.
- To improve liaison with customers and to determine customers requirements and their level of satisfaction
- The customer survey is performed to enable the laboratory put in place strategies to raise the level of customer satisfaction.

Customer satisfaction surveys are great ways of getting feedback from your customers that can be used to drive quality improve of service rendered to customers. Carrying out customer satisfaction surveys and implementing quality improvement suggestions made by customers goes a long way to prove to customers that their opinions and suggestions are appreciated and the service provider listens to the concerns of their customers. Data, comments and suggestions from customers should be objectively and impartially analyzed and corrective actions implemented to increase customer satisfaction. It is important to put a measure in place to ensure that quality of product and service continually increase and improve. Ways of carrying out such surveys include:

- Use of printed questionnaires (short, relevant and straight to the point). It should include open ended questions on what customers like about your product, what their definition of a good product of service, ways they think the present product or service can be improved.
- Face to face or one on one customer interviews
- Electronically via e-mails
- Online
- Telephone interview
- Postal

LABORATORY ORGANIZATIONAL GOAL AND MISSION STATEMENTS

Every result oriented organization (including the laboratory and hospital) must have a mission statement. A mission statement is a statement of the purpose of a company and organization. The mission statement spells out the overall goal, provide a sense of direction, and guide decision-making. It provides the framework or context within which the company's strategies are formulated. Simply put, an organization's mission is the organization's reason for existence, and what it sets out to do. Effective mission statements commonly clarify the organization's purpose. The mission statement ultimately seeks to justify the organization's reason for existing. An organization's mission statements must include the following information:

- Purpose and aim(s) of the organization
- The organization's primary stakeholders (who are your clients/customers).
- How the organization provides value to these stakeholders, for example by offering specific types of products and/or services.

An organizational statement is made up of 5 essential components:

1. Define what the company is
2. Key market—Who are our target client/customer?
3. Contribution—What type of service or services do you intend to deliver to your customer?
4. Distinction—What makes your product or service unique, so that the client would want to choose you despite other competing brands?
5. Must be stated in clear terms so that it is understood by all.

EXAMPLES OF MISSION STATEMENTS THAT CLEARLY INCLUDE THE 3 ESSENTIAL COMPONENTS:

Nelson Biomedical Laboratories mission statement

"Our highly motivated staffs are poised to provide a continually improving and cost effective laboratory and diagnostic service and report accurate laboratory test results in a timely manner which is communicated promptly for the effective management of patients and clients."

- Key Market: The medical and biomedical customers' world-wide.
- Contribution: Cost effective, accurate and timely laboratory test result.
- Distinction: Delivered consistently (world-wide) in a continually improving fashion.

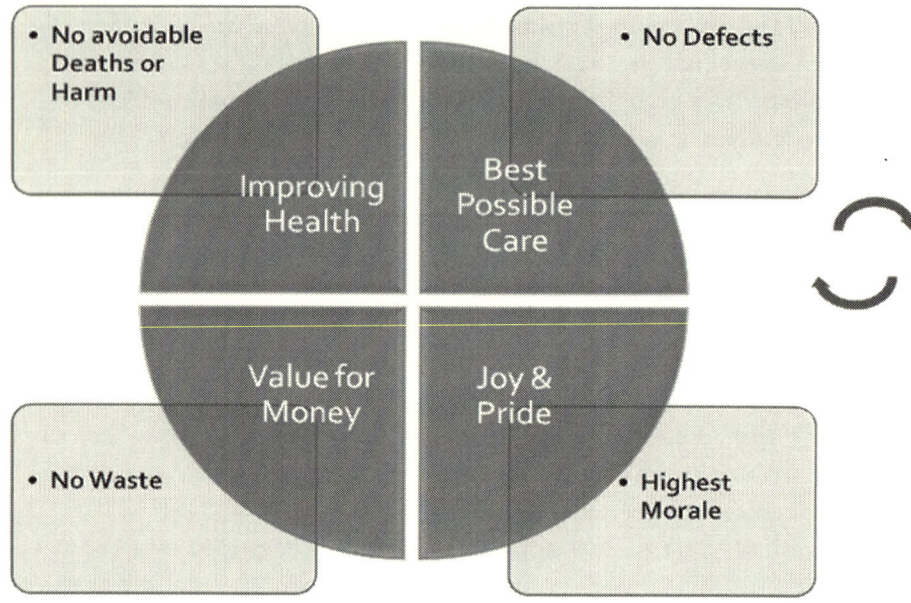

Figure : Mission statement of Nelson Biomedical Laboratories

McDONALDS MISSION STATEMENT

"To provide the fast food customer food prepared in the same high-quality manner world-wide that is tasty, reasonably-priced and delivered consistently in a low-key décor and friendly atmosphere."

- Key Market: The fast food customer world-wide
- Contribution: tasty and reasonably-priced food prepared in a high-quality manner
- Distinction: delivered consistently (world-wide) in a low-key décor and friendly atmosphere.

MARRIOTT HOTELS MISSION STATEMENT

"To provide economy and quality minded travelers with a premier, moderate priced lodging facility which is consistently perceived as clean, comfortable, well-maintained, and attractive, staffed by friendly, attentive and efficient people"

- Key Market: economy and quality minded travelers.
- Contribution: moderate priced lodging.
- Distinction: consistently perceived as clean, comfortable, well-maintained, and attractive, staffed by friendly, attentive and efficient people.

CHAPTER 14

PRINCIPLE OF GOOD LABORATORY PRACTICE (GLP) AND ITS APPLICATION IN THE DIAGNOSTIC LABORATORY

PRINCIPLE OF GOOD LABORATORY PRACTICE (GLP)

Good Laboratory Practice (GLP) embodies a set of principles that provides a framework within which studies are planned, performed, monitored, recorded, reported and archived. Laboratory testing carried out by Biomedical Scientist are generally recognized as affecting decisions literally concerned with life and death issues. There is therefore the need to adopt sound laboratory practices directed at assuring the quality of service delivered. The primary product of a transfusion laboratory is laboratory results of analysis carried out on a blood specimen.

Quality assurance (QA) of such a laboratory must include all of the activities associated with insuring that biologic testing is done properly, interpreted correctly, reported with appropriate estimates of error and confidence levels and communicated effectively and timely to the requesting clinician to facilitate the offering of best possible care to customers. QA activities also include those maintaining appropriate records of sample origins and history (sample-tracking), as well as procedures, raw data, and results associated with each sample. The various elements of good laboratory practice include:

- Use of Standard Operating Procedures (SOP's).
- Availability of Statistical procedures for data evaluation
- Availability and use of personal protective equipment
- Availability and use of infection control equipment
- There is effective management of waste including sharps
- Post exposure prophylaxis
- Staff are up-to-date for the protective vaccination
- Instrumentation validation

- Reagent/materials certification
- Analyst certification
- Laboratory facilities certification
- Specimen/Sample tracking

STATISTICAL PROCEDURES

Data generated by a laboratory will need to be evaluated for the purpose of:

- Showing a trend in workload
- Justification for employment of more staff
- Justification of need for a higher throughput equipment procurement
- Scientific research
- Quality and process improvement.
- Maintenance of optimum stocking of reagents, consumables and blood products.

Laboratories may adopt certain standards which are deemed acceptable within that field (for example using 95% or 99% confidence levels for particular tests) or they may adopt specific statistical analysis procedures for defining detection limits, confidence intervals, analyte measurement units.

STANDARD OPERATING PROCEDURES (SOP's)

SOPs are a written document or instruction detailing all steps and activities of a process or procedure. ISO 9001 and 15189 principles essentially require the documentation of all procedures used in any manufacturing process that could affect the quality of the product. Standard Operating Procedure (SOP) is a set of written instructions that document how a routine or repetitive activity should be a laboratory. The development and use of SOPs are an integral part of a successful quality system as it provides individuals with the information to perform a job properly, and facilitates consistency in the quality and integrity of a product or end-result.

SOP Preparation

Those SOPs should then be written by individuals knowledgeable with the activity and the organization's internal structure. These individuals are essentially subject-matter experts who actually perform the work or use the process. A team approach can be followed, especially for multi-tasked processes where the experiences of a number of individuals are critical. Characteristic of a good SOP.

- SOPs should be written with sufficient detail so that someone with limited experience with or knowledge of the procedure, but with a basic understanding, can successfully reproduce the procedure when unsupervised.
- SOPs should be reviewed (validated) by one or more individuals with appropriate training and experience with the process. It is especially helpful if draft SOPs are actually tested by individuals other than the original writer before the SOPs are finalized.
- The finalized SOPs should be approved as described in the organization's Quality Management Plan. Signature approval indicates that an SOP has been both reviewed and approved by management.
- SOPs need to remain current to be useful. Therefore, whenever procedures are changed, SOPs should be updated and re-approved. If desired, modify only the pertinent section of an SOP and indicate the change date/revision number for that section in the Table of Contents and the document control notation.
- SOPs should be also systematically reviewed on a periodic basis (every 1-2 years) to ensure that the policies and procedures remain current and appropriate, or to determine whether the SOPs are even needed. The review date should be added to each SOP that has been reviewed. If an SOP describes a process that is no longer needed, it should be withdrawn from the current file and archived.

SOP general format

SOPs should be organized to ensure ease and efficiency in use and to be specific to the organization which develops it.

Title Page

The first page or cover page of each SOP should contain the following information: a title that clearly identifies the activity or procedure, an SOP identification (ID) number, date of issue and/or revision, the name of the laboratory to which this SOP applies, and the signatures and signature dates of those individuals who prepared and approved the SOP as well as signature of those who have read, been trained and are committed to following the SOP in carrying out the process/task. Electronic signatures are acceptable for SOPs maintained on a computerized database.

Table of Contents

A Table of Contents may be needed for quick reference, especially if the SOP is long, for locating information and to denote changes or revisions made only to certain sections of an SOP.

Text

Well-written SOPs should first briefly describe the following:

- The purpose of the work or process and the scope to indicate what is covered.
- Denote what sequential procedures should be followed, divided into significant sections; possible interferences, equipment needed responsible person, personnel qualifications, limitation, calculations, reporting, manual handling issues, risk assessment and health and safety considerations.
- Describe all appropriate QA and quality control (QC) activities for that procedure, and list any cited or significant references.

AVAILABILITY AND USE OF PERSONAL PROTECTIVE EQUIPMENT

GLP principle stipulates that laboratory staff wear appropriate personal protective equipment (PPE) when working with biological agents and all potentially infectious materials. Personal protective equipment (PPE) is specialized clothing or equipment worn by a worker for protection against a hazard. The hazard in a health care setting is exposure to blood, saliva, or other bodily fluids or aerosols that may carry infectious materials such as <u>Hepatitis C</u>, <u>HIV</u>, or other blood borne or bodily fluid <u>pathogen</u>. PPE prevents contact with a potentially infectious material by creating a physical barrier between the potential infectious material and the healthcare worker. Personal protective equipments include:

LABORATORY COATS

- Anyone working in a containment laboratory should wear a laboratory coat.
- The lab coat must be fastened at one side, to the neck with close fitting cuffs.
- Coats should be flame retardant and sufficiently impermeable to protect clothing underneath.
- Laboratory coats **must** be removed before leaving the laboratory and hung on appropriate hooks.
- Contaminated laboratory coats should be autoclaved before being sent for washing.

GLOVES

- Gloves should be worn if indicated in the risk assessment for the task being performed. Gloves should be worn for all work with biological agents or potentially infectious material (cell cultures, HIV, HBV, HCV, TB).
- Gloves must be worn when working in a category 3 laboratory. A range of sizes and materials (latex and nitrite) should be available for users to use. Latex gloves must not be used unless justified in a written risk assessment.
- Gloves should be removed before leaving the laboratory, and before using items that may be used by others not wearing gloves such as telephones and computers.
- *Heat resistant gloves must be worn when using the autoclave or handling a hot material.*

EYE GOGGLES

- If the risk assessment indicates that splashes of blood or body fluids are likely, and work is not carried out in a microbiological safety cabinet, then suitable eye and/or face protection (goggles) or a visor should be worn to protect mucous membranes.
- Eye protection may also be required for work with chemicals that can harm the eyes.

RESPIRATORY PROTECTIVE EQUIPMENT (RPE)

Suitable RPE, that has been fit-tested, must be worn when working with airborne hazardous substances. Exposures to airborne hazardous substances can be reduced by either:

- Substituting with less toxic material
- Enclosing the process
- Ventilating the laboratory where the task takes place to ensure an acceptable concentration.

Important point to note with use of RPE equipment:
- Must be used if other means of controlling substances hazardous to health are inadequate.
- Should be used in addition to using other means of control.
- RPE equipment are only effective if used and maintained properly.
- Training should be given to all persons performing task on its use and maintenance.
- The type of protection used should have an appropriate protection factor in relation to the anticipated concentration of hazardous substance(s).
- The PPE should be comfortable for users to wear and a good seal to the face.
- All RPE equipments (except single use disposable types) should be tested regularly and must be in optimum stock levels at all times.

Disposable aprons

Aprons must be worn over laboratory coats when carrying out a task that is associated with risk of spillages.

Availability and use of infection control equipment

- Infection control addresses factors related to the spread of infections within the health-care setting (whether patient-to-patient, from patients to staff and from staff to patients, or among-staff) including prevention (via good hand hygiene/ hand washing, cleaning/disinfection/sterilization, vaccination, surveillance), monitoring/investigation of demonstrated or suspected spread of infection within a particular health-care setting (surveillance and outbreak investigation) and management.
- It is well documented that the most important measure for preventing the spread of pathogens is effective hand washing. Hand washing is mandatory in most health care settings.
- Employers must provide readily accessible hand washing facilities, and must ensure that employees wash hands and any other skin with soap and water or flush mucous membranes with water as soon as feasible after contact with blood or other potentially infectious materials (OPIM).
- Drying of hand is also an essential part of the hand hygiene process. Warm air hand dryers and modern jet-air hand dryers.

There is effective management of waste including sharps

Infectious waste (Clinical waste) and is mainly produced by hospitals, health clinics, doctors' surgeries and veterinary practices, but can come from residential homes, nursing homes and collection of blood for transfusion, which may cause infection to any person coming into contact with it.

Laboratory or clinical waste is made up completely or partly of:

- Human or animal tissue
- Blood or other bodily fluids

- Excretions
- Drugs or other pharmaceutical products
- Swabs or dressings
- Syringes, needles or other sharp instruments
- Also includes drugs or other pharmaceutical products

All sharps must be appropriately disposed into sharps bin. Sharps bins should not be overfilled must have information on source, the signature of staff that put the sharps bin together and the staff that closed it for final incineration and must be kept in a safe place, disposal should be through a registered waste carrier. Sharps are items that can cause cuts or puncture injuries and include:

Examples of sharps used in the laboratory

- Syringes
- Lancets
- Scalpels
- Stitch cutters
- Razor blades
- Glass ampoules
- Other sharp instruments
- Needles

Figure: Sharps commonly encountered in the laboratory

All producers of waste their employees and service carriers, have a duty of care to ensure all waste is being disposed of legally. A duty of care is imposed on all those who produce, carry, keep, treat and dispose of controlled waste or have control of such waste.

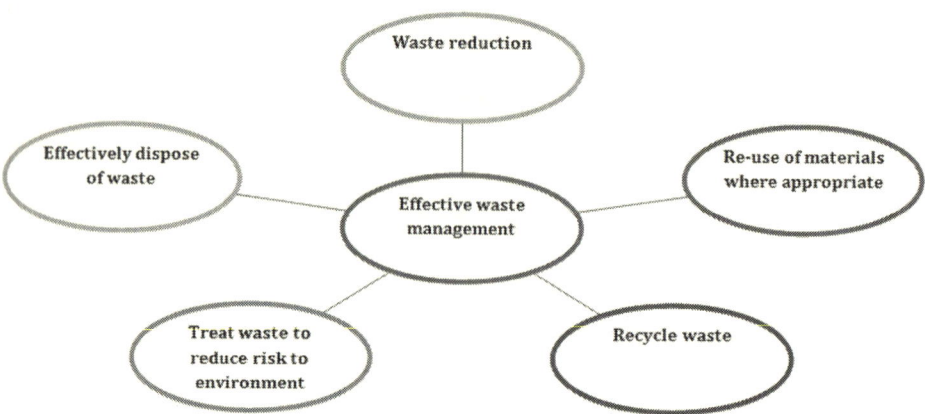

Figure: Effective management of laboratory waste

POST EXPOSURE PROPHYLAXIS

Post-exposure prophylaxis (PEP) is any prophylactic treatment started immediately after exposure to a pathogen (such as a disease-causing virus) in order to prevent infection by the pathogen and the development of disease. In some cases where vaccines do not existent, Post Exposure prophylaxis is another method of protecting the health care worker exposed to a life threatening infectious disease. Management of post exposure prophylaxis includes:

- In case of exposure to blood and body fluid of an HIV-infected patient through needle stick injury, HIV infection can be prevented by giving the exposed healthcare worker post-exposure prophylaxis made up of a course of antiretroviral drugs. This reduces the risk of seroconversion after events with high risk of exposure to HIV.

- The antiretroviral regimen used in PEP is the same as the standard highly active antiretroviral therapy used to treat AIDS. It requires close compliance and can have unpleasant side effects including malaise, fatigue, diarrhea, headache, nausea and vomiting.

- Human Normal Immunoglobulin (HNIG) or hepatitis A vaccine may be used as PEP for staff exposed to blood and body fluid of an hepatitis A positive source patient depending on the clinical situation.

220

- If a healthcare worker who is not previously vaccinated or a non responder is exposed is an HBsAg positive source patient blood or body fluid, HBV vaccine and hepatitis B immune globulin (HBIG) can be administered. But for those already vaccinated and are responders, a booster dose should be given.
- Persons exposed to Hepatitis C should get monthly PCR—if seroconversion then interferon +/- ribavirin

STAFF MUST UP-TO-DATE FOR THE PROTECTIVE VACCINATION

- Health care workers may be exposed to certain infections in the course of their work.
- Vaccines are available to provide some protection to workers in a healthcare setting.
- Depending on regulation, recommendation, the specific work function, or personal preference, healthcare workers may receive vaccinations for hepatitis B; Influenza, Measles, Mumps, Rubella, Tetanus, Diphtheria, Tetanus, Pertussis, Nieseria meningitidis and varicella.
- In general, vaccines do not guarantee complete protection from disease, and there is potential for adverse effects from receiving the vaccine.

INSTRUMENTATION VALIDATION

Instrument validation is a process that is very important for any analytical laboratory. Instrument validation ensures that an instrument is fit for its intended use (fit for purpose). Data produced by faulty instruments may give the appearance of valid data. These events are particularly difficult to detect with modern computer-controlled systems which remove the analyst from the data collection and instrument control functions. Important points on instrument validation include:

- It is essential that some objective procedures are implemented for continuously assessing the validity of laboratory instrument and the data they provide.

- These procedures must be executed on a regular basis to establish the continuing acceptable operation of laboratory instruments within manufacturers prescribed specifications.
- Time-related graphical records of the results of these instrument validation procedures (control charts) must be documented either electronically or as a soft copy.

REAGENT/MATERIALS CERTIFICATION

- GLP guidelines emphasize that all reagents intended for use in the analysis of patient sample must be tested and quality controlled and certified fit for it intended use.
- Certification must follow accepted procedures, and must be adequately documented.
- Each container of laboratory reagent must be labelled with information related to its certification value, date, and expiration time.
- Time expired reagents must never be used for diagnostic purposes on patients samples.
- Reagents must by quality controlled daily before use
- Equipment must be quality controlled with reagents after every major maintenance work is done on it.
- Reagents including temperature dependent reagents must be appropriately stored. Most temperature dependent reagents are stored optimally between 2-8^{0}C.Evidence of temperature monitoring of fridges used for storage of reagents must be kept to show remedial action to be taken when temperature is not maintained within the optimum temperature range.

CERTIFICATION OF ANALYSTS

Certification of analyst is a required part of QA. Some acceptable proof of satisfactory training and/or competence with specific laboratory procedures must be established for each analyst. Execution of these basic procedures will be repeated, if necessary, until satisfactory results are obtained (evaluated based on analytical accuracy and precision).

CERTIFICATION OF LABORATORY FACILITIES

Laboratory certification is normally done by some external agency. For example, an analytical laboratory might be audited by representatives of a federal agency with which they have a contract. An independent laboratory might file documentation with a responsible state or federal agency. The evaluation is concerned with such issues as space (amount, quality and relevance), ventilation, equipment, storage, hygiene, etc. Student chemistry laboratories are generally evaluated by the American Chemical Society, as part of the process of granting approval for the overall chemistry program presented by the college or university. This latter approval process is not as detailed regarding analytical facilities as the certification processes pursued by agencies concerned specifically with quality assurance.

SPECIMEN/SAMPLE-TRACKING

Specimen tracking is an aspect of quality assurance which has received a great deal of attention particularly with the advent of computer-based Laboratory Information Management Systems (LIMS).GLP principle stipulates that:

- Procedures should be in place for assuring adequate specimen/sample-tracking may vary among laboratories; the procedures must however maintain the unmistakable connection between a set of analytical results and the specimen from which they were obtained.
- In addition, the original source of the specimen must be recorded and likewise unmistakably connected with the set of analytical data.
- Finally, in many cases there must be information or an audit trail of a sample (to include when sample was receive, book on the LIMS, when sample was loaded on analyzer, when results was technically validated on the analyzer, when result clinically validated and available to the requesting clinician.
- At every stage of this trails all responsible laboratory staff must make comments on what was done and why.

Documentation and Maintenance of Records.

A central feature of GLP guidelines is the maintenance of records in a clear, accurate and auditable form. Documentation is important for several reasons:

- Specimen origins, chain-of-custody, raw analytical data, processed analytical data, SOP's, instrument validation results, reagent certification results, analyst certification documents and other relevant records must be available and kept safe for a specified period of time.

- Maintenance of instrument and reagent certification records provides for post-evaluation of results, even after the passage of several years.

- Maintenance of all records specified provide documentation which may be required in the event of legal challenges due to repercussions of decisions based on the original analytical results.

- Many vendors are now providing many of these capabilities as part of computer packages for operating modern instruments. For example most modern computer-based instruments will provide for the indefinite storage of raw analytical data for specific samples in a protected (tamper-proof) environment as well as maintenance of historical records of control chart data establishing the operational quality of instruments during any period during which analytical data have been acquired by that instrument.

- The length of time over which laboratory records should be maintained will vary with the situation. The general guidelines followed in regulated laboratories are to maintain records for at **least five years**. In some countries these records are being maintained much longer. The development of higher density storage devices for digitized data is making this kind of record-keeping possible.

Accountability.

- GLP procedures inherently establish accountability for laboratory results. A laboratory organization, the analysts and manufacturers of instruments and reagents are responsible to a larger extent for laboratory results generated by the laboratory.

- Responsibility for all aspects of the laboratory processes leading to technical results and conclusions must be clearly defined and documented. Laboratory organizations have the responsibility to ensure that a robust process is in place to assure the quality of results emanating from the laboratory.
- This situation should place appropriate pressure on analysts to conduct studies with adequate care and concern, laboratory organization to put a process in place to assure quality and instrument manufacturers to ensure that their instruments and reagents are fit for purpose.
- Moreover justify that a process should be in place in the laboratory that ensures the possibility of identifying more quickly and succinctly the source(s) of error(s), identifying the root causes and taking corrective and preventive action to maintain acceptable quality of laboratory data.

INCIDENT REPORTING PROCEDURE IN THE LABORATORY

Clinical Pathology Accreditation (CPA) standards, Blood Quality and Safety Regulations (2005) both of the UK and other regulatory and accreditation agencies worldwide requires that all incidents in laboratory be investigated and reported in a timely fashion to obtain accurate date, ensure optimum learning outcome and to avoid subsequent occurrence of the incident.

The aim and objectives of incident reporting includes:

- To ensure that all incidents relating to quality and safety of blood transfusion are recorded promptly and appropriately in accordance with statutory regulation, principles of Good Laboratory Practice (GLP) and Good Manufacturing Practice (GMP).
- To instil the culture of corrective and preventive action to prevent the re-occurrence of incident.
- It ensures that accurate recorded of incident is available in case of audit and investigation.
- To facilitate the reporting of incidents to statutory authority like the MLSCN.

Method

- Gather all relevant documents related to the incident. This may include documents like patient name, hospital number, and date of birth gender, request forms, compatibility slips, witness statements, root cause analysis information, telephone request documentation, computer records, transport records and temperature records of blood fridges.
- Open an incident/non conformance file with relevant information of the date file opened, date of incident, nature of clinical incident (safety, quality or non conformance).
- Collect information on immediate root cause analysis carried out after the incident, note the remedial action taken, the preventive active and corrective action taken to resolve the incident and prevent a re-occurrence of the incidents.
- Investigate the incident based on information available determine the risk of incident to patient, likelihood of it re-occurring, non-conformances, root causes, the preventive and corrective action the laboratory should put in place to prevent a re-occurrence of incident and a set a date to re-audit the process to ensure that the root causes has been dealt with.

EXAMPLES OF LABORATORY NON-CONFORMANCES

- Equipment and calibration failure
- Quality control failure
- Manufacturers-associated reagent failure
- Sub-optimal cold chain-related issues
- Equipment downtime related issues
- Deviation from Standard Operating Procedure (SOP) with adverse outcome
- Deviation from Standard Operating Procedure (SOP) with no adverse outcome
- Customer complain about quality and safety of blood and blood products
- External Quality Assessment failure or error
- Any non-conformances identified in routine audits carried out in the laboratory.
- Presence in the laboratory inventory of time expired reagents.

EXAMPLES OF CLINICAL INCIDENTS IN THE LABORATORY

- Laboratory testing error.
- Transfusion sample identification error.
- Relevant documentation not signed.
- Traceability-related issues related to non-returns of relevant transfusion documentation.
- Inappropriate transfusion or non-indicated transfusion.
- Incorrect blood component transfused
- Blood component wastage. Blood component (fresh frozen plasma, cryoprecipitate or platelet) ordered but not used and eventually wasted.
- Blood component wastage due to negligent non observance of cold chain management requirement.
- Blood transfusion reaction and other transfusion-related adverse events.
- Blood administration errors
- Issue of wrong component/specification (for example Kell positive unit given to woman of child bearing age, CMV positive unit transfused to HIV or immunocompromised patient and transfusion of non-irradiated blood and blood product for patient in whom it is indicated (patient on purine analogue chemotherapy and patient who are potential candidates for transplant).
- Poor/inappropriate component storage issues such as storage of platelet in the fridge and transfusion of units that has been out of cold storage for greater than 30 minutes.
- Blood component quality problems such as bacterial contamination of blood products.

RISK RATING OF LABORATORY INCIDENTS (SEVERITY)

- None
- Minor
- Major
- Catastrophic

Other GLP Rules

1. Develop SOP for all task, ensure that all staff performing the task are trained to the SOP, sign to the SOP and are following the SOP strictly.
2. Ensure that correct equipment and reagents are being used. Outdated reagents, malfunctioning equipment and equipment that have not been adequately cleaned, calibrated, maintained and quality controlled must not be used for diagnosis on patient sample.
3. Put a robust method in place to avoid mix up of samples as well as labelling errors.
4. Ensure working area is clean, uncluttered and that results are precise and accurate.
5. Report and root cause every mistakes, near misses, errors and bad practices and come up with corrective and preventive action to prevent such errors (Never cover up. Cover up is dangerous and can cause loss of lives).
6. Put in place a mechanism for implementing corrective and preventive action (re-training of staff with deficiencies, modification of process. Records must be clear, accurate and securely kept for several years depending on regulation. Records must identify person responsible, confirm what was done.

CHAPTER 15

Incident Reporting Procedure and Investigation in the Laboratory Medicine

Incident Reporting Procedure

Reducing mishaps from medical management is central to efforts to improve quality and lower costs in health care. Effective feedback from incident reporting systems in healthcare is essential if organizations are to learn from failures in the delivery of care. Risk rating of transfusion incidents (Severity) can either be; None, Minor, Moderate, Major or Catastrophic. The likelihood of a transfusion incident occurring can either be; rarely, unlikely, possible, likely or almost certain. All transfusion incidents, near misses and complaints must be investigated. Clinical Pathology Accreditation (CPA) standards, Blood Quality and Safety Regulations (2005) both of the UK and the MLSCN of Nigeria requires that all incidents in transfusion be investigated and reported in a timely fashion to obtain accurate date, ensure optimum learning outcome and to avoid subsequent occurrence of the incident. The aim and objectives of incident reporting includes:

1. To ensure that all incidents relating to quality and safety of blood transfusion are recorded promptly and appropriately in accordance with statutory regulation, principles of Good Laboratory Practice (GLP) and Good Manufacturing Practice (GMP).
2. To instil the culture of corrective and preventive action to prevent the re-occurrence of incident.
3. It ensures that accurate record of incident is available in case of audit and investigation.
4. To facilitate the reporting of incidents to statutory authority like the MLSCN.

Investigating a transfusion incident

- Incident occurs
- Immediately manage and report incident
- Investigate and review incident
- Identify root causes & agree corrective action
- Change policy/ procedure if applicable
- Change process control & remove bottlenecks
- Communicate change and train staff
- Update documentation (SOP)
- Review process & confirm elimination of root cause
- Close incident

METHOD OF INVESTIGATING A LABORATORY INCIDENT

1. Gather all relevant documents related to the incident. This may include documents like patient name, hospital number, and date of birth gender, request forms, compatibility slips, witness statements, root cause analysis information, telephone request documentation, computer records, transport records and temperature records of blood fridges.

2. Open an incident/non conformance file with relevant information of the date file opened, date of incident, nature of clinical incident (safety, quality or non conformance).

3. Collect information on immediate root cause analysis carried out after the incident, note the immediate remedial action taken, the preventive active and corrective action taken to resolve the incident and prevent a re-occurrence of the incidents.

4. Investigate the incident based on information available determine the risk of incident to patient, likelihood of it re-occurring, non-conformances, root causes, the preventive and corrective action the laboratory should put in place to prevent a re-occurrence of incident and a set a date to re-audit the process to ensure that the root causes has been dealt with.

EXAMPLES OF LABORATORY NON-CONFORMANCES

1. Equipment and calibration failure
2. Quality control failure
3. Manufacturers-associated reagent failure
4. Sub-optimal cold chain-related issues
5. Equipment downtime related issues
6. Deviation from Standard Operating Procedure (SOP) with adverse outcome
7. Deviation from Standard Operating Procedure (SOP) with no adverse outcome
8. Customer complain about quality and safety of blood and blood products
9. External Quality Assessment failure or error
10. Any non-conformances identified in routine audits carried out in the laboratory.
11. Presence in the laboratory inventory of time expired reagents.

EXAMPLES OF CLINICAL INCIDENTS IN THE LABORATORY

1. Laboratory testing error.
2. Transfusion sample identification error.
3. Relevant blood transfusion documentation not signed.
4. Traceability-related issues related to non-returns of relevant transfusion documentation.
5. Inappropriate transfusion or non-indicated transfusion.
6. Incorrect blood component transfused
7. Blood component wastage. Blood component (fresh frozen plasma, cryoprecipitate or platelet) ordered but not used and eventually wasted.
8. Blood component wastage due to negligent non observance of cold chain management requirement.
9. Blood transfusion reaction and other transfusion-related adverse events.
10. Blood administration errors
11. Issue of wrong component/specification (for example Kell positive unit given to woman of child bearing age, CMV positive unit transfused to HIV or immunocompromised patient and

transfusion of non-irradiated blood and blood product for patient in whom it is indicated (patient on purine analogue chemotherapy and patient who are potential candidates for transplant).

12. Poor/inappropriate component storage issues such as storage of platelet in the fridge and transfusion of units that has been out of cold storage for greater than 30 minutes.

13. Blood component quality problems such as bacterial contamination of blood products.

An example an investigated incident in the diagnostic laboratory

Example of an incident Investigation Incident: Issue of time expired product (Novo 7) to patient (X)

Investigator's name: Erhabor Osaro Date of Incident: 3rd April 2010

Give brief information of incident. On the 3rd day of April 2010 an out of time expired unit of batch product (NOVO 7) was mistakenly issued on a patient in HDU who had post partum haemorrhage and had continued to bleed even after the issue of several units of red cells, adult dose of fresh frozen plasma (FFP) and two units of platelet. The Novo 7 had been requested by the consultant to facilitate the immediate arrest of the life threatening haemorrhage. The discovery that the said batch product expired 4 months ago had been noted by the doctors and nursing staff during the pre-product administration checks by the patient bed side. The reconstitution fluid was however in date.

State the reasons for identifying this learning. I had identified this learning (incident) with the aim of carrying out a full investigation of the incident with the hope of determining the root causes, suggesting corrective and preventive measures to prevent the root causes, instigating policy and procedural changes and to enhance our drive as a department for continuous quality improvement.

DESCRIBE THE ROOT CAUSES OF THIS INCIDENT.

1. Poor inventory/stock control management of batch product (Novo 7).
2. Inadequate pre and post product allocation checks before issue of batch product.
3. Absence of SOP on inventory control management of batch products stipulating minimum, maximum and re-order level as well as lead time between order and product availability for use. An SOP is a written document / instruction detailing all steps and activities of a process or procedure. These should be carried out without any deviation or modification to guarantee the expected outcome. Any modification or deviation from a given SOP should be thoroughly investigated and outcomes of the investigation documented according the internal deviation procedure. All quality impacting processes and procedures should be laid out in Standard Operating Procedures (SOPs). These SOPs should be the basis for the routine training program of each employee. SOPs should be available, followed strictly in laboratory analysis and regularly updated to assure compliance to CPA Standard F (Examination process) and sub standard F2 (Examination procedures) requirements. Changes of SOPs are in general triggered by process or procedural changes / adjustments.

DESCRIBE THE IMMEDIATE REMEDIAL ACTION TAKEN TO PREVENT HARM TO PATIENT:

1. Removed all remaining time expired Novo 7 out from stock to prevent re-occurrence of incident.
2. Rang the transfusion manager on call for advice.
3. Conveyed advice of consultant Haematologist to consultant managing the said patient in the high dependency unit.
4. On advise of the consultant Haematologist, requested an in date unit of the batch product from the nearest sister Hospital.

Non-compliances identified:

1. Issue of time expired batch product. This observation constitutes a non-compliance to CPA Standard D (Equipment, information system and materials) and sub standard D3 (Management of reagents, calibration and quality control).
2. Absence of SOP on inventory control management of batch products. This observation constitutes a non-compliance to CPA Standard F (Examination process) and sub standard F2 (Examination procedures).
3. Inadequate pre and post product allocation checks before issue of batch product. This observation constitutes a non-compliance to CPA Standard F (Examination process) and sub standard F2 (Examination procedure).

Describe the corrective and preventive action that could be taken to eliminate root cause.

1. Devise a more effective inventory /stock control system for batch products.
2. Draw up a standard operating procedure inventory /stock control system for batch products.
3. Train all employees carrying out the specific activity on the SOP and get them to sign the SOP as an attestation that they are aware of the presence of a standard procedure for the task and that they will continue to carry out the task based on the Standard operating procedure.
4. Re-iterate in the continuous improvement meetings held every morning the need to do a pre and post batch product allocation checks before despatching products to the wards or satellite fridges.
5. What steps should be taken to implement the corrective actions arising from this investigation and how has lessons learnt from this incident enhanced the department quest for continuous improvement?
6. Amend SOP on issue of batch products (Novo 7) to reflect suggested change with regards to separating the batch product (Novo 7) from the diluents.

7. Communicate change to all staff performing task by way of training on new SOP.

8. Devise a more effective inventory control measure for batch products (Novo 7).

9. Draw up an SOP on inventory control management of batch products.

10. Review process in the next 3 months to ensure that the root causes has been eliminated.

CHAPTER 16

ROLE OF LABORATORY MANAGER AND LABORATORY MANAGEMENT IN THE OFFERING OF A QUALITY SERVICE

THE TRUTH ABOUT QUALITY

- Every customer wants a quality good and service
- Quality in an organization is everybody's business and responsibility (from the laboratory manager to the laboratory attendants and clerical staff). A good manager and a quality conscious organisation must always encourage and create an enabling environment for employees to submit quality improvement ideas and suggestions as a way of building a strong culture of continuous quality improvement. These should learn to reward and praise staff when suggestions are made that significantly improve service delivery (pay rise, award of certificate and celebration of staff or unit of the month).
- Everybody makes mistakes. To err they say is human. What matters however is how an organization manages errors and mistakes. To a quality conscious laboratory error and mistakes are opportunities to improve the process.
- Every quality conscious laboratory must build a culture of continuous improvement by doing root causes (objectively asking why error occurred 5 times) when error occur and arriving at immediate remedial actions to obviate the error, arriving at corrective and preventing actions, implementing those actions and agreeing a time in future to re-audit the process to ensure that the corrective actions implemented have eliminated the root causes.

- By regularly identifying small problems, errors and mistakes and carry out a root cause analysis, arriving and implementing corrective actions can a laboratory build a culture of continuous quality improvement and achieving the task of getting things right first time and all the time.
- Getting it right first time and all the time produces a reduction in post production work and cost.
- Help to build confidence of staff
- Help in the improvement in quality of service delivered
- Facilitate knowledge transfer (promote best practices)

THINGS A QUALITY CONSCIOUS LABORATORY MANAGEMENT OR MANAGER SHOULD KNOW

Be adaptive to change (learn to try other suggestions and philosophy). The only thing that is constant on earth is change. Every organization that must grow, make profit and be relevant must be adaptable to change. Customer requirements are always changing. It is only organizations that are flexible and are ready to continually change their processes to enable them meet the changing customer requirement that are likely to remain in business. Laboratory management must ensure that their services remain competitive in terms of quality and price (cost effective). Despite the fact that customer requirements are regularly changing what remain constant is that customers always want a good quality goods and services at prices that are competitive and affordable.

Build a culture for proactive continuous improvement. Laboratory management must build a culture of continuous quality improvement. They must imbibe in their staff the philosophy that continually identifying and removing small wastes from the process and by continuously finding out why errors occur and implementing small corrective actions, an organization can continually improve their service and grow their profit. Organization must avoid quick fixes as they only provide immediate remedial solution without necessarily removing the root causes. Management should make long-term plans. They must continually envision what the future state they desire and care out A3 study on how to move from their current state to their envisioned future state. Strive to discover better and smarter ways to do things. They must avoid being ensnared by old unproductive culture and traditions. They must not allow good to stand on the way of best. They must learn to predict and prepare for future challenges and must have a making it better mentality or philosophy.

Don't wait for accreditation and inspections before you rush to improve. Build the culture of regular and small continuous improvement. Preparing for accreditation and inspections from regulatory agency can be costly and may not necessarily lead to improvement in the quality of service delivered. What makes the difference is making sure the organization is process driven, have a well defined and standardized process, continually looks for better ways to get task done and building a culture of proactive quality improvement by making regular, consistent small improvements. Big and non-continuous changes is not what grows an organization but rather it is the continual and consistent identification of waste and unexpected outcomes, errors and mistakes and objectively performing root cause analysis and consistently identifying the root causes and implementing the corrective action that an organization is able to build a culture of proactive improvement. Such organizations do not need to spend so much money preparing for accreditation or inspection. They are always ready anytime and any day for inspection because they have already institutionalize the culture of proactive continuous improvement.

Be consistent particularly with equipment and reagents that are fit for purpose and are not associated with recurrent downtimes and repeating of test. Delivering a quality service requires consistency. Applying things that work and causes less variation is critical. This includes the use of suppliers whose analyzers are rugged and are associated with fewer downtimes and whose maintenance team are accessible as well as using reagents that are consistent and are not associated with wastages associated with re-doing a test. Supplier's product must also be cost effective to enable the laboratory break even and make profit.

Strive to continually improve your staff, service delivery and customer satisfaction. By using Kaizen model to reduce waste and to improve productivity, the laboratory as an organization can render effectiveness, cost effective and safe service that meet the requirements of her customers. Laboratory management must strive to standardize their process. Use SOP's to run your process and Train staff carrying out task based on the SOP to prevent ensures that there is no inter staff variation in service delivery. Be a process driven laboratory. Standardise your processes, training staff to the SOP allow for consistency and reduce inter-staff variation. Create an enabling environment for all staff to appreciate their peculiar role in the service delivery in the department. Invest in your staff and encourage them to be actively involved in continuous professional development (CDP). Ensure that staff is appraised yearly and that a personal development plan (PDP) is agreed with staff at yearly appraisal. Management must also strive to provide all the support that staffs need (including staffs that are not performing at their optimum) to enable them perform at their best potential. Managers should strive to build a formidable team. Lead by example, don't cast blame, learn from mistakes and have a zero tolerance for gossip. Management should create an enabling, friendly and stress free environment to allow staff to work safely and effectively. They should take decision that are team build and not team breaking. They should learn to maximize the use of staff creativity, utilize staff more in the area of their strength. Managers should strive to identify ways to help staff attain their full potential and encourage staff to be participative.

Be Objective in all that you do. Be purposeful and not fearful. Encourage creative idea and suggestions as a way of of creating an enabling environment for staff to freely express creative ideas suggestions and concern they may have. Never cast blame even when things go wrong or there is a negative unexpected event but rather encourage and build a culture of always objectively finding out why things go wrong (do a root cause analysis or cause and effect analysis) to enable the laboratory determine the root causes of incidents and put corrective measures in place to eliminate and prevent further occurrence of such error or incident. Build a culture and a process that facilitate the principle of getting things right first time and all the time (prevent re-do).Continually identify the presence of stressors in the system to enable their removal and to enhance staff morale and productivity. Staffs are an organization's greatest asset. Every effort should be made to appreciate staff and make them feel valued to ensure that their morale are high at all times and that they are highly productive. Laboratory management must have a team building spirit. They must be approachable and show empathy when required. Management should be honest in their dealing with their staff. They are encouraged to use open, fair and honest communication to remove fear from the mind of staff to enable the organization function as one big team. Break down barriers between teams, units and departments. Make decisions that facilitates team work among the various subunits. Encourage shared vision, collaboration; maximize staff potential by encouraging secondments across the federating units as well as the sharing of knowledge and best practices

Make sure task are clear and that there are no ambiguity. Every laboratory organization must have a mission statement (slogan). All staff must be aware of the organization's mission statement and be committed to play their peculiar role to ensure that commitments made to customers are continually met. Collect relevant data and analyze it to objectively improve the process even if it has cost implications. Laboratory management must be adaptive to change. They must strive to look out for better and smarter ways of achieving customer requirements by collecting relevant data, analysing those data objectively and using information gathered to improve the process. Management must ensure that staffs are provided with support and resources to enable staff provide a safe and effective service that meets the requirements of the users of the service.

GETTING IT RIGHT FIRST TIME AND ALL THE TIME (RE-DO AND COST IMPLICATION)

Every laboratory organization must always strive to put in place a process in their laboratories to ensure that staffs get it right, first time and all the time. Getting it right first time and all the time from a laboratory point of view means getting the right result from the right sample drawn from the right patient, in the appropriate container, transported in the optimum condition, labelled and effectively booked onto the Laboratory information management system, processed in the right condition (pre-examination phase), analysed by properly trained, competent, occupational health compliant laboratory staff, working in a health and safety conscious laboratory strictly following the standard operating procedure (SOP), using reagents that are optimally stored and in date on equipments that are proactively maintained, calibrated and quality controlled (examination phase), to generate accurate and precise laboratory results that is appropriately communicated in a timely fashion to the requesting clinician to enable a prompt and evidenced based management of patients.

RE-DO AND COST IMPLICATION

Re-doing a laboratory test has cost implications. It is important that a diagnostic laboratory put in place a process to ensure that laboratory test is done right (right result) first time and all the time. Ways to avoiding re-do of laboratory testing include:

- Employment and retention of qualified, competency tested and competent laboratory staff.
- Use of appropriately stored and in date reagents (time expired reagents must never be used to test patient sample)
- Equipment used for testing patients sample must be pro-actively maintained, calibrated and quality controlled before use (equipment must not be used for diagnostic purpose if the quality control material has not met the manufacturers requirement (failed).
- There must be a standard operating procedure for all investigations. Staff performing task must be trained on the SOP and found competent (to prevent inter analyst variation in testing).
- Laboratory must be enrolled in external quality assessment programme and be seen to be performing optimally along with their peers.
- Have a process in place to identify and deal with sample integrity issues that can affect diagnostic results (haemolysed sample, under filled and over filled sample, clotted sample, lipaemic, jaundiced, effects of cold agglutinins).

Cost implications of re-doing laboratory testing

- Cost of reagents to re-do laboratory test
- Cost of wear and tear of equipment
- Cost of manpower in repeat testing
- Delay in turnaround time and by extension delay in treatment of patients and prolonged hospital stay.
- Errors, mistakes, wrong results and post production fixes are annoying to customers and can results in loss of customers and income available to laboratory.
- Human resource cost
- Effect on service delivery and patient care

The power of the concept of aappreciative intelligence *(praise and recognition)*

- Every continuous quality improvement organization and leader needs to become a kind person that others will want to follow.
- It does not necessarily cost much to implement the philosophy of appreciative intelligent (recognition and praise) but the benefit to an organization is however innumerable.
- Most staff don't receive anywhere near the amount of praise that should be receiving. As a result, they become less productive and in most cases, become completely disengaged in our jobs. Most people leave their jobs because they don't not feel appreciated. Staffs that have bosses that are unappreciative and those who dislike their bosses have been shown to be at a higher risk of developing a significantly higher blood pressure, organizational or boss-induced hypertension, and heart diseases (resulting from long-term hypertension).

The principle of appreciative intelligence (concepts of recognition and praise) are two focal issues required to stir up innovative and positive emotions in an organizations. Praise and recognition is a vital tool in an organization. The advantages appreciative intelligence includes:

- Increase staff productivity
- Increase engagement among teams

- Facilitates staff retention. An appreciated staff is more likely to stay with his organization
- Can potentially translate to better service delivery and happy customers
- Staffs that are recognized and appreciated are better safety records (health and safety conscious) and have fewer job-related accidents.

PRINCIPLE OF APPRECIATIVE INTELLIGENCE

Appreciative intelligence is spotting and harnessing what is valuable and positive in a situation or in people. Managers must be able to envision how the positive aspects can be used to create a better future. Building a culture of appreciative intelligence can potentially cause motivation and can skyrocket staff morale. Every worker desires to be appreciated for work well done. Sometimes just mere appreciation is appreciated equally as wage rises. Employees have been found to leave organization because of lack of praise and recognition. Most employee are ready to work even for less pay in an environment where they feel valued, praised and appreciated for job well done. The advantages of praise and recognition in an organization include:

- Makes staff feel valued, and appreciated
- Create a sense of belonging and bonding between managers and their subordinate staffs
- It encourage staff to show gratitude and commitment to the organization (enhances productivity)
- It breeds fairness and equal opportunities. (To whom that is faithful in a little more shall be given and to whom who is unfaithful even that which he has shall be taken away).
- Recognition and praise (genuine compliments) brings out the very best in staff. An appreciated employee is often willing to go an extra mile for an organization. They are often ready to go through the thick and thin with their employer.

IMPORTANT FACT BY PRAISE AND RECOGNITION

- Some time praise does not cost an organization anything (sometimes a mere certificate, appreciation note, word of mouth just to say thank you and well done may be all that is required). It often takes less than a minute to say, "I appreciate the time and effort you have put into this report. It is exceptional brilliant. Thank you or well done.

- Praise should never be withheld. Showing staff that managers and management care about their needs should top first in a manager's to do list. There is no need for delay. When staff anything that is worthy of praising, do so promptly and genuinely after the event.

- Praise and recognition is a moment of honour and heightens staff value

- Appreciating the talents and gifts of employees opens us an organization to greatness.

- It creates a sense of belonging among staff irrespective of how low they are in the organization's organogram.

- It can potentially help put employees in the driving seat. They feel a sense of ownership of the organization and builds commitment to playing staff little role to achieving organizational goals and objectives.

- He that watereth shall himself be watered. Managers who make their staff feel great and honoured will potentially reap the dividends (bonuses and promotion by management and board member) as well when praise transcends to increased staff morale, increased productivity, excellent service delivery to customers and more profit for the organization.

EXAMPLES OF PRAISE AND RECOGNITION PHRASES

- Thank you so much for being you and all that you do for us. It really takes such an amazing person to do what you do.
- Your team has been very amazing. I appreciate the excellent job you guys are doing. Keep it up.
- Take you very much for a job well done. The effort of your team is well appreciated.
- You guys have made our unit proud. I got a letter from the chief executive today congratulating you guys for a job well done. Thank you all. I am honoured to be a member of your team
- In the past one year we have seen a remarkable improvement as shown in our recently concluded customer's satisfaction survey. This could only have been possible because of the dedication of members of our team. Many thanks to you all. Let as keep the flag flying.
- In the last one year we have seen our profit as an organization double. I want to personally thank you guys for working smartly and efficiently in identifying wastes and all non-value added task from our process. The chief executive has asked me to convey his appreciation to us all. Well done guys.

THINGS LABORATORY MANAGERS SHOULD NEVER DO

Instruct rather than order members of your team. A dictator orders their subordinate but a manager instructs members of his team. Managers must realize that employees are not soldiers neither are they children and should not be ordered about. Managers must learn to be polite often treating others the way he will want to be treated. Although managers have the right to hire and fire. They can discipline staff when they err strictly following the organization's laid down discipline rules. However managers stand the risk of losing their productive staff if he acts as a dictator and order his staff around.

Failure to recognize that the organization's business is all about customers and meeting their requirements. Sometimes managers get carried away in their own ego (it is all about me) and lose focus on why an organization exists. A hospital irrespective of how sophisticated it is or how endowed it is with manpower resources will cease to exist if there are no patients to be treated. Managers must always put the aims and objectives of the organization before their own interest. They must continue to strive to offer a continually improving quality service that will encourage the patients to keep patronising the organization. Organization must work hard to meet the requirements of their customers. The customer has choices. They have the right to take their business elsewhere if they are not getting the quality service they desire.

Managers must not be arrogant but rather they must be humble: Arrogance is defined as conceit, self-loving and egotistic. Over-inflated sense of one's position and value, combined with an attitude that somehow you are above everyone else. An arrogant manager cultivates an atmosphere of intimidation. Such manager often portrays a know-it-all approach often refusing to entertain other points of view, tend to have a "just do as I say approach, likely to run a dysfunctional, ineffective team, quick to blame others as incompetence errors are made, goals are not achieved and outcome is not favourable. Arrogant managers often surround themselves with sycophants, busy bodies and yes-men. When an arrogant manager encourages the status quo and discourages change, he stagnates the organization. Such managers often employ the threat tool. Threats don't work. It encourages staff to develop a thick skin and can potentially diminish the authority of the manager. Arrogant managers tend to behave like little children. They often acting out, throwing tantrums, and generally making life miserable for their subordinate staff.

THE DISADVANTAGES OF MANAGERIAL ARROGANCE INCLUDES

- Arrogant bosses never gain employee's respect.
- Arrogant bosses are viewed as dictators, insensitive, rulers and tyrants.
- They have a tendency to control rather than supervise
- Arrogance can devalue what others have to offer

- Arrogant manager or supervisors undermines opportunities for sound sharing, feedback and support of management among teams initiatives
- Working with arrogant manager can have negative effects on the quantity and quality of work generated by employees.
- Arrogant managers are not good team players neither are they team builders.

DEALING WITH AN ARROGANT MANAGER OR SUPERVISOR

- Arrogant managers don't play by the rules. You must be ready to be transferred indiscriminately from one department to another. He tends to blow problems out of proportion. Staff must be ready to meet deadlines, be professional, punctual and play by the rules.
- Start the process of looking for another job or possible seek a transfer to another department headed by somebody else. Avoid using him as a referee for job application if you can.
- Play to win. Try and understand the likes and dislikes of your boss. Learn to play by the rules. Try not to do things he dislikes. Be your best. Make yourself a valuable asset to your department.
- Avoid confrontation.
- Avoid doing things that will cause negative reactions and crate confrontation. You must never be verbally abusive. Keep a written log of all negative situations as well as documentary evidence to buttress your point. It should contain dates, what the situation was, what you did and what the response of your boss was. Documentary evidence may be required if his arrogance gets investigated by a disciplinary committees.
- If his actions becomes bullying, you may have to discuss and send an official complain to your divisional manager to which your boss is answerable. If he is unable to resolve the issue, you may need to send an official complaint to human resources department as well as contact your union representative.
- Whatever happens just keep in mind that your boss is not an island to himself but is answerable to senior managers. Keep enjoying the work and opportunities will come up.

THINGS A QUALITY CONSCIOUS MANAGER SHOULD NOT SAY OR DO

- Never use the phrase that's impossible' or that suggestion will not work here. Use of such a negative phrase can discourage creativity and may prevent staff who make such suggestion to refrain from making suggestions that can potentially improve the process
- Don't encourage gossip. Gossip can kill team spirit and cause crack in relationship between team members. Organizations must have a zero tolerance for gossip. Managers must encourage to discuss and problem they may have with the appropriate person—privately and in a constructive way.
- Avoid giving ultimatums but rather explain to staff to make them understand the urgency in getting task done. Ultimatums like this one don't usually solve anything but rather it opens up threats and often leads to grievances and sometimes litigation.
- Managers should rely on the organization's grievance policy if a a member of staff is insubordinate. He may need to seek advice from HR to ensure that the right steps are followed. Manager must try their best help an insubordinate staff improve.
- Never use the phrase 'I'm always right'. Such phrases portray a manager as being distant, haughty and self-aggrandized.

ATTRIBUTES OF A GOOD LABORATORY MANAGER

A good manager should be a team player that creates an enabling environment for staff to learn from error and mistakes. He is one that builds a culture of continuous quality improvement by encouraging staff to be involved and make suggestion they think can improve the process. He creates room for staff to identify problem and waste in the system, promote the philosophy of doing root cause analysis when things go wrong with the hope of arriving at corrective and preventive action to eliminate the root causes and optimize service delivery. There are things a continuous improvement conscious laboratory manager or organization should do to *make-it-happen*. They include:

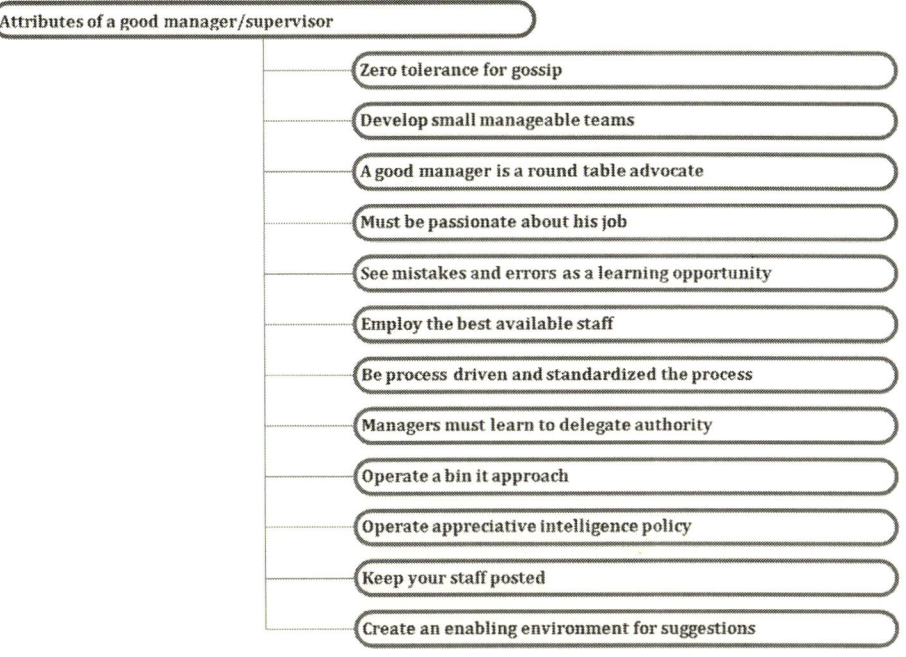

Figure: Attributes of a good manager/supervisor

Zero tolerance for gossip. Every continuous quality improvement laboratory should have a zero tolerance policy for gossip. Gossip is a killer of team spirit and work. Gossip and blame should never be allowed to thrive. A good laboratory manager instead of laying blame on his staff when mistakes, error occur or the expected outcome is not achieved should rather encourage his staff to do a root cause analysis on why the error occurred. By building a culture of carry out objective root causes and arriving at a corrective and preventive action, they can gradually put a place to process to eliminate those root causes and by extension preventing a future occurrence of such error. Gossip destroys the internal ties that exist among members of a team. The negative effect of gossip includes:

- It kills staff morale and productivity
- It has a negative effect on team building
- It makes staff feel inferior and non-valued
- It is practically impossible to have unity with a group in the midst of gossips.

Develop small manageable teams. Team building allows employees to see themselves as members of interdependent teams rather than as individual workers. Teams should be made up of a manageable number of effective individuals. These are people who are experienced, have problem solving ability, openness to addressing the problem, action oriented and charismatic personal style. Every team should have a competent leader who is focused on the goal, create an enabling environment for collaborative effort, builds confidence of team members, sets priorities, demonstrates sufficient know-how of task expected and manage performance through effective feedback. Small team working together on a regular basis does a better job. It is easier to effective communicate and understanding how best to work together.

These advantages of having manageable teams include:

- Increased flexibility in skills and abilities
- It promotes collective responsibility for work done rather than individual mindset
- More beneficial in times of organizational change
- Encourage both individual and team development and improvement
- Allows for collective ideas and brainstorming
- Focuses on group goals and accomplishments
- Enhances employee morale and productivity
- It discourages the blame culture

Successful teams depend on successful team leaders. Good team leaders qualities include:

- A team leader should be goal-oriented and keep the team focused.
- They must create and promote an enabling environment to allow members to confidently suggest ways to do their work better and smarter to provide a continually improving quality service to their customers.
- A team leader is like the captain of a ship. He must build confidence and earn the trust of his team members
- A good team leader must learn to delegate authority and responsibilities to team members. By so doing, team members

develop management skills and learn to take responsibility for delegated work.

- A leader should be technically competent in matters relating to team tasks and goals. A good team leader should be worth his salt. A good team leader does not delegate any responsibility that he himself is not capable of doing. He can potentially loose the respect of his team mates if he does.

- A team leader should be able to effectively manage and prioritize work that needs doing.

- A good leader must learn to praise his team when they make an effort to make things better. He must learn to reward excellent performance (learn to say thank you and well-done to members of his team) and provide feedbacks.

- He should not cast blame but must create an opportunity for the team to use mistakes, errors and near misses as a learning tool (do root cause analysis) and arrive at preventive and corrective actions.

- Leaders should strive to collect useful data to allow for an evidenced-based decision making.

A good manager is a round table advocate. A continuous improvement conscious laboratory manager is a round table advocate. He rally people around a table regularly to identify and discuss problems, issues, waste, possible unfavourable outcomes, near misses to allow for corrective and preventive action to be implemented to enable a continuing improving service delivery. Round table meeting is not often a time to moan over problems, find fault but rather a time to objectively deal with issues as a team. It is a time for brainstorming ahead of a project take off, deal with problems, to discuss quality improvement, waste identification and to plan future development programs.

Must be passionate about his job. Iron they say sharpeneth iron and so does a man sharpen the countenance of his friend. An unenthusiastic and un-motivated team leader can potentially lose the team's interest. The productivity, creativity, innovation, commitment and motivation of team member can only be optimized by a manager who is passionate, enthusiastic and a good example (role model).He is one who does his work as if his life depends on it. A manager with a poor work ethics (comes to work late, leave before official closing time, spend more time than is officially allowed for breaks) and does not keep to team agreed rules) cannot command the respect nor unleash the productivity of his team members.

Employ the best available staff: Staffs are an organization's greatest assets. Effort must be made to recruit the best quality and highly motivated staffs. One of the ways managers or organizations can be on their toes and be at their best always is to employ the best available staff. When interviews are held to employ new staff, managers are encouraged to hire staffs that are good enough for their own job. By so doing even the manager suddenly realizes that he has to optimize his performance to stay on the job. Employing a cream of seasoned goal getters, every member of the team are compelled to be the best they can creating no room for excuse or failure.

See mistakes and errors as a learning opportunity: Managers in a quality conscious organization should avoid a blame culture or name calling when thing goes wrong. Mistakes must be seen as an opportunity to put things right by doing a root cause analysis and improving the service delivery by implementing the corrective action arrived at. Name calling and criticism is a killer of innovation, it destroys staff morale and productivity as well as make staff feel inferior. Even when things go wrong managers should avoid name calling and criticism as it can potentially blocks learning and imagination and can cause staff to blank out. Managers must learn to show empathy even in the midst of unpleasant outcome. *Manager must never be tempted to use words such as:*

- Bugger how can you be so daff to make such mistakes
- How can so be so stupid
- You are suppose to have known better
- Even a child cannot make such a silly mistake
- How can an educated person make such a silly mistake

Be process driven and standardized the process (no ambiguity). Managers must be very specific in their dealing (no ambiguity).For an organization to succeed, it must be process driven. There must be standard procedures in place for the entire task performed. Staff performing those procedures must be trained and certified to carry out such procedures. Staff must sign to attest their commitment to abide by the rules. The process and procedure must be plain, simple to understand and leaves no ambiguities for interpretation. Staff in a process driven organization with standard produces knows what to do at any material time. This leaves no room for variation since everybody is carrying out the procedure in the same correct and generally accepted way. *Then the LORD answered me and said, write the vision, and make it plain upon tables, that he may run that readeth it. (Habakkuk 2:2)* [1].

Managers must learn to delegate authority. Usually managers *have a long* list of tasks that needs doing. Managers can prevent burning out (overwhelmed) by break activities into small sections and delegating the responsibility of getting them done to members of his team feed staff pieces at a time. Time is your most precious commodity. No matter how hard a manager try, he can't do everything by himself. It is a wrong notion that "If you want something done right, does it yourself." Many managers erroneously fear and believe that delegation of responsibilities puts them at risk of being outshined by their subordinate staff. They want to be an island and be seen to be indispensible. Managers and supervisors need to understand that they are coaches. Coaches are known to pass on knowledge, teaching, and motivating their subordinate staff. When you delegate responsibilities to subordinate staff, you are:

- Teaching them to take responsibility for their actions
- You are bringing out the managing skills in them
- You are building their morale, confidence and increasing their productivity.
- Delegation of authority facilitates accountability, responsibility, builds organizational culture, coaching, teamwork, incentives and goal setting.

TRUTHS ABOUT DELEGATION OF DUTIES

- Never delegate sensitive task : Very sensitive and highly confidential task that required the expertise of a management staff or supervisor and which can have a significant negative impact on service delivery and the organization must never be delegated.

253

- Only delegate task to staff you are confident can do it 9individuals best suited for task). The manager must always remember that he is responsible and accountable for negative effect or unexpected outcome that arises from the delegated duty.
- Consideration must be given to staff skill level, motivation, and dependability. This is however not an excuse not to give opportunities to team member not to broaden their horizons and become a more valuable asset to the team.
- Write down the delegated task in plan and easy to comprehend format.
- Managers must be specific about task he wants doing, explain and make it as plain and detailed as possible (provide standard work for task) such that there is no room for ambiguity.
- Be ready to measure the performance and offer supervisory guidance if needed. Managers must explain to staff to which task is delegated how their performance would be measured. Make sure all that materials the staff require to complete task is available. Be available to clarify and monitor task perform if there are grey areas. Remember that you are accountable if things go wrong.
- Manager should see delegated duties as a learning process for staff:
- Delegation of task is a way of building the confidence of staff. Delegated task is a managers was of motivating staff and showing that you have absolute assurance that they are capable of performing delegated task. Once completed manager must give feedback. He must praise staff for areas of best practice while offering explanation on areas that could have been done better. By so doing staffs are motivated, feel valued and useful and can become a potential mentor in the task.
- Delegation of duty can be a useful tool to get an unproductive staff up to speed. Managers must realize that it is the desire of every right thinking individual to be successful in what they do. Sometimes certain situational factors can prevent a staff from being productive. It is the responsibility of managers to identify those situational issues during staff appraisal to enable him removes the hindrances that is preventing staff from being productive:

- Suggestions made by staff in the past have not always taken seriously.
- Staffs has been told he makes too many mistakes in the past
- Unlike other staff in the team duties are not always delegated to him.
- Staffs have always performed sub-optimally in external quality assurance testing.

One of the ways managers can build the confidence and improve the morale of underperforming staff is by delegating task starting from small easy to perform task and gradually stepping up to more challenging task. Manager must be ready to provide feedback as well as make adequate use of the principle of appreciative intelligence (praise) to help build the confidence of staff. Gradually the staffs feel valued, morale increases and staffs becomes more productive

Operate a bin it approaches. Challenges are part of life. Challenges occur as organization provides her goods and services to customers. Once they occur they must be dealt with immediately and appropriate. The best way is to do a root cause analysis when issue is still fresh and all the information associated with the challenges is still available. This is to allow for immediate remedial action to be taken and preventive and corrective action to be implemented to ensure that the root causes are dealt with despatched and binned. Managers must never put aside problems that can be solved today to tomorrow. If they do problems pile up and can have a snowball effect on the team.

Operate appreciative intelligence policy (learn to be polite and appreciative): To whom respect is given, respect is expected. Respect is reciprocal. If you demand it, you must also be ready to give it. There is no harm in a smile, saying good morning, thank you and well done. Being polite, having respect for your staff, having a sense of humour and being appreciative (use of words) can be a morale booster and make your staff honoured and valued. High morale staffs are a productive staff. Managers must take a minute in the morning during staff meeting to greet his staff and appreciate them for the work of the previous day or week. Managers must learn to you the eight letter word (thank you and well done) as often as they possible to appreciate staff for excellent work and effort put into offering a quality service to their customers. Most managers tend to frown rather than smile. Smile on the face of a manager eases tension and apprehension among teams and boosting morale. There is no harm in sending a thank you card w*hen your team does well. Some of such card ends up as memorial for some staff.* People like evidential proofs when they have made a difference.

Keep your staff posted (up to date). It is the responsibility of managers to carry their subordinate staff along. Weekly team briefs (meetings or via e-mails) are very important. It is an opportunity for staff to be kept informed of the direction that service delivery is taking, the goals and aspirations, challenges being faced and what is been done to enhance joy and pride at work for staff.

Create an enabling environment for suggestions. Only a mad man keeps doing things the same way year in year our and expect a different result. If you expect an improvement in your service delivery, then you must be ready to do things differently incorporating the useful quality improvement suggestions from staff involved in the process. Managers make policy and require the help of staff to run with policy. The success story of Toyota Corporation was borne form the 20 million doing it better suggestions made by her staff within a forty years period. Those who carry out daily tasks know where the bureaucracies are in the process. Staff will only be confident to make suggestion if management are seen to have a listening ear. By listening and taking on board the implementation of useful suggestion from staff management can creates trust, understanding, involvement, true dialogue, and a shared team vision that is required for organisation growth. All quality improvement suggestion should be taken seriously. There should be brainstorming of it to see the practicality and workability for possible implementation. Laboratory managers can learn from the Toyota experience. The Toyota's creative idea suggestion system involved the use of a grassroots method to potentially turn every employee into a manager generating 20 million quality improvement suggestion and creative ideas in 40 years. Toyota believes that continuous improvement comes from the bottom from those who are involved in the day to day process up through the suggestion system that involved and motivated staff to contribute creative ideas and suggestion that contributes to the success of the organization. Laboratory managers that are continuous improvement conscious must refrain from using words that kill creativity and does not create an enabling environment for staff to contribute creative ideas and suggestion that can potential help improve the service delivery in the laboratory.

Words that kills creativity that laboratory managers must never use

- That suggestion will not work here
- We have done that before
- What have we not done to improve this service? I am sure that suggestion will not work.
- What a suggestion? That cannot work here
- We have been doing it this way even before you were born or employed.
- This suggestion is outdated
- Even a child will know that your suggestion is not feasible
- I will not waste my time and resources implementing your suggestion because I know it will not work.
- What we need is a serious suggestion that can potentially improve our process not this one you are postulating
- This theory cannot work
- Your suggestion is baseless we won't even bother implementing it
- There is no substance in your suggestion
- We have heard this before
- You are not the first to make this suggestion and I am sure you will not be the last

References

1. Holy Bible. King James Version. Then the LORD answered me and said, write the vision, and make it plain upon tables, that he may run that readeth it. (Habakkuk 2:2).
2. Mike Pedlerw, John Burgoyne, Tom Boydell. A manager's guide to self development. McGraw-Hill Professional 2007.
3. Richard Templar. The Rules of Management, Expanded Edition: A Definitive Code for Managerial Success. Person Education Inc, 2011.

CHAPTER 17

EFFECTIVE LABORATORY INVENTORY CONTROL MANAGEMENT OF EQUIPMENT, REAGENTS AND CONSUMABLES

Laboratory services play a significant role in the delivery of quality health services. Managing effective inventory control of laboratory supplies to support laboratory services is critical to the provision of an effective laboratory service delivery to facilitate the timely treatment of patients by clinicians. Laboratory results is vital to supporting clinical practice by providing important information that clinicians require to make differential diagnosis to facilitate the delivery of appropriate treatment regimens and treatment monitoring. Effective inventory control management ensures that laboratory equipments, reagents, and other consumables required for the diagnosis and monitoring of diseases are delivered in the right quantities, in the right condition, to the right place, at the right time and for the right cost effective price.

EFFECTIVE INVENTORY MANAGEMENT OF LABORATORY EQUIPMENT, REAGENTS AND CONSUMABLES

- Reagent and consumables delivered in the right quantities
- Reagent and consumables delivered in the right condition
- Reagent and consumables delivered to the right place or location
- Reagent and consumables delivered at the right time (Just in time)
- Reagent and consumables delivered at the right cost-effective price

Effective inventory control management of equipments, reagents and consumables is vital to the rendering of quality diagnostic services as well as optimizing the profitability of medical laboratory. Unnecessary inventory costs can potentially eat up the profit of the laboratory as a business. Profit that could be used to improve the services rendered, to procure new equipments and to introduce new test repertoire is often converted to storage of the unnecessary or excess inventory. Such inventory constitutes waste for the following reasons:

- The laboratory will require space to store the excess or unnecessary inventory.
- The laboratory will have to meet the cost of cold storage of temperature dependent reagents.
- There is a high tendency for such inventory to expire before being used by the laboratory.
- The laboratory will need to pay for the disposal of such time expired reagents.

COMPONENTS OF INVENTORY CONTROL MANAGEMENT

- Inventory costs
- Optimum stocking and replenishing
- Effective management of reagent (storage)
- Ensuring that there is no outdating challenges associated with overstocking
- Ensuring that incidence of reagent stock out of reagent is avoided to prevent the inability to render services to customers on demand (Use of visual control using the Kanban system (color coded cards to demonstrate stocking level to easily when stock level gets to re-order level).This allows replenishment to be done based upon real-time demand.
- Ensure that the incidence of emergency ordering are minimized to prevent extra cost associated with emergency order
- Ensuring that there is appropriate evidenced based budgeting and forecasting of reagent and consumables
- Ensure that the principle of first in first out is implemented (using reagents with closest expiration date earlier than those with longer expiration to prevent reagent outdates.
- Effective management of vendor contracts (ensuring that vendors are prompt and consistent).
- Determine the minimum, maximum stocking levels as well as re-order and emergency order stock levels.
- Calculation of lead times (times between reagents and consumable ordering and delivery in a ready to use state in the laboratory)

Good practice in laboratory inventory control management

- Monitor storage condition (temperature, humidity and protect from direct sunlight).
- Ensure that inventory does not obstruct the aisle and that store is not cluttered.
- Keep an eye on stock levels, conduct physical inventory and update inventory control records at least weekly.
- Dispose of time expired reagents appropriately and safely
- Protect storage area from insects, rodents and reptiles (snake)
- Arrange stock in a way to ensure that reagents with close expiration date are used in preference to those with longer expiration based of the principle of first-to-expire, first-out (FEFO).
- Keep storage space clean and uncluttered
- Identify, remove from inventory and safely dispose damaged and expired stock.
- Avoid storing liquid reagents and chemicals on lower shelves
- Store flammable and hazardous chemical and reagent in access-controlled Flammable Liquids Cabinets.
- Ensure there is functional and appropriate fire extinguisher required to deal with fire from flammable chemicals.
- Remember to always store corrosive chemicals and reagents from flammable chemicals.
- Every reagent or chemical should have a stock card with the following vital information; Date column, chemical or reagent name, stock at hand, stock received, stock issued, transaction reference number (voucher number), special storage requirements, lot numbers, expiry dates.

NELSON BIOMEDICAL STOCK CARD

Name of Reagent/Consumable: Prothrombin Time reagent

Special storage requirements: Store at 2-8 ⁰C

Unit of Issue: Box of 10

Maximum Stock level:

Minimum Stock Level:

Re-Order Level:

Date	Supplier/User	In	Out	Balance	Entry By	Transaction Reference Number

Figure: Example of an inventory control or stock cards

Common Terms Used in Inventory Control Management

Terms	Definition
Minimum stock level	The minimum stock level is the stock level which once reached should trigger a re-order of inventory to maximum stock level. For effective inventory control it is important to determine this level based on evidence gotten from data of reagent used over a period taking into consideration the seasonal variation in the request for certain diagnostic test. This is also known as the Re-order Level. Once stock levels gets to this level, the item must be re-ordered to set maximum stock level
Maximum stock level	This is the optimum stock level. It is the highest level that the stock of a particular item must get to. The maximum stock level is calculated based of data on the number reagents used over a period taking into consideration seasonal changes that may affect the request for certain laboratory test.
Stock review	This is the time set for the regular reviews of stock. Depending on the amount of stock held, this can be weekly, bi-weekly or monthly. At every review, it is the duty of the inventory control officer to determine inventory that has gotten to the minimum stock (re-order) level to facilitate the placing of an order to return stocks to a pre-determined maximum stock level.
Re-order lead time	The re-order lead time is the time between the placing of an order and receiving the supply in a palpable ready to use state. The re-order lead time is critical in setting the minimum or re-orders stove level.
Emergency order level	This is the stock level at which an order must be place as a matter of urgency. Emergency order comes with extra cost as the supplier most times will have to depend of courier agency that can deliver same day, next day or within a period less than the original re-order lead time. It is imperative to place an order urgent when stock levels get to emergency order level to ensure that service is not interrupted.

Challenges associated with reagent stock out

- Turnaround time for laboratory test are not met
- Treatment of patients are delayed
- Can lead to significant loss of revenue due to cancellation of surgeries, unnecessary prolonged stay in hospital
- Can negatively affect service delivery and result in customer dissatisfaction in service.
- Result in the interruption of service

Keys to effective inventory control of laboratory equipment, reagents and consumables

Key	Features
Avoid excess inventory	Excessive inventory constitutes waste to laboratory because of extra cost require storage, warehousing and risk of reagent becoming out of date. Use of software that tracks inventory in real-time can potentially obviates challenges associated with overstocking of laboratory reagents and consumables.
Implement the principle of just in time	Just In Time principle can potentially facilitate the efficient management of laboratory reagent and consumables, cost reduction (cold chain management and warehousing) and enables inventory to be triggered by demand. The potential disadvantage of this principle however that is there is a risk of reagent stock out of stock. The JIT principle is only practicable when the supplier of reagent or consumable is capable of delivering in a timely fashion to prevent interruption of service.
Determine what the effective cost is per test and determine the profitability per test	Ideally a laboratory should be able to calculate effectively and accurately the cost of each test using variables such as cost of kits, number of test per kit, cost of warehousing and inventory control management, number of control test done per kit. Using the above information a laboratory should be able to calculate how much it is effectively costing them to carry out a unit test as well as be able to determine how much profit the laboratory is making per test.

Build a culture of effective and efficient management of reagents and consumables	It is expedient that all staff responsible for inventory control management of laboratory reagents and consumables are appropriately trained on the optimum storage requirements for different laboratory reagents. Storage of reagent that should be stored at 2-8^0c in the fridge can potentially render the reagent unsuitable for testing. Also storage of reagent that requires cold chain management at room temperature can potentially affect its potency. Effective control of inventory costs in a laboratory involves the implementation of standard inventory-control best practices.
Implement the principle of first in first out	First in, first out principle is a system that ensures that perishable stock is used efficiently to prevent storage-related deterioration or loss of potency. Under this principle, stock is identified by date received and expiration date enabling inventory received earlier and with shorter shelf life to use in preference to inventory received later and with longer shelf life to be used later.

EFFECTIVE INVENTORY CONTROL USING KANBAN VISUAL MANAGEMENT SYSTEM

The term Kanban comes from 2 Japanese words kan (visual) and ban (card). A kanban is a visual colour coded card that acts as a trigger, signals or provides a clue that a particular inventory needs replenishment. It is a associated with a pull system where supply is determined by the need. Kanban system is based on the Just In Time Principle that supply should be available when they are needed. The use of Kanban discourages the keeping of unnecessary or excess inventory because of the transport, storage related cost and the fact that funds that could be invested into other gainful ventures by the laboratory (procure new equipment, expand the test menu available in the laboratory, facilitate continuous professional development of staff and improve staff welfare) are tied down in unnecessary inventory. Kanban is a concept associated with the use of color coded card for inventory control. It is related to lean and Just In Time (JIT) principle. It involves the uses of color coded cards to signal when stock is optimal, when stocking levels has gotten to a re-order or emergency order level. Kanban is a simple but effective way for visual inventory control (VIC) of laboratory reagents and consumables using color coded cards as triggers for replenishment.

OPTIMUM STOCKING OF LABORATORY REAGENTS AND CONSUMABLES

How much of reagents and consumables a laboratory decides to stock is dependent on a number of factors; the size of the laboratory, the nature of laboratory (localized or have affiliated), the type of stock involved, storage space available and the relative number of test done in the laboratory. There are advantages and disadvantages associated with keeping large and little stock levels of laboratory reagents and consumables.

ADVANTAGES AND DISADVANTAGES OF KEEPING LOW STOCK LEVELS

Advantages	Disadvantages
Allow for efficient and flexible management of inventory (order on demand)	Risk of stock out and inability to deliver service promised to customers is high particularly if there is any challenge associated with delivery.
Risk of reagent getting expired is reduced.	Risky. It puts the laboratory at the mercy of their suppliers
Cost of warehousing and cold chain management is reduced	It may be more expensive to run the service if the supplier is unable to meet their obligation because of challenges beyond their control. This may be weather-related (snow) or disaster-related (crash) or other factors (ash clouds).
Is ideal for highly expensive and short shelf life reagent	Can potential put the lives of patients at risk
Ideal for stock that is easy and quick to replenish	

Advantages and Disadvantages of Keeping Excess Inventory

Advantages	Disadvantages
It may be more cost effective to buy reagent in bulk and enjoy a significant discount from the manufacturers	Waste associated with extra cost of ware housing and cold chain management.
The risk of reagent stock out is significantly reduced	There is the risk of losing reagent due to expiration
There is better flexibility with management of inventory	Extra cost in incurred in securing extra storage space to accommodate excess inventory.
Guarantee for uninterrupted service delivery to service users	In the event of natural disaster that result in power outage and affect the cold chain management of product, can potentially result in huge loses to the laboratory.
Allow for seasonal increases or disaster-related (avian influenza outbreak) needs of increases in certain request to be met with ease.	Capital that could have been invested in other profitable venture is potentially tied down in unnecessary inventory.

Rule of 5's (Doing 5 quality improvement tasks every day can potentially improve the quality of your service delivery and grow your business).

If you want better results from your marketing as a laboratory, you need a marketing plan. Once you've decided how you plan to market your product or service, then you need to execute the steps. To get the most from your marketing plan though, you need to be consistent. One of the ways to be consistent as a business is to implement the the rule of 5. Basically, the idea is to do five quality improving marketing activities every day to promote your products or services. This will be five marketing tasks. You can select these from your marketing plan, or you can create new tasks to do. The idea is to market consistently. On day number one, you could contact five new potential contractors. The next day you could visit 5 potential customers to introduce your products and services to them. On day number three you can put an advert on five professional magazines to target potential customers. On the fourth day, you can attend the annual meeting of general practitioners and target 5 potential customers to discuss your product and service with. On day number 5 attend a lunch time seminar organized by one of regional meeting organized by a professional group who are potential users of your service to talk about the special qualities of your product or service that make you better than your competitors. The basic principle is based on the fact that carrying out small but consistent marketing and quality improving activities daily, you gradually build a culture of continuous improvement as well as improve your marketing potential and help you maximize your profit. The key factor is in being consistent about your marketing efforts. Real success in marketing comes from doing it regularly. Rule of 5 leads to success and increased profitable. It is all about being there for your customers and being responsive to the requirements and needs. Other potential 5 daily activities include:

- Call 5 potential customers on a daily basis
- Post information on the internet about your products and services targeting at least 5 potential customers.
- Send copies of your product and services brochures to 5 potential customers
- Visit 5 customers every day.

CHAPTER 18

LABORATORY INFORMATION MANAGEMENT SYSTEM (LIMS)

LABORATORY INFORMATION MANAGEMENT

Laboratory Information Management System (LIMS) solutions which improve performance and business effectiveness. Laboratory information management system (LIMS) is a software-based laboratory and information management system that offers a set of key features that support a modern laboratory's operations. Those key features include:

- Workflow and data tracking support
- Flexible architecture and smart data exchange interfaces (particularly in a regulation conscious diagnostic laboratory).

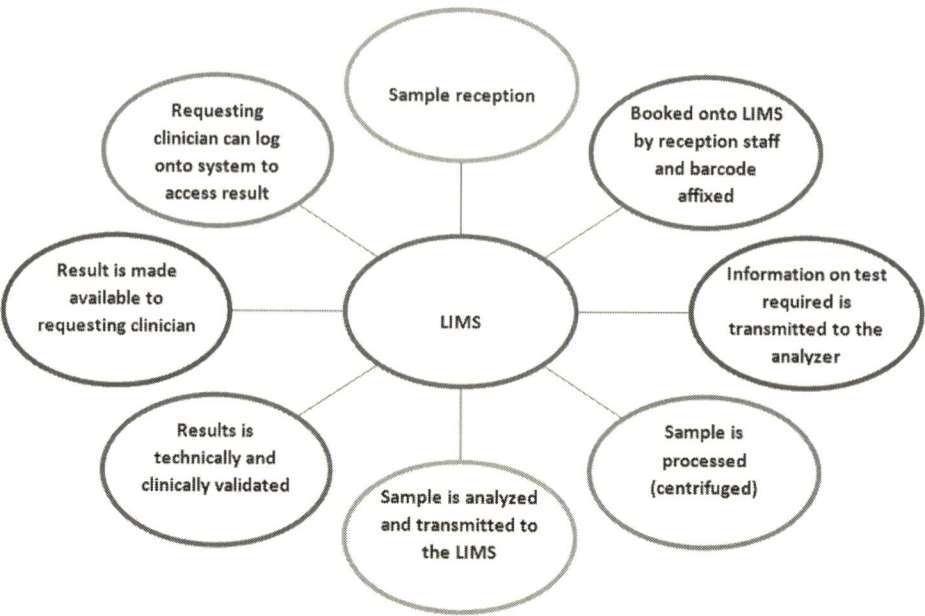

Figure: Overview of the LIMS

One of the greatest advances in diagnostic laboratories over the years has been the implementation of laboratory information management systems (LIMS). A laboratory information management system (LIMS) can make a major contribution to the quality and therefore to the efficiency and competitiveness of a laboratory. As a tool, LIMS permits the laboratory to input and use its own know-how and experience to optimize the total organization (internal and external) and workflow of generated information. Laboratory information management systems have become a necessity in modern laboratories as it helps in integrating and synchronizing the functions of all the software and equipment in the lab. Apart from this core function, a laboratory information management system is also responsible for managing and tracking lab samples and maintaining a user database and laboratory working standards. Before discussing the importance of such laboratory information management systems, let's first look at what they are all about.

Laboratory information management systems have been designed to carry out the function of managing laboratory samples, analysis by analyzers and transmission of results to the LIMS for final clinical validation. Once validated the requesting clinician can log into the LIMS and be able to access the laboratory results as well as print off copies. The role of a laboratory information management system begins right from the time the sample enters the lab, where it receives a barcode and the patient details are booked onto the LIMS. The sample is recorded and registered, and its every element and usage is tracked by the laboratory information management system. The LIMS captures when sample was received booked on the system, when it went on the analyzer when results was transferred from the analyzer to the LIMS, when results was technically validated and by who and when result was available to the requesting clinician. It provides an audit trail of patients sample as it goes through the laboratory. The LIMS also gives the laboratory scientist the opportunity to compare present results with previous to help in monitoring of patients on treatment. It also facilitates the detection of a significant deviation in patient's results over time. In the transfusion medicine it can potentially detect miss-matches of patient sample often when patient blood group determined does not match the previous blood group of the patient.

DR. ERHABOR AND DR. ADIAS

IMPORTANCE OF LIMS

Laboratory information management systems are important to a modern laboratory in the following ways:

- It simplifies data and sample management—Sample management and data management have been two of the biggest challenges for modern laboratories. These two functions require a considerable amount of working hours, but laboratory information management systems have simplified it to a very large extent. With these systems, the manpower in the lab can be utilized for the core activities, not for data management. This improves the productivity of the entire laboratory

- It synchronizes with other laboratory applications. Another major challenge for laboratories, especially the large ones, has been the management and integration of multiple applications. In a large modern lab, there are bound to be different instruments and application software used for various purposes and a laboratory information management system can integrate with all of them so that the laboratory functions as one unit. This significantly increases the efficiency of the laboratory.

From all this, it is clear that laboratory information management systems play a vital role in modern laboratory settings. In fact, laboratory information management is a requirement in modern high-tech laboratories.

LABORATORY INFORMATION MANAGEMENT OPERATIONS

The LIMS is an evolving concept, with new features and functionality being added often. As laboratory demands change and technological development improves, the functions of a LIMS will likely also change. Despite these changes, a LIMS tends to have a base set of functionality that defines it. That functionality can roughly be divided into five laboratory processing phases with its associated software functions:

- The reception and log in of a sample and its associated customer data
- The assignment, scheduling, and tracking of the sample and the associated analytical workload

- The processing and quality control associated with the sample and the utilized equipment and inventory
- The storage of data associated with the sample analysis
- The inspection, approval, and compilation of the sample data for reporting and/or further analysis

SAMPLE MANAGEMENT BY THE LMIS

- A lab worker matches blood samples to documents. With a LIMS, this sort of sample management is made more efficient.
- The core function of LIMS has traditionally been the management of samples. This function commences the moment a sample is received in the laboratory and is booked onto the LIMS. This registration process may involve accessioning the sample and producing barcodes to affix to the sample container.
- Various other parameters such as clinical or patient information (name, date of birth, hospital number, age, gender, address, source of sample, requesting clinician, clinical details and diagnostic test required).
- The LIMS then tracks chain of custody as well as sample location. Location tracking usually involves assigning the sample to a particular freezer location or on a shelf, rack, box, row, and column.
- It can also track events such as freeze and thaw cycles that a sample undergoes in the laboratory may be required.
- Modern LIMS have implemented extensive configurability. LIMS are adaptable to individual environments.
- LIMS help users to meet the requirements of regulatory authorities and compliance (MLSCN, CPA, MHRA, FDA and GLP).

INSTRUMENT AND APPLICATION INTEGRATION

- Modern LIMS offer an increasing amount of integration with laboratory instruments and applications. A LIMS may create control files that are "fed" into the instrument and direct its operation on some physical item such as a sample tube or sample plate. The LIMS may then import instrument results files to extract data for quality control assessment of the operation on the sample. Access to the instrument data can sometimes be regulated based on chain of custody assignments or other security features if need be.

- A relatively new development in LIMS products is the ability to import and manage raw assay data results.
- Allow for the status of a sample to be changed from routine to urgent and allow analyzer to prioritize the analysis of such samples
- Modern targeted assays such as qPCR and deep sequencing can produce tens of thousands of data points per sample.
- In drug of abuse testing as many as 12 or more assays may be run per sample.
- In order to track this data, a LIMS solution needs to be adaptable to many different assay formats at both the data layer and import creation layer, while maintaining a high level of overall performance.
- Allow for inputs of reference ranges for assay as well as an opportunity to flag results that are abnormal and require urgent attention.

ELECTRONIC DATA EXCHANGE

- The exponentially growing volume of data created in laboratories coupled with increased business demands and focus on profitability have pushed LIMS vendors to increase attention to how their LIMS handles electronic data exchanges.
- Attention must be paid to how an instrument's input and output data is managed
- How remote sample collection data is imported and exported, and how PDAs and tablet technology integrates with the LIMS

ADDITIONAL FUNCTIONS OF THE LIMS

- Aside from the key functions of sample management
- Facilitate management of increased work load
- Evidence of good laboratory practice (GLP)
- Prevent waste of quality time and facilitates excellent service delivery to patients. Requesting clinician can see results

272

immediately sample is tested and result is available even in remote areas like theatre without having to physical walk to the lab to collect test result.

- Facilitate service delivery in accident and emergency, intensive care units and high dependency units where results are needed urgently to allow for the effective management of patient.
- Allow for electronic requesting of laboratory investigations
- Facilitates instrument and application integration and electronic data exchange
- Facilitate audit management
- Allow for effective sample tracking and maintain a complete audit trail
- Barcode handling and specimen identification
- Assign one or more data points to a barcode format; read and extract information from a barcode
- Allow for a chain of custody
- Prevent unauthorized access to patients records and results
- Assign roles and groups that dictate access to specific data records and who is managing them
- Facilitate compliance to requirements by regulatory authorities
- Follow regulatory standards that affect the laboratory customer relationship management
- Handle the demographic information and communications for associated clients.
- Facilitate patient identification
- Process and convert data to certain formats; manage how documents are distributed and accessed
- Instrument calibration and maintenance
- Schedule important maintenance and calibration of lab instruments and keep detailed records of such activities
- Facilitates the audit process
- Facilitate inventory control management of equipment and reagents.
- Measure and record inventories of vital supplies and laboratory equipment
- Allow for manual (results that are done manually) and electronic data entry (interface between analyzer and LIMS)
- Help prevent transcription errors by direct transfer of test result via interface between analyzers and the LIMS

- Provide fast and reliable interfaces for data to be entered by a human or electronic component
- Method management
- Facilitate document control
- Help with accreditation
- Provide one location for all laboratory process and procedure (P&P) and methodology to be housed and managed
- Help with identification and management of urgent samples
- Personnel and workload management
- Organize work schedules, workload assignments, employee demographic information, and financial information
- Quality assurance and control
- Gauge and control sample quality, data entry standards, and workflow
- Creates an opportunity to clinically and technically validate test results before release to requesting clinicians
- Audit trails in case of investigation of incidents and near misses
- Facilitate reporting of investigations
- Create and schedule reports in a specific format; schedule and distribute reports to designated parties
- Time tracking
- Calculate and maintain processing and handling times on chemical reactions, workflows, and more
- The LIMS system should contain maintenance records of the equipment used in testing so that notifications can be generated to perform regular preventive maintenance

EXAMPLES OF LIMS

- Analytik Jena
- Clinysys
- LabLynx, Inc
- Labvantage
- LabWare
- Mincom
- PerkinElmer
- Sapio Sciences
- STARLIMS
- Thermo Fisher Scientific
- The Weaver Group Inc.
- Waters Corporation

LIMS OPTIMIZES PATHOLOGY SERVICE DELIVERY.

- Allows for laboratory instrument interfaces.
- Paper reporting of pathology results.
- Allow for easy order communications for pathology tests within the hospital and other satellite laboratories linked to the LIMS.
- Patient demographics (ADT) updates for patients can be added.
- Order communications for laboratory tests, for GP practices.
- GP electronic reporting of pathology test results
- Data analysis, billing, ad hoc reports for the laboratory

CHAPTER 19

PRODUCT DEVELOPMENT AND CUSTOMER SATISFACTION ISSUES ASSOCIATED WITH THE LABORATORY

KANO MODEL OF PRODUCT DEVELOPMENT AND CUSTOMER SATISFACTION

The Kano model is a theory of product development and customer satisfaction developed by Professor Noriaki Kano. Kano classifies customer preferences into five categories:

- Attractive
- One-Dimensional
- Must-Be
- Indifferent
- Reverse

These categories have been translated into English using various names

- Delighters/exciters
- Satisfiers
- Dissatisfiers

Attractive Quality: These attributes provide satisfaction if available in a product or service. Their absence however does not result in any customer dissatisfaction in the product or service. These attributes are not normally often expected by customers. However if the manufacturer of the goods or provider of the service goes out of their way to include it in their product or service, customers get excited by their presence. For example a car with cruise control or a fridge on board. These quality attributes are unexpected attributes. They are often unspoken. Their presence however comes as a delight to customers. Such products or service are likely to be accepted over competing brands that lacks such attributes.

One-dimensional Quality: These are attributes which if present in a product or service can potentially translate to customer satisfaction. However their absence leads to dissatisfaction when not fulfilled. These attributes are often spoken of or required by customers. The move of these attributes a product or service has the more receptive the product is likely to be to customers. Example is fruit juice that is said to contain 10% protein and sugar free, buy that actually contain 2% protein and sugar, eggs that are claimed to be range when actually they are not, fruits that are said to be organic when actually they are not and buy one get one free offer for orange juice only to find out that quality of the fruit juice has been compromised by poor storage. These attributes if present will lead to customer satisfaction. However, customers are likely to feel misled and dissatisfied if these claimed attributes are not available.

Must-be Quality: These are basic attributes that customers expects from a product or service. Their absence however results in dissatisfaction when not fulfilled. Every customer expects a hotel room to contain at least a bed with a pillow and bed sheet. These attributes are basic requirements. However a customer will be dissatisfied if he checks into a hotel room only to find out that there is a bed but no pillow of bed sheet. Customers in a temperate country like Siberia will expect a car to have heating facility as an unspoken basic requirement but they will be dissatisfied if this requirement is not met. Since customers expect these must-be quality attributes and view them as basic. They are often unspoken when asking enquiring for quality attributes of a good or service.

Indifferent Quality: These attributes refer to aspects that are neither good nor bad, and they do not result in either customer satisfaction or customer dissatisfaction. These attributes are however subjective because what one customer sees as good may be seen as bad by another or vice versa. Example is side where the fuel tank is located, shape of mirrors and presence of sun roof in a car.

Reverse Quality: These are attributes of a product that indicates a high degree of achievement but which result in dissatisfaction based on the fact that customer requirement differs. An example is a high tech phone with internet access, 14 megapixel camera and other high tech qualities may be dissatisfying to an unsophisticated (basic) customer who is not technological inclined and just require a basic with which to make and receiving call. This factor is indicative of the fact that not all customers are alike and that customer requirements can vary from one individual to another.

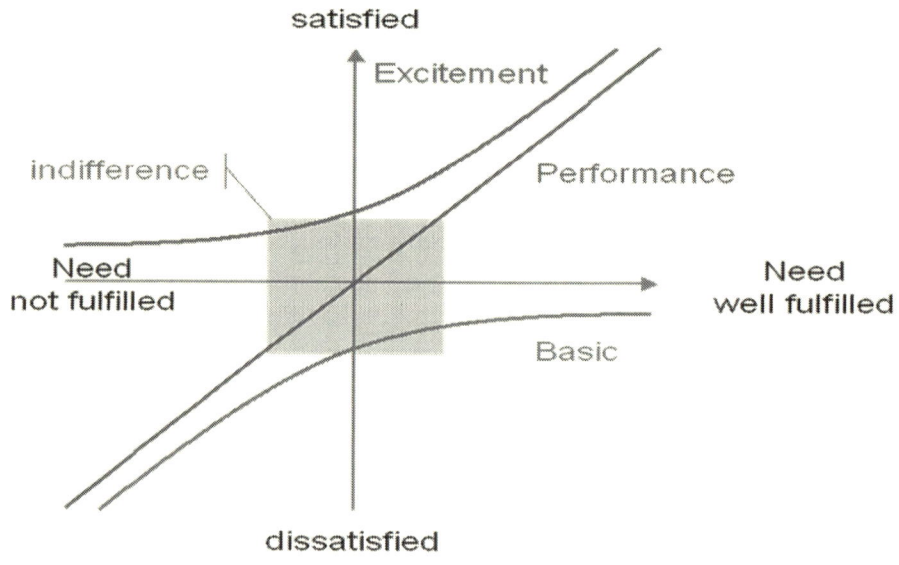

Figure: Kano Model

THRESHOLD OR BASIC ATTRIBUTES

One of the main points of assessment in the Kano model is the threshold attributes. These are basically the features that the product must have in order to meet customer demands. This is a crucial part of product innovation. Threshold attributes are simple components to a product. However, if they are not available, the product will soon leave the market due to dissatisfaction. Example is a car without a break, wiper or a steering wheel. Such cars will not be fir for purpose.

PERFORMANCE ATTRIBUTES

These are attribute of a good or service that makes up the behavioral characteristics that drives the performance of a product. For example it is reliability and perfection to Lexus, comfort, quality and prestige to Jaguar, low prices or cost and availability to ASDA or Wal-Mart. The more of performance attributes a product or service has, the better the customer satisfaction and acceptance of the product or service (more is better).Most customer requirements for a product falls under performance attributes category. The price a customer is willing to pay for a product is dependent on the product's performance attributes. So the higher the performance attribute, the higher the customers will be willing to pay for the product.

EXCITEMENT ATTRIBUTES

Excitement attributes are usually unforeseen by the customer. They are often unspoken. Their absence may not make any difference. However their presence yield paramount satisfaction. If a customer were to make a choice between competing brands, they are likely to go for the brand with the added excitement attributes. Excitement attribute has the tendency to spur a potential consumers' imagination. They can potentially be used to help the customer discover needs that they've never thought about before (unknown need). A manufacturer that must stay relevant in the market must earnestly seek to discover and introduces attributes (exciters) that causes them to stand out against competing brands. The more exciters (WOW factors) a product has, the more significant its competitive advantage over competing brands and the more it is likely to trigger impulsive wants and needs in the mind of the customer. Of all the attributes introduced in the Kano Model, the excitement ones are the most powerful and have the potential translate to significant more profit to the manufacturers.

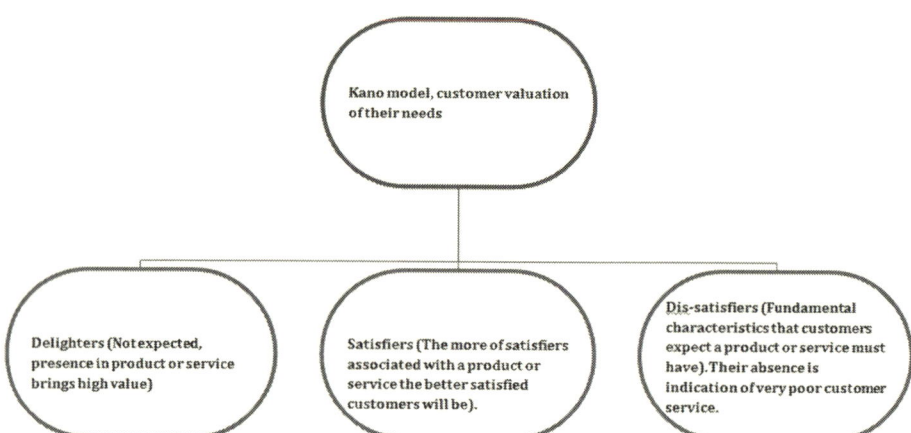

Figure: Kano model of customer valuation of their needs

- **Dissatisfiers:** Fundamental requirements that are expected as part of a package. For example, when buying a car, everyone expects the car to have brakes. If these fundamental characteristics are not there, the company needs to focus immediately on delivering them, otherwise it will likely not be able to remain in business. Because these are "must-have" requirements, they do not make the customers happy; however, their absence **produces dissatisfied and** unhappy customers.

- **Satisfiers:** These are requirements that the customers are not necessarily expecting. However the more of them that the producer can include, the more satisfied and happier the customer becomes. For example a car having heated seats (customers in temperate countries), orthopedic seats, keyless operation, hands free telephone use adds additional satisfaction. Customers can live without these satisfiers. However when it comes to make choices between competing brands, the satisfiers becomes a major factor for consideration. The products with more satisfiers end up being chosen.

- **Delighters:** These are characteristics that are not expected, so they do not cause dissatisfaction if they are not available. However their presence makes a customer highly delighted. It is often seen as a mean of competitive advantage. Example is the presence of cruise control (autonomous cruise control) commonly seen in some luxury cars that enable a driver to set his speed and just cruise along on that speed without using the throttle pedal, senses when traffic stops and then brakes the car even before the driver has noticed that the vehicle in front of them has stopped. Delighters normal exceed customers expectations (breakthrough features, competitive differentiators).When considering the changes needed in your organization, it is important to perform an honest assessment of where your company is and where it wants to be:

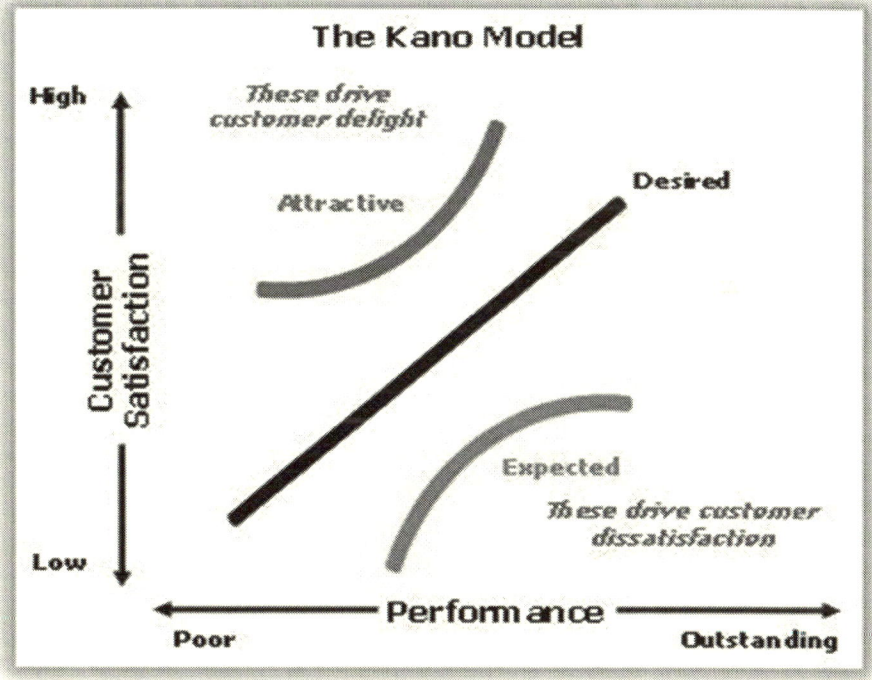

Figure: Kano Model of valuation of customer needs

REFERENCES

1. Kano Noriaki, Nobuhiku Seraku, Fumio Takahashi Tsuji. Attractive quality and must-be quality. Journal of Japanese Society for Quality Control 1984; 14(2):39-48.
2. Cadotte ER, Turgeon N. Dissatisfiers and satisfiers: suggestions from consumer complaints. Journal of Consumer Satisfaction and Complaining Behaviour 1988; 1:74-79.

CHAPTER 20

OCCUPATIONAL HEALTH ISSUES ASSOCIATED WITH WORKING IN THE LABORATORY

OCCUPATIONAL HEALTH ISSUES

Occupational health involves the evaluation and control of factors within work environment that can potentially affect the health and well being of the staff. People have the right to expect and ensure that there is an adequate level of control over those environmental factors that affect their state of health. Occupational Health and Safety issues relating to the personal safety, protection and welfare of staff is a very important in employer-employee relationship. Hospitals also play an integral role in community protection through wider public health issues including injury and illness prevention, health surveillance and disease notification and disaster management. Occupational health involves the management of the effect of work on health, and the effect of health on work. It plays a vital role in helping employers care for and understand the needs of their employees, enabling businesses to reduce sickness absence levels and optimize staff performance and productivity.

ROLE OF OCCUPATIONAL HEALTH DEPARTMENT

Every hospital should have an Occupational Health department. It is the responsibility of the Occupational Health department to provide all employees with confidential advice and support on any health issues.

- Pre employment health assessment.
- Provision of protective vaccines and post exposure prophylaxis to exposed staff.
- Management of accidental exposure to infectious materials (blood borne and chemical).
- Management of job-related accidents and follow up accidents at work.
- Monitoring of medically certificated sickness absence

- Promotion of workplace health
- Maintenance of staff health records
- Advice on workplace health issues
- Advice on rehabilitation after accidents or ill health
- Health monitoring of staff at special risk or those required by Health and Safety legislation.
- Management of health problem in staff that have been caused by or exacerbated by their work and those that is affecting the work or task assigned.

OCCUPATION EXPOSURE TO SHARPS AND PROVISION OF POST EXPOSURE PROPHYLAXIS

Health care workers particularly in resource-limited settings in sub Saharan Africa are at risk of acquiring and transmitting parenteral infection including HIV, HBV and HCV. Sharp injuries and other exposure of staff to source patient blood and body fluid carry a risk of transmission of blood borne viral infections.

Health, Safety and Environment (HSE) provides services and leadership in the areas of medical surveillance and environmental monitoring, the treatment of occupational illness and injuries, fire safety, biological safety, chemical safety, laboratory safety, facility and equipment safety, employee safety training programs and the payment and adjudication of worker's compensation claims.

PREVENTIVE MEDICINE (DISEASES IN WHICH PROTECTIVE IMMUNIZATIONS ARE AVAILABE)

- Hepatitis B
- Rubella (German measles)
- Rubella (measles)
- MMR (mumps, measles, rubella)
- Varicella (chickenpox)
- Tetanus
- Smallpox
- Rabies
- Influenza (flu)

Table: Infectious agents or diseases to which laboratory workers may be exposed.

Blood-borne pathogens and Infectious agents to Laboratory staff are exposed

Mode of transmission	Infectious agent/Disease
Blood and body fluids	Hepatitis B, Non-A, Hepatitis C, Acquired Immunodeficiency Syndrome (AIDS) and Cytomegalovirus (CMV).
Faeces	Hepatitis A, Salmonella, Shigella, Campylobacter
Urine and stool (virus shedding)	Rubella (German measles)
Sputum and airborne droplets	Pulmonary tuberculosis, Varicella zoster virus (VZV) (Chickenpox only).
Respiratory secretions	Rubella (German measles), Rubella (measles), Mumps, influenza, Respiratory syncytial virus (RSV).
Saliva	Mumps, Herpes simplex virus (HSV)—Type I, Type II, Herpetic whitlow, Varicella zoster virus (VZC) (chicken pox & shingles).

Surveillance

- Tuberculosis screening for employees particularly those working in microbiology that is exposed to TB. Screening should be done annually as required by regulations and for exposures to TB.
- Respirator Program to medical assesses staff whose job roles involve wearing a respirator to ensure pulmonary function.

Communicable disease exposure in the hospital laboratory

It is a normal requirement for staff whose role exposes them to communicable or contagious diseases such as HIV, HBV, HCV, TB, Varicella, Meningitis and Pertussis to be evaluated and vaccination provides as part of a pre-employment requirement. Pre-Employment Health Screening often includes:

- Blood work for full blood count
- Antibody titres for diseases such as; Hepatitis Rubella and Varicella
- Vision check
- Urinalysis and drug screening if indicated
- HIV Testing
- Hepatitis B antibody titre
- TB testing
- Blood pressure
- Pulse rate
- Review of health history

HBV EXPOSURE AND MANAGEMENT

Current recommendation iws for staffs that are prone to occupation exposure to contaminated blood to receive post exposure prophylaxis (PEP) (be vaccinated against HBV using hepatitis B immunoglobulin (HBIG) which provides passive immunity). HCWs are also expected and have a significant anti HB-s titre of >100 IU/mL. Testing is recommended for those at risk of occupational exposure (particularly healthcare and laboratory workers). Antibody titres should be checked one to four months after the completion of a primary course of vaccine.

HBV VACCINATION AND ANTIBODY TITRE REQUIREMENTS

- The standard course of immunization involves three injections at 0, 1 and 6 months.
- An accelerated course of 0, 1 and 2 months is also possible.
- Adults who are accidentally exposed and need protection very quickly can have a schedule of 0, 7 and 21 days started within 48 hours of exposure. After an accelerated course, a booster at one year is often recommended.
- Responders with anti-HBs levels greater than or equal to 100 IU/mL do not require any further primary doses. Further assessment of antibody levels is not indicated. They should then receive the reinforcing booster dose at five years.

- Responders with anti-HBs levels of > 10 but less than 100 IU/mL should receive one additional dose of vaccine. Further assessment of antibody levels is not indicated. They should however receive a booster dose at five years.

- Healthcare workers with an antibody titre of <10 IU/mL are classified as a non-responders. It is advisable to test such staff for markers of current or past infection. In non-responders, a repeat course of vaccine is recommended followed by a determination of the antibody titre after one to four months of completing the second course. HCW who still does not respond and continue to have anti-HBs levels <10 U/mL, and show no markers of current or past infection, will require hepatitis B immunoglobulin (HBIG) for protection if exposed to the virus.

POST-EXPOSURE EVALUATION & FOLLOW-UP PROCEDURES

- Exposure (eye, mouth, mucous membrane, non-intact skin or parenteral surface) to potentially infectious (blood or other potentially infectious material) by staff must be reported, investigated and appropriate post exposure prophylaxis administered.

- The exposed staff must also be report the incident to their laboratory manager The Laboratory manager and the employee will promptly complete the incident report form. The employee will need to take the incident report to the Occupational Health department.

- Occupational health department will need to counsel the exposed staff and offer any necessary post-exposure evaluation, treatment, and follow-up.

- If the source patient is in a high risk group for viral infection such as HIV, HBV and HCV, consent can be sought from the source patient to have their sample screened to enable an evidenced based approach in the administration of the post exposure prophylaxis. If source patient refuses to offer consent then universal prophylaxis will need to be provided.

- Exposed staff may need to be tested for HIV, HBV and HCV upon offering consent. However if the individual refuses to offer consent for testing, a blood sample will need to be collected and held for 90 days (save sample) to allow time for the sero-conversion to possibly occur.

- The test results for both the individual and the source patient are confidential medical information.
- HBV immune globulin and/or HBV vaccine as well as prophylaxis for HIV will be offered when indicated after discussion of potential risks and benefits.
- Laboratory managers is expected to investigate the circumstances surrounding the incident and take appropriate remedial and corrective action including modifications of the physical environment, working practices and instruction regarding safe working practices as it affect the incident.

CHALLENGES OF EFFECTIVE POST EXPOSURE MANAGEMENT IN DEVELOPING COUNTRIES

- Absence of occupational health policy
- Lack of adequate training on universal precaution
- Lack of effective modification of procedures that have high risk,
- Absence of institutional policy for handling of sharps
- Lack of universal access to post exposure prophylaxis for exposed HCWs
- Suboptimal segregation and disposal of sharps

HIV EXPOSURE AND MANAGEMENT

Although preventing exposures to blood and body fluids is the primary means of preventing occupationally acquired human immunodeficiency virus (HIV) infection, appropriate post exposure management is an important element of workplace safety. The average risk for HIV transmission after a percutaneous exposure to HIV-infected blood has been estimated to be approximately 0.3% and after a mucous membrane exposure, approximately 0.09%. Episodes of HIV transmission after non-intact skin exposure are estimated to be less than the risk for mucous membrane exposures. The risk for transmission after exposure to fluids or tissues other than HIV-infected blood is also considerably lower than for blood exposures. Factors that affect risk for HIV infection following accidental exposure includes:

- Exposure to a larger quantity of blood from the source person
- Exposure to a sharp device such as needle and lancet that are visibly contaminated with the infected patient's blood.
- A procedure that involved a needle being placed directly in a vein or artery or a deep injury that exposes A HCW to an HIV positive source patient's blood.
- The stage of HIV infection in the source patient (exposure to blood from source persons with terminal illness with higher titre of HIV viral RNA in blood such as those with full blown AIDS

POST EXPOSURE MANAGEMENT

Antiretroviral agents from five classes of drugs are currently available to treat HIV infection. These include the nucleoside reverse transcriptase inhibitors (NRTIs), nucleotide reverse transcriptase inhibitors (NtRTIs), non-nucleoside reverse transcriptase inhibitors (NNRTIs), protease inhibitors (PIs), and a single fusion inhibitor. The recommendations are to provide exposed HCWs with highly active antiretroviral therapy made up of two-or-more drug PEP regimens. The expectation is that a combination regimen with three or more antiretroviral agents with activity at different stages in the viral replication cycle is superior to monotherapy and dual-therapy regimens combination of drugs and might offer an additive preventive effect in PEP. PEP should be initiated as soon as possible, preferably within hours rather than days of exposure. PEP should be administered preferably for 4 weeks, if tolerated by the exposed HCW. Exposed HCWs should receive follow-up counselling, post exposure testing, and medical evaluation regardless of whether they receive PEP. HIV-antibody testing by enzyme immunoassay should be used to monitor seroconversion risk for about 6 months after occupational HIV exposure. After baseline testing at the time of exposure, follow-up testing could be performed at 6 weeks, 12 weeks, and 6 months after exposure.

POSSIBLE HIV PEP TREATMENT OPTIONS TO PREVENT HIV INFECTION IN EXPOSED HCWS

Regimen	ART combination	Dosage	Advantages	Disadvantages
Basic PEP Regimen	Zidovudine (AZT), + Lamivudine (3TC) or Combivir	AZT : 600 mg per day, in two or three divided doses, and 3TC : 150 mg twice daily	AZT is associated with decreased risk of HIV transmission the CDC case-control study of occupational HIV infection, It has been used more than the other drugs for PEP in HCP, serious toxicity is rare when used for PEP, side effects are predictable and manageable and can be given as a single tablet (COMBIVIR™) twice daily	Side effects are risk of poor adherence, risk that source patient virus might have resistance to this regimen and potential for delayed toxicity.
Alternative Regimen	Lamivudine (3TC) + Stavudine (d4T)	3TC: 150 mg twice daily, and d4T: 40 mg (if body weight is <60 kg, 30 mg twice daily) twice daily	Well tolerated in patients with HIV infection, resulting in good adherence, serious toxicity appears to be rare and twice daily dosing might improve treatment adherence.	Source patient virus might be resistant to this regimen and potential for delayed toxicity

CHAPTER 21

HEALTH AND SAFETY ISSUES IN THE LABORATORY

HEALTH AND SAFETY ISSUES

Employers have responsibilities for the health and safety of their employees as well as those of visitors to their laboratory (customers, suppliers, contractors and the general public. They are to ensure that the department is effectively sign posted in case of fire or other incident where there are needs to evacuate. All employers, whatever the size of the business, must ensure that the workplace is safe.

Staffs who do not work safely and carefully can potentially endanger themselves as well as put their colleagues at risk. It is the duty of all laboratory staff to take reasonable care for their own health and safety as well as those of other staff that may be affected by their actions and inactions. They are expected to collaborate with their employer to ensure compliance to health and safety legislation. They must not interfere with or misuse equipment and materials provided for promote their health, safety and welfare. They are required to abide by departmental safety policies and health and safety regulations.

THE LABORATORY AND WASTE MANAGEMENT

In an increasingly cost conscious world concerned with the long term environmental effects of pollution, there is an increasing expectation that laboratory as producers of potentially hazardous waste and products should be responsible for them from the point of generation to their safe disposal. To allow for the effective use of limited and diminishing resources and to maximize use of resources there is increasing pressure for waste minimization and recycling despite the costs involved. Effective waste management principles encourages: Waste reduction, re-use when appropriate, recycle, treat and effectively dispose.

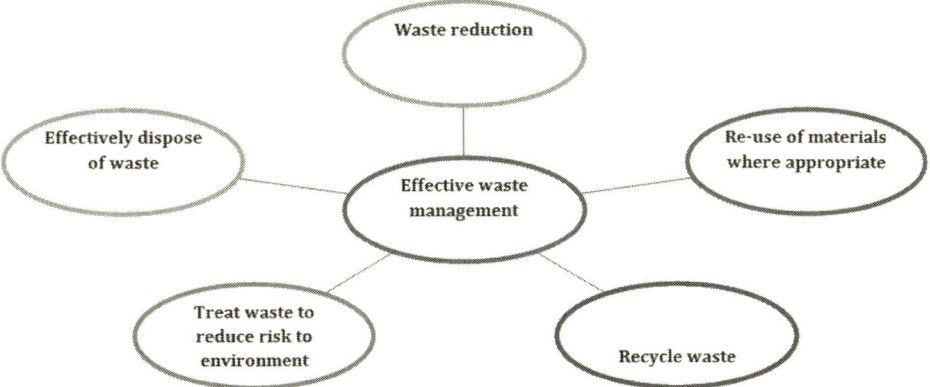

Figure: Principle of Laboratory waste management

The major components of such a laboratory waste management system should include:

- Waste segregation at the source (sharp containers, biohazard bins, general waste bin all standardized and color-coded.
- Storage and transport of laboratory samples in safe and leak proof containers.
- Sterilization of contaminated laboratory waste treatment prior to final disposal (autoclave and incineration).

EMPLOYER'S RESPONSIBILITIES AS IT AFFECT HEALTH AND SAFETY

- Employers are to ensure that the equipment and other materials that employees require to work safely are provided.
- They must ensure that personal protective equipment that staff require to safely carry out designated task (laboratory coats, hand gloves, aprons, nose mask, eye goggles and ear muff) are provided.
- Ensure that the right warning and safety signs are provided.
- Employer has a duty of care to look after, as far as possible, your health, safety and welfare while you are at work. They are expected by law to carry out regular risk assessments to identify and eliminate health and safety hazards and reduce risk.
- Provide regular mandatory health and safety training for staff.
- Have a process in place for documentation and investigation of accidents, incidents and near misses.

- Have a formal health and safety policy to include arrangements to protect the health and safety of staff and visitors to the department.
- Have a policy on waste management to ensure that all waste materials generated are handled, stored and safely disposed.
- Have a nominated competent person responsible for all health and safety related issues in the department.
- Provide adequate first aid facilities
- Inform staff, training and supervise the use of any potential hazards associated with chemicals and other substances.
- Ensure that that adequate ventilation, temperature, lighting, toilet, washing and rest facilities are available and that they meet health, safety and welfare requirements
- Have a process in place to ensure that the right equipment is provided and is properly used and regularly maintained.
- Manage and control exposure to substances that may damage the health of staff
- Take reasonable precautions against the risks caused by flammable or explosive hazards, electrical equipment, noise and radiation. Ensure that all electrical appliances in use are Pat tested to reduce fire risk.
- Ensure that appropriate tools are available for manual handling of potentially heavy equipments and other materials to reduce the risk of injury.
- Ensure the provision of materials to enable staff deal effectively and safely with spillages.
- Ensure that workrooms are big enough to allow easy movement as well as ensure that benches are not cluttered. Ensure that physical hazards such as noise and vibration are minimal.
- Ensure that floors, walkways, stairs, roadways etc are safe to use. Provide suitable washing facilities and clean drinking water.
- Have a clean area with all necessary amenities set aside for rest breaks, meals and relaxations.
- Ensure that staffs are adequately instructed in the correct, appropriate and safe use of equipment.
- Ensure that visitors to the laboratory complete a visitor's note book to indicate their presence in the laboratory as well as ensure that they are equipped with appropriate safety equipment.

- Ensure the provision of post exposure prophylaxis for laboratory staff that are accidentally exposed to high risk source patient blood and body fluid (Engerix-B' is indicated for active immunization against hepatitis B virus infection and a course of Highly Active Anti-Retroviral Therapy (HAART) for the prevention of HIV seroconversion in exposed staff).
- Ensure that there is availability of protective vaccination and that staff are up to date with their protective vaccination (Hepatitis B and Tuberculosis).
- Obsolete materials and equipments must never be allowed to accumulate and must be disposed of following appropriate procedure.

STAFF RESPONSIBILITIES FOR HEALTH AND SAFETY

- Must not interfere or misuse materials provided to ensure the safety and welfare of staff (personal protective equipment).
- Use the personal protective equipment provided by the employer (gloves, goggles, face shields, laboratory coats, aprons and hearing protection equipment).
- Abide by applicable health and safety rules as provided by the employer.
- Report all unsafe conditions to the laboratory manager or assistant director of laboratory services.
- Must attend mandatory annual health and safety lectures.
- Report all incidents, accidents and near misses to the laboratory manager.
- Adhere to standard work in operational to address health and safety issues in the laboratory.
- Must complete and be compliant with all recommended occupational health screening.
- Staff must be conversant with the layout of the laboratory as well as location, and operation of the health and safety equipment in the laboratory.
- Show zero tolerance for eating, drinking and smoking in the laboratory. Food must never be stored in the refrigerators and freezers used for storage of reagents and blood.
- Must use equipment for the appropriate and designed purpose

- Show Zero tolerance for mouth pipetting. Use appropriate pipetting devices
- Must use personal protective equipment provided.
- Ensure that fire doors are kept closed at all times.
- Ensure that all exposed cuts and grazes are covered with a water proof dressing before handing any specimen or working on the bench.
- Always seek advice and clarification from laboratory manager if in doubt about the use of any equipment. Report defective equipment to laboratory manager.
- Ensure that all containers are appropriately labeled with the name of the content.
- Never operate electrical equipment with wet and damp hands.
- Wash hands after completion of task and remove all protective equipment before leaving the laboratory.
- Consult the material safety data sheet of laboratory chemicals and reagent prior to using a new chemical and reagent and strictly follow the manufacturer's prescribed procedures.
- Use steps, ladders or kick-stools when reaching high objects. Other inappropriate laboratory furniture must never be use for this purpose.
- Ensure that laboratory waste are appropriately segregated and safely disposed following employers standard procedures.
- Must not consume food and beverages in the laboratory.
- Must be health and safety conscious in the shoes and clothing worn, use of cosmetics as well as their hair. Use of cosmetics in the laboratory other than emollient hand crème used after hand washing must not be used or kept in the laboratory work area.
- Must carry out a risk assessment to determine potential hazards and appropriate safety precautions are in place before implementing a new procedure or operation.
- Avoid exposure to aerosols, gases, vapors and particulates by carry out applicable processes in a functional fume hood.
- Ensure that laboratory equipments are maintained as required and that up-to-date records are kept of such maintenance.
- Ensure that spillages are dealt with immediately, appropriately and safely using spillage kits provided by employer.

- Access to emergency equipment and exit must never be blocked.
- Ensure that all hazardous agents and chemicals are appropriately stored.
- Use of open flame in the laboratory should be avoided if possible.

MANAGEMENT OF ACCIDENTS AND INCIDENTS IN THE LABORATORY

Accident: An accident is an undesired and unfavourable event which results in harm to laboratory staff and or damage to property. Accidents include minor cuts, scratches, splash accident, needle stick injury and falls. Accidents can be minor (minor cuts, scratches, splash accident) or major (needle tick injury, fracture loss of sight, amputation, burns, electric shock, ingestion or adsorption of chemical or biological toxin, loss of consciousness and any work-related accidents that results in admission and hospital stay for ≥ 24 hours. All accidents that require immediate medical attention must be promptly reported to the laboratory manager and accident and emergency department for immediate attention. Where appropriate, minor cuts and injuries should be cleaned, dresses as required. Every laboratory must have a first aid box containing all appropriate first aids materials located in a place that is assessable to all staff.

MANAGEMENT OF NEEDLE STICK INJURY AND SPLASH INJURY

Needle stick injuries are injuries caused by the piercing of the skin or body by needle or other sharps (lancet, cannula and others).In the event of such accident occurring, wash the contaminated area with warm running water, allow cut to bleed freely and dress the wound once the bleeding has stopped. Identify the contaminating material, report to the laboratory manager and complete an accident form and trigger off appropriate post exposure prophylaxis as required. For splash injury, use eyewash or rinse the mouth with clean water.

Dealing with Laboratory Chemicals and Reagents

All chemicals in use in the laboratory must have a Control Of Substances Hazardous to Health (COSHH) risk assessment before being put to use. It must contain the name of the chemical, the hazard group, rating, storage, safe handling and safe disposal information. The manufacturers safety data sheet (MSDS) must be provided with all chemicals supplied to the laboratory. Chemicals, Hazard Information and Packaging (CHIP) regulation recommend manufacturers of all laboratory chemicals display hazard warning labels and other relevant information on containers of chemicals. Common information required is shown in the table below.

Table: Chemicals, Hazard Information and Packaging (CHIP) Regulation

CHIP Classification	Hazard code	Nature of hazards	Symbols
Corrosive	C	These are chemical that can potentially destroy living tissues. Examples of corrosive chemicals include; Acetic acid, Aluminium bromide, Ammonia solution, Ethylene diamine, Ferric chloride, Formic acid, Phosphoric acid and Hydrochloric acid.	
Explosive	E	These include substances that have the potential to explode when subjected to heat, shock and friction particularly when dry. Explosive chemical exhibit all of the following: Rapid expansion (rapid production of gases or rapid heating of surroundings), produces heat, reacts rapidly and is spontaneous in initiation. Important explosives include; trinitrotoluene (TNT), dynamite, nitrocellulose, nitro-glycerine, and picric acid.	

Flammable	F	These include chemical which becomes hot and inflames when in contact with air or a source of ignition. These chemicals tend to produce inflammable gases when they come in contact with water or damp air. Flammable is a property of a material relating how easily the material ignites or sustains a combustion reaction. Inflammable (flammable) chemicals include most hydrocarbons such as methane and butane, alcohols, and some metals such as magnesium	
Harmful	X_h	Harmful chemicals are substances that are associated with risk of limited seriousness when inhaled, swallowed or are exposed to the skin. Examples of harmful chemicals include; Strong Acids (Hydrochloric acid and Sulphuric acid) and Alkalis (Sodium Hydroxide and Potassium hydroxide), Gases (Nitrogen Dioxide, Carbon Monoxide and Sulphur Dioxide), Potassium Cyanide and Hydrogen sulphide.	
Irritant	X_i	Irritant chemical are substances which although are non-corrosive, but can cause inflammation when there is prolonged or repeated contact with the skin or mucous membrane. Examples include: Hydrochloric acid, sulphuric acid, sodium hydroxide, potassium hydroxide, Dichloromethane and N-methyl pyrrolidine.	

Oxidising	O	Chemicals that have a strong exothermic reactions with other chemicals (particularly flammable substances) are called oxidising chemicals. Oxidizing chemicals are materials that spontaneously evolve oxygen at room temperature or with slight heating or promote combustion. This class of chemicals includes peroxides, chlorates, perchlorates, nitrates, and permanganates.	
Toxic	T	Toxic chemicals are substances that can be harmful or fatal when ingested. Toxic chemicals are chemicals that can produce injury or death when inhaled, ingested, or absorbed through the skin. Damage may result from acute or chronic exposures and involve local tissue or internal organs. Common examples include; ethanol, methanol, mercury, carbon disulfide, and tetraethyl lead acetone, methyl ethyl ketone, and chloroform.	

THINGS LABORATORY STAFF MUST KNOW ABOUT DEALING WITH HAZARDOUS CHEMICALS.

- Avoid direct contact with the skin. In case of contact drench with water and wash with soap and water.
- Treat all chemical and reagents as potentially dangerous taking universal precaution.
- Avoid direct contact with spillages or breakages and never inhale or breathe in solvent vapours.

- Wash your hand with soap and water after handling and transporting any laboratory chemicals
- Wear appropriate protective equipment when dealing with chemicals and never mouth-pipette any chemical solution (use safety pipette or measuring cylinder).
- There must be biohazard containers for disposal of chemicals and other substances that cannot be dispersed into the regular sink.
- Use fume hood when dealing with chemicals that have potential harmful vapours.
- Do not pick up or move flasks or other containers holding chemicals unless absolutely necessary. Fewer mistakes mean fewer accidents.
- If you have to move chemicals from one point to the other, use both hands to make sure you have a firm grip, and always make sure your travel path is clear.
- Always consult the manufacturers Material Safety Data Sheet (MSDS) which contains the hazard rating, normal storage conditions, safe handling and disposal information before using any new chemicals. This information enables a COSHH risk assessment to be carried out.
- Label all chemicals appropriately and extra caution and care must be exhibited when removing chemicals from its container (especially strong acids, alkalis and ammonia).
- Chemical containers must be securely closed after use and any spillage must be safely dealt with following manufacturer's instructions.
- Handle chemicals in a well ventilated room (especially organic solvents).
- Apply principles for controlling chemical hazards such as; elimination (use an alternative process or strategy such as use of disposable chemical reagents, substitution of more toxic chemicals with less toxic chemical, and isolation of toxic chemicals in a safe and less exposed area.

Control of Substances Hazardous to Health (COSHH) Assessment Form

Ward /Department Assessed:

Assessed By:

Job Title of Assessor:

Date Assessed:

General description of work/activity assessed:

Staff grade that normally carryout activity:

How many times per week does staff carry out activity:

Is there a standard work for carrying out activity:

Is standard work being adhered to:

Is substance being assessed hazardous to health:

Name of chemical and hazard associated (blood borne, flammable, harmful irritant e.t.c):

Is it compulsory this substance must be used for this activity: Yes: ⬭ No: ⬭

Is there any less hazardous alternative to this substance: Yes: ⬭ No: ⬭

Evaluate risk associated with substance assuming that no control is in place:

Circle as appropriate

Severity	Likelihood of risk occurring	Risk Rating	Risk score
Minor	Rare	Low	1-3
Serious requiring medical treatment	Unlikely	Moderate	4-7
Major associated with excessive injury	Moderately likely	Significant	8-12
Fatal	Likely	High	13-25
Catastrophic	Certain		

List all control in place to avoid risk: (e.g. Automated testing, PPE, Spill kits, Dedicated storage area):

If control is in place to manage substance, re-evaluate risk:

Severity ☐

Likelihood ☐

Risk Score ☐

Is there any procedure for managing spillage:

Summary and conclusion (is exposure to substance adequately controlled):

Yes: ☐ No: ☐

If no what are the root causes:

Corrective action required by laboratory manager:

Signature of assessor: [   ]

Date for next review:

Signature of Laboratory manager/Date:

FIRE SAFETY IN THE LABORATORY

All fires and smell of smoke must be reported. Even though a fire may appear to be extinguished, the fire department still needs to respond to verify it's out as well as complete a report. Fire is a chemical reaction called combustion. Fire needs 3 principal agents (fuel, oxygen and heat) in order to burn. Fire extinguishers apply an agent that will cool burning fuel or restrict or remove oxygen so the fire cannot continue to burn. Small fires can be quickly controlled by a portable fire extinguisher. Fire extinguishers must be located throughout the laboratory. To properly use an extinguisher, staff must be trained effectively, be familiar with what type of fire each extinguisher is appropriate for as well as know how to operate it.

Figure: Fire triangle

DEALING WITH FIRE IN THE LABORATORY

Report the fire: Break the fire alarm trigger box. Report the fire to switch board, the fire department and the fire service.

Fight the fire: Attempt must only be made to fight small fires with available and appropriate fire extinguishers. Staff must always ensure that they have a safe exit. It is advisable to report the fire first and then attempt to fight it.

Escape: If the fire becomes is large escape through the safest fire exit.

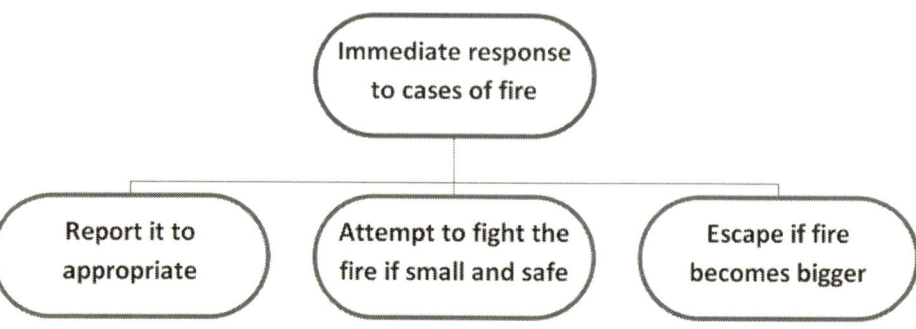

Figure: Immediate response to cases of fire

FIRE CLASSIFICATIONS

All fires are grouped into classes, according to the type of materials that are involved. The classes of fire differ from one continent to another. The following is a quick guide to the different types of fire.

Class A fires involve combustible materials such as paper, wood, cardboard, and most plastics.

Class B fires involve flammable or combustible liquids such as petrol, kerosene, paraffin, grease and oil.

Class C fires involve flammable gases, such as propane, butane and methane.

Class D fires involve combustible metals, such as magnesium, titanium, potassium and sodium.

Class F fires are specific to cooking oils and fats

TYPES AND USE OF FIRE EXTINGUISHERS

Fire extinguishers are remarkably sophisticated items of firefighting equipment, and each type has been specially designed to tackle different types of fire. Fire Extinguishers display a fire rating which indicates the size and type of fire that they can extinguish. The letter is the type of fire it is capable of extinguishing and the number is the size of fire it can extinguish under test conditions. Generally, the larger the number, the larger the fire it can extinguish. Some fire extinguishers are suitable for tackling different types of fire and are often referred to as Multi Purpose Fire Extinguishers. For example, all fire extinguishers capable of extinguishing both class A and B fires carry a Fire Rating which is indicated by a number and letter (**8A/34B**). This rating indicates the extinguisher is capable of extinguishing a Class-A fire to the size 8 and a Class-B fire to the size 34 under test conditions. Fire extinguishers are categorized into; water, dry powder, foam, CO2 and wet fire extinguishers.

Water Fire Extinguishers: Water fire extinguishers are filled with ordinary tap water. They are ideal for use on Class-A fires involving everyday materials such as paper, wood, fabric, furnishings, etc. Water fire extinguishers are solid red in color.

Dry Powder Fire Extinguishers: Powder fire extinguishers are excellent all-round fire extinguishers suitable for use on Class-A, Class-B and Class-C fires. They are also are safe to be used on fires involving electrical equipment. Powder fire extinguishers are painted red with a blue panel above the operating instructions. A variety of specialist fire extinguishers are required to tackle the various Class-D flammable metal fires. All specialist flammable metal fire extinguishers are categorized as powder extinguishers.

Foam Fire Extinguishers: Aqueous film forming foam fire extinguishers (AFFF) are very popular due to their all-round abilities and are suitable for use on Class-A and Class-B fires. Foam fire extinguishers are red with a cream panel above the operating instructions.

Carbon Dioxide (CO2) Fire Extinguishers: Carbon dioxide or CO2 fire extinguishers are suitable for Class-B fires involving flammable liquids and are also recommended for fires involving live electrical equipment. Carbon dioxide fire extinguishers are painted bright red with a black panel above the operating instructions, and have a distinctive horn-shaped nozzle at the side or a hose with a horn on the larger models.

Wet Chemical Fire Extinguishers: Wet chemical fire extinguishers were developed specifically for use on Class-F deep fat cooking fires. Wet chemical fire extinguishers are red with a yellow panel above the operating instructions.

Symbols found on fire extinguishers & what they mean	Water	Foam spray	ABC powder	Carbon dioxide	Wet chemical
A Wood, paper & textiles	✓	✓	✓	✗	✓
B Flammable liquids	✗	✓	✓	✓	✗
C Flammable gases	✗	✗	✓	✗	✗
Electrical contact	✗	✗	✓	✓	✗
F Cooking oils & fats	✗	✗	✗	✗	✓

Figure: Classification of fires and use of appropriate fire extinguisher (www.fireextinguishersguide.co.uk).

HOW TO USE A PORTABLE FIRE EXTINGUISHER

The easiest way to remember how to use a portable fire extinguisher is to remember the acronym: PASS. Effective use of fire extinguishers includes; pulling the safety pin, aiming the extinguisher nozzle at the base of the flames, squeezing the trigger while holding the extinguisher upright and sweeping the extinguisher from side to side ensuring that the fire extinguishing agent cover all areas of the fire.

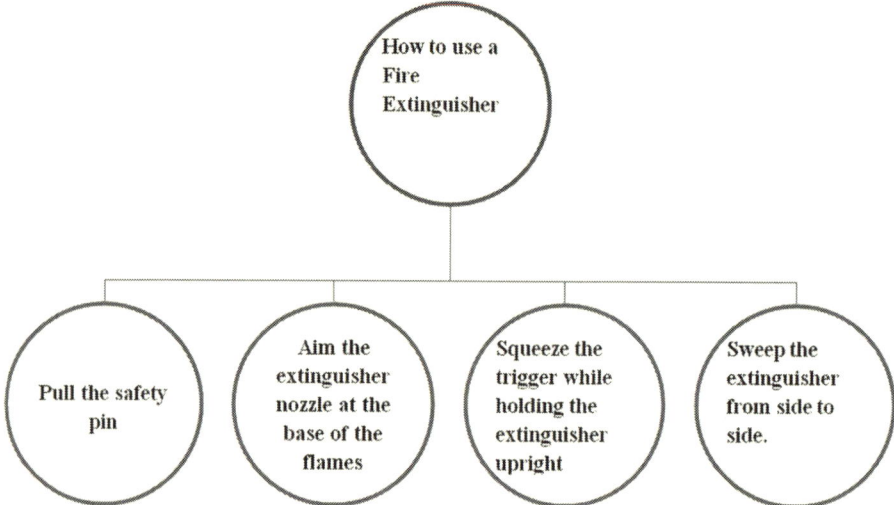

Figure: How to effectively use a fire extinguisher

THINGS LABORATORY STAFF MUST KNOW ABOUT DEALING WITH FIRE

- Know the different types, location of the nearest operable fire extinguisher and know how to use it.
- Must attend annual mandatory fire lecture
- Before using the fire extinguisher, evacuate the building by pulling the fire alarm. Never wait until the fire gets out of control. Even if you smell smoke, you must raise an alarm
- Only attempt using the extinguisher to manage a small fire. If one extinguisher doesn't put out the fire, you must evacuate immediately.
- While attempting to fight a fire, every attempt must be made to ensure that the fire exit does not become blocked by fire.
- After an extinguisher has been successfully put off, you must still contact the fire unit to follow up on the probable causes and arrive at corrective action as well as ensure that the fire extinguisher is replaced.
- Be aware of what to do in dealing a fire as well as know the exit route and the muster point.

- Know the location of emergency eye wash station, emergency showers, spill cleanup and the alarm pull box.
- Laboratory staff should never overload sockets with multiple plugs, Use of extension cords should be avoided, only use multi outlet devices that have their own self contained circuit breaker.

CHAPTER 22

CARRYING OUT RISK ASSESSMENT IN THE LABORATORY

RISK ASSESSMENT

A risk assessment should be carried out on all processes in the laboratory. It is a legal requirement and an important step in protecting staff. It is a way of identifying and managing all the risks that can potentially cause harm to staff working in the laboratory. It is a way of putting simple, cheap and effective measures in place to ensure that staff work safely and are protected from potential harm. A risk assessment is simply a careful examination of substances or condition in the laboratory that can cause harm to staff to ensure that adequate precautions are in place to prevent harm. Employers are potentially liable if staffs suffer harm and it is proven that the employer have not put enough reasonable control measures in place to prevent harm in the workplace. If any potential risk is identified risk is identified, the chances of it causing harm must be evaluated (low, medium or high).It is also important to state existing control measure in place to reduce the likelihood of it causing harm. Risk assessment should be carried out before the introduction of a new procedure or following an incident. Risk assessment cannot and is not expect to eliminate all risk, but it requires that measures be put in place as far as is 'reasonably practicable' to reduce the likelihood of identified risk causing harm. Reviewed after 12 months to ensure that the risk identified in previous assessments has been eliminated or reduced to the barest minimum.

HAZARDS AND RISKS

Hazard: A hazard is defined as anything that has the potential to cause harm. Hazards include; contact with electricity, a chemicals, radiation, working from ladders, exposure to needle stick injury, exposure to hot surfaces and others.

Risk : A risk is defines as the chances (Low, medium or low) that a person (staff, patients, visitors and contractors) could be harmed by any hazards as well as an indication of how serious the harm could potentially be.

STEPS INVOLVED IN A RISK ASSESSMENT

- Identification of hazard
- Decision of staff that are potentially at risk of being harmed and a description of how they can possibly be harmed.
- Evaluation of the risks and identification of precautionary and control measures in place to minimize risk.
- Recording of any risk identified, carrying out of root causes, suggesting corrective measures for implementation
- Review of the assessment at a future stipulated date (12 months after initial review) and implements any further corrective measures if necessary.

NELSON BIOMEDICAL LIMITED RISK ASSESSMENT FORM

Name of Unit/Department:	Assessed by:	Date Assessed:
Description of activity under assessment:		
Hazard	List Existing Control Measures in place	Risk Evaluation (Low/Medium/High)
Manual handling		
Slip, Trip, fall on same level		
Slip, Trip, fall from a different		
Fall from height		
Struck down by object		
Struck by a moving or falling object		
Contact with cold of hot surface or liquid		
Chemical exposure-related burns		
Cut with sharp object (including needle stick injury and other non-medical exposure to sharp objects)		
Trapped between surfaces		
Contact with electricity and risk of electrocution		
Exposure to a hazardous substance or chemicals (COSHH risk assessment)		
Exposure to radiation		
Physical and verbal assault		
Other risk (specify)		
Persons potentially at risk: Staff: ☐ Patient: ☐ Visitors: ☐ Contractors: ☐		
Is a signficant risk assessment required for procedure: Yes ☐ No ☐		
Name /Signature of manager/Date:		

DEALING WITH BIO-HAZARDOUS AND CHEMICAL SPILLAGES IN THE LABORATORY

Spillages involving chemicals and bio-hazardous substances can occur in the laboratory. Potential hazards associated with spillages include; the broken container, aerosol release and the spillage material itself. If the spilled material is blood or body fluid, there is a risk of possible infection or contamination. Spillage involving chemicals are associated with potential hazard of corrosion, flammability, harmful, and oxidising (associated with the release of noxious and poisonous gases).When dealing with chemical spillages, you isolate the area and PPE such as rubber gloves, eye goggles, all purpose respirators and rubber boots should be worn. Absorbent granules or sand can be used to absorb and liquid while dust pan and brush can be used to sweep up pieces of broken glass. Neutralize acids with sodium carbonate. Dispose of spillage waste following manufacturer's instruction in the MSDS for the chemical involved. For bio-hazardous spillages (blood and other body fluid), isolate the area, put on appropriate PPE, use absorbent paper soaked with a disinfectant (Virkon) to absorb the spill, all soiled absorbent paper and other contaminated materials including hand gloves should be place in a plastic bag and disposed into yellow clinical waste bin. The area should be disinfected using a suitable disinfectant. Hand should be washed thoroughly with soap after dealing with a spill.

ACCIDENT REPORTING

All accidents, injuries and near misses no matter how minor or insignificant must be reported investigated (to determine the root causes to allow for corrective actions to be taken to remove the root cause) and monitored. It must be reported to the laboratory manager. An incident form must be completed, investigated by carrying a root cause analysis, taking immediate remedial action and corrective action to eliminate root cause as well as provision of post exposure prophylaxis if appropriate. It is the responsibility of staff completing the accident report form to ensure that the form is completed correctly as soon as practically possible after the accident. In some countries such as the UK, certain types of accident must be reported to appropriate external authorities such as the Health and Safety Executive (HSE) as required by law (Reporting of Injuries, Disease and Dangerous Occurrences Regulations). An example of an accident, incident and near miss form is shown below.

NELSON BIOMEDICAL LIMITED ACCIDENT/INCIDENT FORM

Name of staff :

Occupational group:

Date of accident/incident:

Time of accident/incident:

Time work began:

Location of accident/incident:

Description of accident/incident:

List of staff present during accident/incident:

Manager to which accident/incident was reported:

Immediate remedial action taken:

Possible root causes:

Corrective action to eliminate root cause:

_____   _____

Employee name and signature   **Laboratory managers signature**

For Occupational health department use

Incident number:

Disposition of staff (full duty, restricted duty, off duty or referral for medical management):

Does accident fall into that reportable to regulatory agency:

Is safety investigation or risk assessment require:

_____

Signature of Occupational health officer

Date _____

CHAPTER 23

HOUSEKEEPING ISSUES ASSOCIATED WITH THE LABORATORY

HOUSEKEEPING IN THE LABORATORY

Laboratories are categorized based on the type of biohazard handled into pathogen or protection level P1 to P4. The laboratory is a high risk environment for exposure to hazardous chemical and bio hazardous material. Good laboratory housekeeping is essential in the laboratory to ensure a clean, safe and pleasant environment required for effective service delivery. Good housekeeping in the laboratory in the laboratory is essential to prevent accidents and harm to staff and visitors. Work in the laboratory is associated with three categories of hazards encountered; chemical (most laboratory chemicals have the potential to cause harm or injury if they are misused or if appropriate precaution are not taken), biological (microbes, toxins, recombinant organisms, and viral vectors) and physical (electrical safety hazards, ergonomic hazards associated with manual material handling and equipment use, handling sharps, and basic housekeeping issues). Fire, property loss, injury and loss of life are often associated with poor laboratory housekeeping.

CLASSIFICATION OF LABORATORIES BASED ON THE BIOHAZARD LEVEL

Biohazard level	Inclusive organisms/diseases
Biohazard level 1	Bacteria and viruses including non-infectious bacteria, Escherichia coli, Varicella (Chicken pox), canine hepatitis, cell cultures and Bacillus subtilis.
Biohazard level 2	Bacteria and viruses that cause only mild disease to humans and are difficult to contract via aerosol in a laboratory setting including hepatitis A, B and C, HIV, Lyme disease, Salmonella, measles and, influenza A

Biohazard level 3   Bacteria and viruses that can cause severe to fatal disease in humans, but for which vaccines or other treatments are readily available exist including West Nile virus, yellow fever, malaria, anthrax, tuberculosis, Rocky Mountain spotted fever, SARS virus and Venezuelan equine encephalitis.

Biohazard level 4   Viruses and bacteria that cause severe to fatal disease in humans, and for which vaccines or other treatments are *not* available. Organisms handled in category p4 laboratories includes; Ebola virus, Bolivian and Argentine haemorrhagic fevers, Marburg virus, Lassa fever, Dengue haemorrhagic fever, Hantaviruses and Crimean-Congo haemorrhagic fever.

HOUSEKEEPING DON'TS

- No mouth pipetting is allowed
- No eating, chewing of gum and smoking is allowed in the laboratory
- Floors, aisles, exits, fire-extinguishing equipment, eyewashes, showers, electrical disconnect and other emergency equipment shall remain unobstructed.
- Storage of food and drink is prohibited in the laboratory
- Never lick labels of chew pens in the laboratory
- Never handle the phone, computer mouse or keyboard with hand gloves on
- Wash your hands before leaving the laboratory
- Never block emergency exit
- Never resheath needles
- Never smell or taste any chemicals
- Long hairs, loose clothing and high heeled shoes are not indicated in the laboratory particularly when working with moving equipment and machine.
- Never use electrical equipment in a damp environment
- Never add water to a concentrated acid solution but rather always add acid to water slowly.
- No horseplay is allowed in the laboratory
- Never temper with equipment provided for health and safety
- Observe universal precaution all the time when working in the laboratory

HOUSEKEEPING DO'S

Dispose of all chemicals, broken glass and other lab materials into the proper containers

- Reduce the risk of slips, trips, and falls by cleaning up liquid or solid spills immediately.
- Ensure you protect your own health and safety as well as those of your co workers
- Label all containers appropriately (content and sate of reconstitution)
- Wear personal protective equipment when required (hand gloves, goggles, apron, laboratory coats, ear and nose protector)
- Must be up-to-date with all appropriate protective vaccinations (Hepatitis B, TB, etc)
- Segregate appropriately all laboratory waste and dispose safely
- Keep work benches clean and uncluttered
- Store heavy items on the lower shelves, lighter items on the upper shelves
- Use appropriate manual handling tool for all manual handling related task
- Wash your hands before leaving the laboratory
- Store flammable and combustible chemical in appropriate flammable cabinet or box
- Ensure the laboratory is sign posted with necessary hazard warnings where necessary.
- Ensure that rooms where chemicals are handles are properly ventilated
- Keep work benches clean and uncluttered
- Reduce cosmetic use in the laboratory particularly area where chemicals are handled
- Store inflammable chemicals in flammable box or cabinet
- Report all accidents, incidents and near misses to appropriate staff
- Use fume hood when dealing with chemicals that have potential harmful vapours
- Know the location of all safety and emergency equipment used in the laboratory
- Be up-to-date with mandatory annual fire, infection control, health and safety and manual handling training.
- Know fire drill procedures and locations of fire extinguishers and all fire exits.

- Never use any equipment that you have not be trained and certified competent on
- Know the location of all safety and emergency equipment used in the laboratory (Alarm systems with pull stations, fire blankets, eye washes, first-aid kits and deluge safety showers
- .Properly dispose of broken glassware and other sharp objects into sharps containers provided
- Wear shoes that adequately cover the whole foot; low-heeled shoes with non-slip soles are preferable. Do not wear sandals, open-toed shoes.
- Remove any protective equipment (gloves, laboratory coat, apron and chemical splash goggles) before leaving the laboratory.
- Check the label to verify it is the correct substance before using it

CHAPTER 24

PSYCHOLOGICAL HAZARDS AND STAFF MORALE-RELATED ISSUES ASSOCIATED WITH WORKING IN THE LABORATORY

PSYCHOLOGICAL HAZARDS ASSOCIATED WITH WORKING IN THE LABORATORY

Workplace stress is the harmful physical and emotional response that occurs when the environment is not conducive (human and material resources endowment) and when, there is a poor match between job demands and the capabilities. There are different kinds of hazard associated with working in the hospital environment that can potentially cause stress that can affect the general well-being of staff. The hospital environment is a difficult, challenging and stressful place to work. Hospital work often involves caring for sick and injured patients and their families. There are factors that can make the working environment in the hospital very stressful. Working in a stressful environment predisposes staff to conditions which may lead to poor work performance, higher absenteeism, less work morale, productivity or even <u>injury</u>. Job-related stress is also associated with various biological reactions that may lead ultimately to compromised health (hypertension and other <u>cardiovascular disease</u>s, diabetes or in extreme cases <u>death</u>.

TABLE: PSYCHOLOGICAL HAZARDS ASSOCIATED WITH WORKING IN THE HOSPITAL LABORATORY

- Lone working, shift work and on call duty work is often associated with fatigue, burn out, depression, anxiety and emotional strain (dissatisfaction and tension).
- Negative workload associated with high workload and demand but with sub-optimal human and material resources to manage workloads.

- Unrealistic turnaround times set be most hospitals management despite suboptimal staffing put staff under so much stress.
- High or unrealistic patient expectations can be very demanding particularly in the atmosphere of job cuts being implemented in most hospitals.
- Verbal abuse or threats from mental health or intoxicated patients.
- High or unrealistic expectations from supervisors and managers.
- Poor management associated with poor application of appreciative intelligence.
- Challenging interpersonal work relationships particularly in organization where rumor mongering is tolerated.
- Frustrations due to limited resources (equipments and sub-optimal staffing levels
- Lack of supervisory support particularly during shift and call duty during out of hour's period.
- Poor organizational climate with low staff morale and reduced productivity.
- Extensive work hours that is non-compliant with European Working Time Directive and other relevant legislation.
- Burden of a high turnover of staff and the loss of trained staff
- Toxic, sub-optimal and non-health and safety friendly work environments
- Management bullying and harassment in the workplace.
- Lack of opportunities or motivation to advancement to encourage staff development.
- Job insecurity associated with the willingness of hospital to swiftly lay off workers to cope with changing economic environments and unrealistic demands from government.
- Low morale of staff associated with decision by hospital to de-band (demote) staff as a cost saving measure.
- The decision by most hospital management to replace more qualified high level staff with low level less qualified and experienced staff as a cost saving measure.

MANAGEMENT OF ABSENCES AND FINANCIAL IMPLICATIONS ON AN ORGANIZATION

Employee absence is a significant cost to businesses. Annual employee absence survey should contain data on sickness absence costs, causes and the average number of working days lost. It also looks at trends and current practices in managing absence. Effective absence management involves determining the root causes of sickness absences and implementing corrective actions to eliminate root causes, finding a balance between providing support to help employees with health problems stay in and return to work and taking consistent and firm action against employees who try to take advantage of organizations' occupational sick pay schemes. Every organization must have an absence policy to effectively manage absences from work. There are many reasons why people take time off work.

COMMON REASONS FOR WORK ABSENCES

- Short-term sickness absence
- Long-term sickness absence
- Unauthorized absence or persistent lateness
- Other authorized absences
  - Annual leave
  - Maternity
  - Paternity
  - Adoption or parental leave
  - Time off for public or trade union duties
  - Carer's leave for dependents
  - Compassionate leave (Bereavements)
  - Educational leave.

WHY ABSENCE FROM WORK MATTERS

Apart from genuine ill health, work-related stress is a a major cause of absences and a serious problem for businesses with cost implications. Employers are encouraged to focus on prevention, rather than after stress occur. Work-related stress is one of the largest causes of ill health in the workplace in most countries and a major cause of revenue losses. In

2007/08 the British government lost an estimated 13.5 million working days to work-related stress, depression and anxiety. On the average, when stress, anxiety or depression leads to absence from work, the average length of sick leave per case is about 30.6 days. Employers must realize that. It is a legal requirement for employers to assess risk of work-related stress. Employers have a general duty to ensure, so far as is reasonably practicable, the health of your employees at work. Absences from work have a serious effect on service delivery, meeting set turnaround times and drives up the cost of rendering the service. In the long term, such stress can lead to physical, medical (cardiovascular diseases, hypertension and diabetes) and mental ill health problems. Employers to implement the Management Standards approach (Risk assessment). This should involve the following steps:

- Identify the stress risk factors
- Decide who might be harmed and how (Gather relevant evidenced based and unbiased data).
- Evaluate (carry out a root cause analysis) to determine route causes and explore the corrective measures (develop solutions).
- Record your findings (implement corrective action)
- Monitor and review (Carry out a periodic monitoring and review action plans and assess effectiveness)

COMMON FACTORS THAT CAUSES STRESS IS THE WORK PLACE

- Job demands (Unreasonable demands on staff by their employers and government, unrealistic goals, lack of enabling working environment, workload and lone working out of hours or on call).
- Control over work (increased workload with sub-optimal staffing levels).
- Lack of support from managers, supervisors and colleagues (poor communication between colleagues or between employees and management and lack of senior staff support out of hours)
- Relationships at work (bullying, discrimination and a poor work-life balance and gossip).
- Job Role and Organisational Change (De-banding of staff, job cuts, pay freezes, salary cuts, job insecurity, burden of a high

turnover of staff, the loss of trained individuals and lack of support for continuing professional development).

COMMON SIGNS OF WORK-RELATED STRESS

- Uncharacteristic mood swings
- Failure to communicate
- Lack of zeal
- Low staff morale and productivity
- Failure and lack of contribution in departmental quality improvement meetings
- Evidence of continuous fatigue and tiredness
- Loss of confidence
- Loss of concentration
- Reduced work output and quality
- Social isolation and a loss of interest in their work
- A high level of sickness absence
- Changes in the behaviour of an employee

DEALING WITH WORK-RELATED STRESS

It is in the interest of an organization that issues that causes staff stress in the work place are identified and dealt with. If the work-related stress is associated with a particular staff, it is important for the laboratory manager and the individual suffering from stress to have a formal discussion to try and solve the problem. If either party requires help or advice, then a union representative and employee representative (Human resources department) may be involved. However, if excessive pressure has led to ill health or absence from work, the individual's doctor, psychiatrist or other relevant health professional should be involved. It is expected that an employer strive to do the following;

- Understand the situation, including the root causes and possible corrective actions (solutions).
- Provide adequate support to the individual
- Develop a plan in conjunction with the affected staff to tackle the root causes of stress that is acceptable to all (the individual and their laboratory or line manager)

- Assess whether any other members of staff is experiencing similar problems and if a broader organisational intervention is required.

Breaks requirements in the laboratory

Most workers have the right to take breaks, but whether or not you are paid for them depends on the terms of your employment contract. Employers should ideally be entitled to a minimum of 30 minutes break for every 4 hours worked. The European Working Time Directive is a directive from the Council of Europe (93/104/EC) to protect the health and safety of workers in the European Union. It lays down minimum requirements in relation to working hours, rest periods, annual leave and working arrangements for night workers. Working time shall mean any period during which the worker is working, at the employer's disposal and carrying out his or her activity or duties, in accordance with national laws and/or practice. The directive is a European Union initiative designed to protect workers from exploitation by employers. Countries in sub Saharan African countries can learn from this evidenced based best practice by tailoring the implementation of this directive to meet their peculiar needs as a way of ensuring that staffs are productive and health and safety requirements are compromised.

Advantages of regular breaks

Importance	Details
Enhances staff productivity	Most workplace studies have reached the conclusion that workers are more productive if they have several shorter breaks a day as opposed to one much longer one. For most jobs which are full time based, two shorter breaks either side of longer lunch break is often adequate and enhances staff productivity and alertness as well as reduces chances of making a mistakes or being involved in accident and injury.
Prevent impaired blood circulation	Being static for a long time can potentially affect blood flow and can cause circulation to be impeded. Suboptimal blood flow to an active muscle can result in impaired oxygen supply which can impair muscle function with resultant fatigue

Reduces risk of errors	For example, where a job requires lots of physical exertion, several much shorter breaks will often help to keep fatigue at bay and keep production levels up. Those who work in extreme environments which are either very hot or very cold should also be given the opportunity to spend their break times outside of these extreme temperatures where possible to avoid the effects of either excessive heat or cold.
Prevent Burnout	People who work continually face complete burnout and physical exhaustion which can lead to problems such as chronic headaches, fatigue, lack of concentration, and insomnia (lack of sleeping at night). Staff can use their break time to wind down and refresh themselves and feel more energized the rest of the work day.
Enhances staff morale	Many studies have revealed that workers who take breaks are of higher morale and generally more productive during the day as opposed to those who do not. Performance levels have been shown by several studies to increase dramatically so that you can tackle tasks again with renewed vigor, alertness and finish them accurately. Staff involved in monotonous or repetitive task as well as those whose role involves constant monitoring or inspection will need to be given short breaks to prevent boredom and reduces chances of mistakes and errors.
Reduces heart disease and thrombosis risk	Scientific research has shown that being static for long hours without physical activity, mobility and rest can potentially predispose staff to thrombosis (clot formation in blood vessel due to stasis) and cardiovascular disease. Staffs who do not take out time to go on break and relax periodically are prone to build up of plaques in their arteries which contribute to potential heart attacks, deep vein thrombosis and strokes.

Reduces stress and stress-associated mistakes and accidents	Spending long time carrying out a tedious task without adequate break can result in physical and mental exhaustion and stress. Stress can predispose staff to illness (hypertension, diabetes high blood sugar, poor fitness, low resistance to viruses, and other serious illnesses). It is always advisable for staff carrying out stressful task to take time out for breaks to enable them unwind. There is the tendency that staff comes back after the break calm, more alert, with high morale and more productive. Mistakes are also made more when staff does not have time to refresh their mind and body.
Prevent repetitive Stress Injuries	Repetitive stress injury is particularly common among secretariat staffs and other staff whose jobs involve long time staring at a computer and typing. Such staffs are more prone to repetitive stress injuries (eyes strain from staring at a computer screen, Carpal Tunnel injury which can develop from spending long time during the working day typing particularly when done in the wrong posture. Improper posture can potential cause back and neck pain (resulting from inadequate lumbar support).
Facilitates the awareness of time (computer-related work)	Worker who work with computers have a tendency not to be conscious of time because they often work for long hours without taking a break. This can potentially affect their productivity the longer they go on working for hours without taking adequate break. An easy way to eliminate this problem is to make sure people take regular breaks by using time reminders.

BREAK ALLOCATION

Where possible employers are encouraged to allocate appropriate breaks for their employees ensuring that the service delivery is unhindered when staff are on break. Most organization tends to have a set of staff go on break while the second set is at work on the bench. The second set can go their break once the first set returns from theirs. Other factors that be taken into consideration in determining when and for how long break time last include:

Factors that may affect break requirements by staff

- Age and gender
- Nature of the job
- State of health of staff
- Environment in which the job is performed
- Level of physical activity involved
- Degree of repetition or monotony of a particular job
- Experience of the worker in that particular role
- Based on medical advice from a medical officer
- If minimal exposure requirement to a particular agent to which staff is exposed in their daily work.
- Based on advise of the occupational health department

General requirements under European Working Time Directive

Rest and Break requirements under EWTD

- A minimum daily consecutive rest period of 11 hours
- A minimum rest break of 20 minutes when the working day exceeds six hours
- A minimum rest period of 24 hours in each seven day period (or 48 hours in 14 days)
- A minimum of four weeks' paid annual leave
- A maximum of eight hours' work in any 24 hours for night workers in stressful job

- A person's average working week must be no longer than 48 hours in seven days. Working time includes job-related training, travelling time and paid overtime, but excludes normal travel to work, breaks when no work is done and voluntary unpaid overtime.
- Not more than 40 hours a week. Except if the employee signs to do so on their own volition not compelled by their employers.
- Workers are entitled to a minimum rest period of 11 consecutive hours in every 24, as well as a rest break during working time if they are on duty for longer than six hours. They are also entitled to a minimum uninterrupted rest period of 24 hours in every seven days.
- Night workers are entitled to extra protection. Average working hours must not exceed 8 hours per 24-hour period and employees are entitled to free health assessments and, in some cases, a transfer to day work.
- All employees must be given paid annual leave of at least four weeks per year.

TYPES OF BREAKS AND ENTITLEMENTS

Staff will normally have a variety of different breaks from work. These can be broken down into three types:

Rest breaks	Rest breaks include lunch breaks, tea breaks and other short breaks during the day. This type of breaks are often paid except otherwise stated in the employee's contract
Rest day	This involves a break between finishing one day's work and starting the next. Rest days are often given after a 12 hours night work within a working week days by most employers. Rest days are almost never paid unless you have to remain 'on call' and are available to work if called out.
Weekly rest	This are whole days when employee don't come into work (usually at weekend).Most employee who are a shift rota in departments that run a 24 hours service this may not apply. This type of break is almost never paid unless you have to remain 'on call and are available to work if called or otherwise stated in the contract.

Break entitlements   The amount of break time an employee gets is a function of what is agreed with your employer and stated in the staff contract or might be part of your employer's standard practice. Every employer are expected by law to give their staff at least the rest breaks as required by the Working Time Regulations. This is to ensure that staff health and safety is not compromised. Employers may generally be expected have to possible give staff more than what is statutorily expected and set out in the regulations particularly if this reduces a health and safety risk.

REST BREAKS—A BREAK DURING YOUR WORKING DAY

Based on European working time directive and legislation in most developing countries, an adult worker (≥ 18 years) is statutorily entitled to a minimum of 20 minute rest break if you are expected to work more than six hours at a stretch. A lunch or coffee break is often seen as part of rest break by most employers. Additional breaks might be given in the contract of employment. General requirements for rest breaks include:

GENERAL REQUIREMENTS FOR TAKING REST BREAKS

- Cannot be taken in one large block. Taken after every 4 hours work as part of a > 6 hours continuous day work
- Cannot be taken off one end of the working day (preferable in the middle)
- Cannot be accumulated and converted to annual leave
- Employer can say when the break must be taken to ensure compliance to legislation
- Approved break is employee's own time. The employee has the right to do whatever he wants during those times.

CHAPTER 25

DOCUMENT CONTROL AND STANDARD OPERATING PROCEDURES

DOCUMENT CONTROL

Each organization should develop a numbering system to systematically identify and label their SOPs, and the document control should be described in its Quality Management Plan. Generally, each page of an SOP should have control documentation notation, similar to that illustrated below. A short title and identification (ID) number can serve as a reference designation. The revision number and date are very useful in identifying the SOP in use when reviewing historical data and is critical when the need for evidentiary records is involved and when the activity is being reviewed. When the number of pages is indicated, the user can quickly check if the SOP is complete. Generally this type of document control notation is located in the upper right-hand corner of each document page following the title page.

STANDARD OPERATING PROCEDURE (SOP)

An SOP is a written document or instruction detailing all steps and activities of a process or procedure. ISO 9001 essentially requires the documentation of all procedures used in any manufacturing process that could affect the quality of the product. The aim is to ensure that a trained staff can perform task to achieve consistently the desire outcome. It should have a named author and must be validated by a second party, approved by the responsible manage and have information on date issued and statement that photocopied version is not controlled. It should be uniquely identified (document control number) and reviewed regularly. It is a useful tool in the training of new staff. All staff performing the task spelt in the SOP must sign the SOP as an attestation that they have read, have been trained on the SOP and are committed to work consistently following the SOP. The development and use of SOPs are an integral part of a successful quality system as it provides individuals with the information to perform a job properly, and facilitates consistency in the quality and integrity of a product or end-result. In addition, the best written SOPs will fail if they are not followed. Therefore, the use of SOPs needs to be reviewed and re-enforced by management, preferably the direct supervisor. Current copies of the SOPs also need to be readily accessible for reference in the work areas of those individuals actually performing the task, either in hard copy or electronic format, otherwise SOPs serve little purpose. The development and use of SOPs minimizes variation and promotes quality through consistent implementation of a process or procedure within the organization, even if there are temporary or permanent personnel changes. SOPs should be written in a concise, step-by-step, easy-to-read format. The information presented should be unambiguous and not overly complicated. SOPs need to remain current to be useful. Therefore, whenever procedures are changed, SOPs should be updated and re-approved. If desired, modify only the pertinent section of an SOP and indicate the change date/revision number for that section in the Table of Contents and the document control notation. SOPs should be also systematically reviewed on a periodic basis, e.g. every 1-2 years, to ensure that the policies and procedures remain current and appropriate, or to determine whether the SOPs are even needed. Each organization should develop a numbering system to systematically identify and label their SOPs, and the document control should be described in its Quality Management Plan. An SOP should include the following sections:

1. The first page or cover page of each SOP should contain the following information: a title that clearly identifies the activity or procedure, an SOP identification (ID) number, date of issue and/or revision, the name of the applicable agency, division, and/ or branch to which this SOP applies, and the signatures and signature dates of those individuals who prepared and approved the SOP.

2. A table of Contents may be needed for quick reference, especially if the SOP is long, for locating information and to denote changes or revisions made only to certain sections of an SOP.

3. Well-written SOPs should first briefly describe the purpose of the process, including any regulatory information or standards

that are appropriate to the SOP process, and the scope to indicate what is covered. Define any specialized or unusual terms.

4. Denote what sequential procedures should be followed, divided into significant sections; possible interferences, equipment needed as well as state cautions (indicating activities that could result in equipment damage, degradation of sample, or possible invalidation of results; listed here and at the critical steps in the procedure).

5. Procedure (identifying all pertinent steps, in order, and the materials needed to accomplish the procedure such as; Instrument or method calibration and standardization, Sample Collection, Sample handling and preservation, Sample preparation and analysis (such as extraction, digestion, analysis, identification, and counting procedures), troubleshooting, data acquisition, calculations and data entering requirements, data and records management, identifying any calculations to be performed, forms to be used, reports to be written and data and record storage information).

6. State the personnel qualifications/responsibilities (denoting the minimal experience the user should have to complete the task satisfactorily, and citing any applicable requirements (certification).

7. Health & Safety Warnings (indicating operations that could result in personal injury or loss of life and explaining what will happen if the procedure is not followed or is followed incorrectly; listed here and at the critical steps in the procedure). Safety considerations (Risk assessments and hazard identification (Control of Substances Hazardous to Health (COSHH) and Material Safety Data Sheet (MSDS) and manual handling-related risk) must be taken into consideration.

8. Result reporting, reference ranges, calculations, clinical interpretations and interferences (describing any component of the process that may interfere with the accuracy of the result or outcome).

9. Information on risk assessment associated with the procedure, identification of hazards associated and manual handling-related issues.

10. Describe next all appropriate QA and quality control (QC) activities for that procedure.

11. List any cited or significant references and a signature section

CHAPTER 26

Tips in doing a scientific presentation

Presentation should not be done in a hurry if you desire to make a lasting impact. It must be planned weeks prior to actual presentation. It should be rehearsed once or twice prior to actual presentation. You must decide what the main issue the presentation is centred around. You must learn to use a strategy and words to arouse the interest of your audience as well as make the presentation a humorous presentation rather than a grave yard experience. Learn to highlight the following:

- Important findings
- Different interpretations of your data
- Future ongoing work on topic and projected future findings
- Have a clear justification for carrying out the study as well as the aims and objectives.

Presentation proper

The presentation proper should be straight to the point. There should be no ambiguity. It should include the following headings.

- Title of presentation
- Justification why of all the topics in the world, this is priority
- State how you recruited your subjects (no bias in recruitment), the inclusion and exclusion criteria, how you went about getting informed consent from subjects, calculated on the number of subjects that was significant for study, equipment and other materials used.
- Findings from your research or experiments (Results)
- Major findings and statement of fact from your study (conclusion)

    State your plan, discuss your presentation in sub-sections that fits your topic and package the in a form and language that your audience will understand.

Use of visual Aids

Visual aids are useful in a presentation. Avoid using irrelevant tables or figure that does not add value to your presentation. Make your table and graphs as simple and self explanatory as possible. Other points to note include:

- Keep the aids as simple as possible
- Use 24pt as a minimum for your lettering to allow for easy visualization by your audience
- Ensure your slides has bullet point with short sentences of not more that a single line per bullet point
- Minimize row and columns in tables to manageable level (five to 6 rows and columns).To ensure that your audience can glace at your tables and graph while still listening to your presentation.
- Prompt your audience by telling them what to expect in the next slide just before it comes on. Pause a while as soon as it is on and then explain the content.
- Stay by the side. Avoid covering your Aids and preventing your audience from seeing it. You can use pointer to draw attention to point being discussed on the table or graph.
- Never read from a script or from the presentation board. You can have a set of post cards with key words. Learn to from time to time look at your audience to get eye contacts.
- Conclude by thanking your audience for finding time to attend the presentation and informing your audience that you will be delighted to take few questions.

Do's and don'ts in making a Presentations

The goal of doing a presentation is to improve your listener's knowledge on the subject matter. To make a meaningful presentation, it is vital to have an understanding of the following questions:

- Who are in the audience
- What are the interests of people in the audience
- What is their level of knowledge on the subject matter (this is to enable you to come to their level and to endure that people in the

audience understands what you are saying). Phrases like "as many of you will already know," may be quiet useful when the audience are highly enlightened on subject being presented.

- Ensure that your presentation is inspiring, relieved and not threatened by your presentation.

ABOUT THE AUTHORS

DR ERHABOR OSARO

Dr Erhabor Osaro is a chartered scientist and fellow of the Institute of Biomedical Science of London. He holds a doctor of philosophy degree in immunohaematology. He completed the University of Greenwich specialist courses in blood transfusion and laboratory quality management system. His teaching experience spans both Nigeria and the United Kingdom. His work experience includes working as a Specialist Biomedical Scientist at the Royal Bolton Hospital-a continuous improvement conscious and a centre of excellence in the implementation of lean principle in the health sector in Europe. He is the recipient of several awards, including the famous British Blood Transfusion Society Young Scientist Award and the Margaret Kenwright Young Scientist Award. He is a registration portfolio verifier/examiner for the Institute of Biomedical Science of London. He is a member of the editorial board as well as an article reviewer for several scientific journals. A well-published contributor in the field of infectious diseases, immunohaematology, and transfusion medicine, he is chairman of the board of directors of Nelson Biomedical Limited, UK and Nigeria. He is married to Angela, and they are blessed with five children—Emmanuel, Majesty, David, Daniel, and Michelle.

Dr Adias Teddy Charles

Dr Adias Teddy Charles (PhD, FIBMS)

Dr Adias Teddy Charles is the provost of the Bayelsa State College of Health Technology, Ogbia, Nigeria. He holds a PhD in immunohaematology and is a fellow of the Institute of Biomedical Science (FIBMS), London. His current research interest is focused on transfusion immunology, safety and alternatives, and the haematology of infectious diseases. Recent publications have included articles in journals, such as the *Journal of Blood Medicine*, *Transfusion Clinique et Biologique*, *Pathology*, and *Laboratory Medicine International*, amongst others. Dr Adias is happy married and blessed with two children.

Dr Adias Teddy Charles (Ph.D, FIBMS)

2427637R00175

Printed in Great Britain
by Amazon.co.uk, Ltd.,
Marston Gate.